RESEARCH ETHICS IN THE RI

Euro-Western and
Indigenous perspectives

Helen Kara

P

First published in Great Britain in 2018

Policy Press
University of Bristol
1–9 Old Park Hill
Bristol
BS2 8BB
UK
t: +44 (0)117 954 5940
pp-info@bristol.ac.uk
www.policypress.co.uk

North America office:
Policy Press
c/o The University of Chicago Press
1427 East 60th Street
Chicago, IL 60637, USA
t: +1 773 702 7700
f: +1 773-702-9756
sales@press.uchicago.edu
www.press.uchicago.edu

British Library Cataloguing in Publication Data
A catalogue record for this book is available from the British Library

Library of Congress Cataloging-in-Publication Data
A catalog record for this book has been requested

ISBN 978-1-4473-4474-2 hardcover
ISBN 978-1-4473-4475-9 paperback
ISBN 978-1-4473-4476-6 ePub
ISBN 978-1-4473-4477-3 Mobi
ISBN 978-1-4473-4478-0 epdf

Cover design by Robin Hawes
Front cover image: istock
Printed and bound in Great Britain by CMP, Poole
Policy Press uses environmentally responsible print partners

I dedicate this book to my sister Ros and my nephew Jamie, two of the most ethical people I know, who always inspire me to think and act more ethically.

Contents

Part II: Doing research ethically

Contents

Acknowledgements

I would like to thank:

Sandie Hope-Forrest who set my feet on this road with her inspiring ethics lectures when I was an MSc student at Staffordshire University in 1999.

Amanda Taylor and Katy Vigurs for initial encouragement without which I might never have got going on this book.

Les Back who gave me great encouragement at an early stage and sent me helpful literature.

Bagele Chilisa, Deborah McGregor and Helen Moewaka Barnes who put me straight about Indigenous research and inspired the direction of this book. Almost two years later, Deborah McGregor very kindly reviewed an almost-final manuscript and not only waived anonymity but also offered great encouragement along with invaluable suggestions for improvement. I am glad to be able to acknowledge her contributions in the text as well as here.

Sarah Banks, Michaela Benson, Mel Bartley, Jonathan O'Donnell and Alistair Roy who provided much-needed encouragement along the way.

Petra Boynton, Martin Holmes, Mihaela Kelemen, Melissa Terras and Daniel Turner who gave practical assistance.

Bagele Chilisa for alerting me to Walter and Andersen (2016) *Indigenous Statistics*, which I might not otherwise have found.

Christine Soltero who kindly reached out through the magic of the internet and bought me a copy of Strega and Brown (2015) *Research an Resistance: Revisiting Critical, Indigenous, and Anti-Oppressive Practices* (2nd edn), which I couldn't afford and was very glad to have.

Roxanne Persaud for the sand drawings of Vanuatu.

Emma Uprichard for helpful comments on an early draft of Chapter 5.

Philomena Horsley for a very interesting and helpful conversation in Melbourne in December 2016.

All the people who agreed to be interviewed for this book, for sharing their knowledge and experience so generously.

Two sets of anonymous proposal reviewers and one set of anonymous manuscript reviewers who provided helpful suggestions and good food for thought. This is a much better book as a result of your input.

Ron Iphofen, the members of the UK and Ireland Social Research Association (SRA) ethics support group, Graham Farrant, and everyone who served on the SRA Board with me between 2012 and 2018, for helping to refine my ethical thinking.

The UK's National Centre for Research Methods for taking me on as a Visiting Fellow and for giving me writing space. In particular: Eva Nedbalova, Alex Frosch and Penny White for practical support and help; Ros Edwards for terrific mentoring in general and for pointing me to cognitive sociology in particular;

and Rachel Ayrton for the case study, and for helpful comments on an earlier draft of Chapter 1.

I would like to thank my family and my friends for their love and encouragement.

My family: Mark and Julie Miller, Ros Round, Jamie Round, Pauline Ward, Clare Miller, David Miller, Vicki Miller, Harry, Fi, Emma and Jess Miller, Bob Denyer, Lauren Denyer, Marie-Claire Denyer, John McCormack, Sophie and Joe Denyer McCormack, Anne-Louise Denyer, Lowell Black and Aaron Stevenson.

My friends: Gilly and Dave Brownhill, Carol Burns, Zoë Clarke, Su Connan, Anne and Mike Cummins, Nick Dixon, Leigh Forbes, Sue Guiney, Radhika Holmström, Hazel Larkin, Narelle Lemon, Sarah-May Matthews, Roxanne Persaud, Lucy Pickering, Janet Salmons, Wayne Thexton, Pat Thomson and Katy Vigurs.

Nik Holmes has made an immense contribution to this book despite only appreciating my writing if it's funny (spoiler: not many laughs in this one) or lucrative (with each book hope wins over experience). Sorry, love – and thanks.

Prologue

This book has three main aims. The first is to set side by side the ethics of the Euro-Western research paradigm and the ethics, or axiology, of the Indigenous research paradigm. The second is to demonstrate that research ethics does not exist in isolation but is linked with other forms of ethics, such as individual, social, institutional, professional and political ethics. The third is to raise awareness of the need for good ethical research practice at all stages of the research process.

The intention of the first aim is not to compare the two paradigms with a view to concluding that one is better than the other. Nor is it to suggest that Indigenous research needs to be compared with Euro-Western research, or to attempt to integrate the two paradigms. The Indigenous paradigm is mature and fully formed; it stands alone. Also, while there are some similarities of method and ethics, the paradigms are based on fundamentally different types of knowledge (Kovach, 2009: 31). 'Research ethics' is not a single or a universal approach in either paradigm, but a diverse collection of theories and practices (Ball and Janyst, 2008: 48). Indeed, research practice that may be ethical in one context, such as academia, may be harmful in another, such as a specific community (Brunger and Wall, 2016: 1865).

Yet it is worth learning about, and reflecting on, other ways of being with research than our own. Learning about other peoples' approaches to research and ethics can be limited by language and translation problems but, even so, I argue that this can expand researchers' options and improve our ethical practice. The benefit of drawing on both paradigms is recognised by some Indigenous researchers (Kovach, 2009: 13; Chilisa, 2012: 7; Okalik, 2013: 243; Wehipeihana et al, 2013: 283; Lambert, 2014: 8). Elder Albert Marshall, of the Mi'kmaw Nation, has named this 'Two-Eyed Seeing' (see this book's companion website: http://policypress.co.uk/resources/kara-ethics). It 'encourages that we learn to see from one eye with the best in the Indigenous ways of knowing, and from the other eye with the best in the Western (or mainstream) ways of knowing ... and, moreover, that we learn to use both these eyes together, for the benefit of all' (Bartlett et al, 2015: 283). While I am primarily writing for Euro-Western readers, I hope my work will enable researchers working in either paradigm to reflect on their ethical stance in the light of a wider range of ethical perspectives than they might otherwise consider.

The intention of the second aim is to help to enrich understandings and discussions of research ethics. In the Euro-Western literature, research ethics is commonly treated as though it exists in isolation. This is not, and cannot be, true. This book demonstrates that research ethics is unavoidably linked with other forms of ethics such as individual, social, professional, institutional and political ethics. I argue that we will be better able to act ethically as researchers if we are more aware of these links and their influences on our behaviour.

The intention of the third aim is to help Euro-Western researchers to understand that ethical considerations need to underpin research throughout. A variety of scholarly exercises have shown that the current Euro-Western system of research ethics governance, incorporating formal ethical approval, is primarily designed to protect institutions from risk (Dingwall, 2016: 27). As a result, this system focuses almost entirely on the data-gathering phase of research. The system also encourages researchers to see ethics as a discrete bureaucratic process, separate from research itself, rather than as a series of principles for continuous application. Furthermore, not all research is subject to formal governance or approval. I argue that researchers in all fields need to develop ethical knowledge and skills, to enable them to design and conduct research ethically and to manage effectively when inevitable unforeseen ethical difficulties arise.

Writers also need to be mindful of ethics. By the end of June 2016 I had done over a year's preparation for this book and was almost ready to start writing. At that stage the book was focused on the second and third aims alone. On 6 July 2016 I attended a seminar on post-colonial and Indigenous research methods at the Research Methods Festival in Bath, England. The seminar was convened by Professor Rosalind Edwards, from the University of Southampton, UK. There were three presentations: from Professor Bagele Chilisa (University of Botswana, Africa), Professor Helen Moewaka Barnes (Massey University, New Zealand) and Dr Deborah McGregor (York University, Canada). All three presenters are Indigenous researchers and their words helped me to realise that I needed to reconfigure part of my own work. I had understood, from previous reading, that decolonising methodologies constituted a transformative research framework akin to feminist, activist and participatory methodologies. I learned from Professors Chilisa and Barnes and Dr McGregor that Indigenous researchers regard Indigenous methods, which include decolonising methodologies, as belonging to a paradigm of their own. This insight led me to rethink this entire book, and to do a further year of preparation before I began to write.

This work offers a response to calls from the Indigenous research methods literature for Euro-Western scholars to include that literature on a par with our own research methods literature (Kovach, 2009: 13, 25; Graham Smith in Kovach, 2009: 88–9; Chilisa, 2012: 56; Bartlett et al, 2015: 280). After the seminar in Bath opened my eyes to the need for this, I collected and read Indigenous research methods and other Indigenous literature. There is an ethical danger here: of being extractive, that is, taking information from Indigenous communities and using it for my own benefit, as countless Euro-Western researchers have done before me (Denzin, 2005: 935; Gaudry, 2015: 244–5). I have tried to guard against this by reading Indigenous literature carefully and representing it respectfully.

I also conducted 18 in-depth interviews with researchers around the world who had a particular interest in research ethics. I offered anonymity to enable them to speak more freely about their experiences in connection with research ethics, and indeed most interviewees were very candid. Towards the end of my interviewing process one interviewee stated a preference for being named, although that person did accept anonymity when I explained that the others had all been glad of anonymity. I found interviewees from my own networks, from the networks of my networks and through social media. I did not try to interview researchers who identify as Indigenous. This was partly because I thought it would be extractive, and partly because most Indigenous researchers, understandably, prefer to support other Indigenous researchers in their struggle for self-determination than to assist privileged Euro-Western researchers. I was able to interview some Euro-Western researchers who work closely with Indigenous communities. Quotes from the interviews are used in this book to illustrate and develop points drawn from the literature and made in the text.

While writing the book I learned through social media that some Indigenous people think it is disrespectful of me even to address this topic. Also, I am sure that there are some Euro-Western people, particularly racist white people, who think this is a stupid and pointless endeavour. It certainly would be pointless if I failed to acknowledge that Euro-Western research has helped to create and perpetuate horrendous injustices affecting Indigenous peoples around the world (Wilson, 2008: 13; Kovach, 2009: 158; Millett, 2013: 318–19; Smith, 2013: 91–2; Dunbar-Ortiz, 2014: 231; Castleden et al, 2015: 1; Strega and Brown, 2015: 6; Rix et al, 2018: 7).

Today, many Euro-Western researchers are still unaware of these injustices (Ball and Janyst, 2008: 34). Also, much of Euro-Western research literature completely ignores the Indigenous paradigm (Brearley and Hamm, 2009: 38). Where Euro-Western researchers do hear of Indigenous research, they may believe it is inferior (Chilisa, 2012: 55–6; Sherwood, 2013: 210). Even some Indigenous people hold this view, having internalised it from Euro-Western teachers (Potts and Brown, 2015: 38). Euro-Western researchers who study Indigenous peoples often start from a 'deficit model', focusing on what they see as the problems, rather than looking at Indigenous peoples' strengths and their positive contributions to the world (Ball and Janyst, 2008: 37; Chilisa, 2012: 175; García et al, 2013: 368; Sherwood, 2013: 204). There is a depressingly long history of Euro-Western people researching Indigenous people around the world in ways that conveyed no benefit to the Indigenous peoples and all benefit to the Euro-Western researchers (Liamputtong, 2010: 3; Rix et al, 2018: 6–7). Also, Euro-Western research ethics often focuses inward, on the processes of the research project itself, rather than outward, on the impact the research could have on structural inequalities (Millett, 2013: 326; Smith, 2013: 96). Overall, this constitutes colonisation in practice: not as Euro-Western people commonly think of it, that is, in terms of moving into other physical territories, but colonisation as 'an attempt by the Western world to order the whole world according to Western standards' (Chilisa, 2012: 81).

In view of all this, the Indigenous research methods literature is far more respectful towards Euro-Western researchers and our methods than we deserve. Despite this, reading Indigenous research literature from a Euro-Western standpoint is uncomfortable, because it gently but inexorably makes visible colonially assembled structures that, if you read only Euro-Western literature, are invisible (Ascione, 2016: 168).

Here are two recent examples of that invisibility. First, an edited collection was published in the UK called *Research and Policy in Ethnic Relations: Compromised Dynamics in a Neoliberal Era* (Husband, 2016), which includes detailed accounts from Europe and Australia. The back cover states that one of the book's aims is to 'kick-start a wider debate about the political context of current research and policy'. Yet this book makes no mention of Indigenous peoples, and mentions colonialism only occasionally, in passing. Second, in the same year a sole-authored collection of 'brief essays on the things that matter', by the Australian philosopher and ethicist Peter Singer, was published in Australia and the US. Singer's book, *Ethics in the Real World*, has a comprehensive index which does not include the words Indigenous, Aboriginal, Torres Strait, native American, First Nation, Indian, colonial or post-colonial. There are eight essays on the rights of animals, but none on the rights of Indigenous peoples. One essay does address racism, and the author acknowledges that he learned the key fact on which the essay is based from his Black students in America (Singer, 2016: 254). Singer speaks of Australians as though they are one homogeneous group, saying 'We truly are lucky to be Australians' (Singer, 2016: 168) without any acknowledgement that some Australians are very much 'luckier' than others.

These kinds of omissions are not exceptional; they are the norm in Euro-Western research and ethics literature. This is colonialist privilege in action (Wilson, 2008: 44). It is probably mostly unintentional that Euro-Western literature serves to reaffirm colonialism (Ascione, 2016: 169), but being unintentional does not make it acceptable. I now find it astonishing that so many really clever Euro-Western people can completely ignore these issues, even though I largely did so myself until July 2016.

Gennaro Ascione is one of the few white Euro-Western scholars engaging with colonialist privilege. He identifies the links between research methods and 'the historically determined relationship between power and culture', and suggests that 'thinking the global' is aligned with 'the political and theoretical problem of how to think the colonial' (Ascione, 2016: 171). I would argue that this applies equally to research ethics. To be truly ethical, among other things Euro-Western scholars have to acknowledge colonialism, its injustices and the resulting benefits we still accrue today.

I have learned a great deal from the words of Indigenous researchers. This prologue itself was inspired by Indigenous scholars Graham Smith and Margaret Kovach (Kovach, 2009: 3). Although I have learned a lot, I am not, and never will be, an 'expert' on Indigenous matters or Indigenous research. I have not used, and would not try to use, Indigenous methods in my own research. Most of my learning about Indigenous research methods has come from books, journal articles and the internet. In writing this book, I tried to work as ethically as possible with all the literature I used in the process: to acknowledge, respect and honour the scholarship of all the authors and contributors. I aim to work within the 'ethical space' (Poole, 1972, cited in Ermine et al, 2004) that can be found in the conceptual hinterland between cultural divides (Ermine et al, 2004: 20). I am accountable for all that I have written. I am writing primarily for Euro-Western readers, although if any Indigenous people find this book useful I will be glad. I hope that my readers will take whatever they find of value in these pages and forgive my mistakes.

Part I
Research ethics in context

CHAPTER 1

Introduction

Introduction

In the real world, ethical research requires an ongoing and active engagement with people and the environment around us. This book argues that research cannot be rendered ethical by completing a one-off administrative task, and explains why and how researchers and evaluators need to work in an ethical way throughout the research process. It advocates for a move away from the 'do no harm' ethical baseline inherited from biomedical research, and towards a social justice approach to research ethics. In doing this, it draws on both the Indigenous and Euro-Western research ethics literatures. The book also draws on interviews with researchers who have an interest in ethics, and a small number of meetings with Indigenous researchers. A further source is my own experience of learning about research ethics during my postgraduate studies for an MSc in Social Research Methods and later a PhD, and my efforts to act ethically in research practice in a wide variety of contexts since 1999.

Generally speaking, social researchers and evaluators are working to make the world a better place. Indigenous researchers acknowledge this (Smith, 2013: 91), and some Euro-Western researchers do too. However, there are economically driven pressures on Euro-Western researchers to stick with 'do no harm'. This approach focuses on protecting the vulnerable, and so is easier and cheaper than the more proactive social justice approach that requires us to address the inequalities that create vulnerability (Williams, 2016: 545).

For researchers in Euro-Western societies, 'truth' is something that can be empirically verified (Alldred and Gillies, 2012: 142), while for researchers in Indigenous societies, 'truth' may exist in stories, experiences and relationships with ancestors (Chilisa, 2012: 116; Blackfoot Gallery Committee, 2013: 18). The Euro-Western approach has been to assert that our way of thinking about truth is the right way, which is in effect another imperialist attempt to colonise the world (Castleden et al, 2015: 12–13). Castleden et al, like Connell, argue that instead we need to aim for respect for and engagement with each other's knowledges between societies. In Connell's view, we need to think about social sciences, arts and humanities in global terms, and to offer to respectfully engage with each other's knowledge systems, as a basis for mutual learning (Connell, 2007: 224). I would build on this to argue that we also need to aim to respectfully engage with each other's knowledges *within* societies as a basis for mutual learning.

Research ethics is rarely a question of right and wrong; it's more a matter of finding a multi-dimensional equivalent of the 'line of best fit'. This book aims to show why research ethics involves more disagreements than agreements and more debate than consensus (de Vries and Henley, 2014: 84). Even the choice of a word can have ethical implications. For example, some Indigenous people are unhappy with the term 'Indigenous' being used to describe them (Passingan, 2013: 361). One danger is that using a single term in this way gives the impression that Indigenous peoples are one homogeneous group, which is certainly not the case (Wilson, 2008: 106; Kovach, 2009: 5; Cram, Chilisa and Mertens, 2013: 21; Ignacio, 2013: 162; Lambert, 2014: 38; Puebla, 2014: 176; Blalock, 2015: 59–61; Bowman, Francis and Tyndall, 2015: 344; Rix et al, 2018: 3). The term itself is contested, so for the avoidance of doubt I am using 'Indigenous' to mean peoples native to lands that have been colonised by settlers from other nations (Cram, Chilisa and Mertens, 2013: 16; Lambert, 2014: 1). Following Linda Tuhiwai Smith's example (2012: 7), I will use the term 'Indigenous peoples' to reflect multiplicity, and 'Indigenous' to reflect the global aspect of my work. Where I refer to a specific nation, community or tribe, I will use its own name.

This book situates the ethical researcher at the centre of a network of connected factors that affect ethical decisions, as shown in Figure 1. Of course this diagram, like all diagrams, is an over-simplification. It would be justifiable to connect each element of the diagram with every other element, but that would make it very hard to read. Also, it is a diagram created from a Euro-Western perspective, as it has an individual researcher placed at the centre. Such a diagram created from an Indigenous perspective might look very different.

Figure 1: The ethical researcher

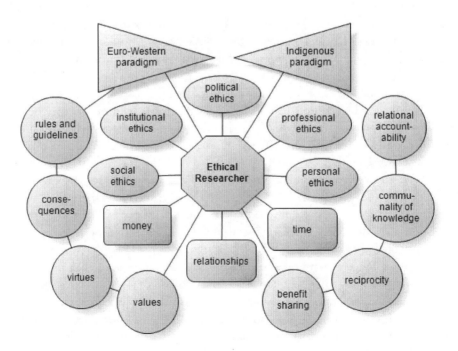

The following case study will show some aspects of how this can work in practice. It is the story of a Euro-Western doctoral student's research in South Sudan, Liberia and Uganda. Although the story is quite long, I have included it in full, as it is a very useful illustration of the interactions and intersections between individual, institutional, social, professional, political and research ethics.

Case study

Rachel Ayrton's background is in community development, where she chose to work because of her own deep-seated concerns about local and global issues of injustice and inequality. These in turn were informed by her Christian faith. Rachel wanted to work internationally, but that is hard to get into, so she started in the UK to get experience. She developed skills in working across differences within UK communities, as an outsider, fostering the values of community development such as self-determination. She learned that it was possible to facilitate something valuable happening for people without doing it for them, and that being an outsider could be helpful in that role. Some community leaders were unable to take a neutral position because they were so embedded in their communities, whereas Rachel was able to encourage without directing.

She also did a couple of short stints of grassroots volunteering overseas, but chose not to continue with that because she concluded that it was more valuable for her than for the people she had intended to help. She decided that she wouldn't work overseas again until she had professional skills to offer, and she thought social research skills might be useful. She had developed a particular interest in sub-Saharan Africa in general and South Sudan in particular, and for her PhD she wanted to study how trust operates in post-conflict zones. She was aware of the impact of colonialism, and of her position as a white British woman. Her experience of community development work in the UK had led to a firmly held conviction that it was possible for her to do ethical research within communities in Africa by developing respectful and productive relationships, and by maintaining a continual and iterative ethical engagement with her work.

Doing this as a doctoral student, though, raised another ethical issue. Rachel had learned, from her community development work, that it was possible to do worthwhile work in communities, as an outsider, without being extractive or abusive or self-serving. However, doing research in communities for an educational qualification had the potential to confer great advantage on Rachel, raising her status massively within South Sudanese society and to some extent in UK society too. South Sudanese people value education highly, and so would be sympathetic to Rachel's cause. This was an interesting dilemma for Rachel, which she intended to solve by ensuring, as far as she was able, that the research she did had maximum potential benefit for her participants and for wider South Sudanese society.

Rachel had done some fieldwork in South Sudan for her MSc dissertation, and had developed relationships with South Sudanese colleagues and friends. While aspects of the role of British colonisers in South Sudan were without doubt morally questionable, the South Sudanese people Rachel met had a lot of positive things to say about the British influences in their country, as well as negative things. This made Rachel feel that being British wasn't as loaded in South Sudan as it would be in other parts of sub-Saharan Africa. Also, being an outsider seemed useful, because everyone in South Sudanese society was implicated by identity in the networks of the Second Sudanese Civil War, which had ended after 22 years in 2005. Rachel was not completely untouched by these networks, because they affected her contacts who introduced her to potential field sites and participants, but she was not implicated by her own identity.

Altogether, South Sudan seemed an obvious place for Rachel to do her doctoral fieldwork: in particular, the city of Juba. In many ways the research would have been better done by a South Sudanese researcher, but opportunities and funding for South Sudanese researchers are very scarce, while Rachel had access to a studentship for her doctoral research. Also, there was little empirical research on South Sudan, which had gained its independence in 2011, becoming the youngest country in the world. Partly for this reason, there was no formal system of research ethics governance for social research within South Sudan.

The South Sudanese people Rachel had spoken with while she was doing her MSc fieldwork were supportive of her research aspirations, stating their belief that her proposed investigation of trust would be important for peace and reconciliation in their country. She made a plan, then, with the help and approval of local people, and a commitment to come back and see it through. In the interests of fulfilling these commitments, Rachel began learning Sudanese Arabic, not because she intended to conduct her research in that language but to help her communicate with people while she was there. Her South Sudanese tutor was so supportive of her proposed work that he sometimes waived his fees when she was in financial difficulty, and took pains to teach her about South Sudanese culture and politics as well as the language.

During the first year of her PhD, Rachel had to suspend her doctoral study for a while, due to outstanding professional commitments. The day before she was due to resume her studies and begin the process of applying for ethical approval from the University of Southampton, a new civil war broke out in South Sudan, beginning with fighting in Juba. This was heartbreaking for Rachel, who was desperately worried about her friends and contacts. Initially it seemed that the conflict might be short lived and containable, but in time it became apparent that it would be a longer-lived crisis. The UK government's Foreign and Commonwealth Office (FCO) gave South Sudan a red rating, which meant that Rachel could not travel there, because her university could not insure her for travel to anywhere that didn't have a green rating. She considered doing her fieldwork with South Sudanese refugees in Uganda, or with South Sudanese people in the UK, but in the end she decided to take her supervisors' advice and choose a different country. This led to some difficult conversations with South Sudanese people, particularly her Sudanese Arabic tutor, whom Rachel did not want to disappoint.

It was also difficult for Rachel to work out where to go instead. She chose to stay in sub-Saharan Africa because she had some knowledge of the region, and looked at conflict data to help her make a shortlist of possible countries. There were also some pragmatic factors: she didn't have time to learn another language, so she needed to choose a country that used English or French for administration, and of course it had to have a green rating from the FCO. While Rachel was doing this work, she had a stroke of luck: a good friend was able to put her in touch with a senior member of staff at the International Federation of Red Cross and Red Crescent Societies (IFRC) who agreed to facilitate contact with the national Red Cross Society in the country she chose. A formal partnership agreement was made between Southampton University and the IFRC on this basis.

The country Rachel chose was Liberia, which again had no formalised system of social research ethics governance. She designed her research, and receiving ethical approval from the University of Southampton was straightforward. She also managed to secure funding for a short orientation and planning trip to Liberia in July 2014. The Liberia National Red Cross Society was very supportive, assigning a member of staff to answer Rachel's questions and help her as far as possible. Rachel identified two communities for her fieldwork: she met local leaders in one, and local Red Cross staff in the other, who helped her to begin to plan her fieldwork. One potential fieldwork site that was under discussion was in Lofa County in the north-west of Liberia, but Rachel and her Red Cross colleagues decided against it because a serious but apparently localised outbreak of the Ebola virus was centred on that area. By the following month the Ebola crisis had taken hold throughout the country and it became apparent, once again, that Rachel couldn't do the fieldwork she had planned, or honour the commitments she had made to local people.

Due to extenuating circumstances, Rachel was able to negotiate an extension to her doctoral funding: technically it was a six-month extension, but as it took two months to negotiate, it was only a four-month extension in practice. The extension enabled her to make a final attempt to do fieldwork in sub-Saharan Africa, this time in northern Uganda. One of her supervisors had a former student who was now an academic in Kampala, and he was able to put Rachel in touch with another academic in the north of the country, close to the border with South Sudan. The conflict between the Ugandan government and the Lord's Resistance Army spanned the border between northern regions of Uganda and South Sudan. One of the participants in Rachel's MSc research had been displaced by this conflict, so she felt as though she was getting close to where she'd started. However, she didn't have the resources to make an exploratory trip to Uganda, and it was difficult to work with people whom she hadn't met, or to work remotely with people who usually work face to face.

Also, unlike South Sudan or Liberia, Uganda benefits from a system of research governance, and Rachel had to apply for ethical approval in Uganda. There are not many research ethics committees; there was one at the university in Kampala that Rachel could have reached with the help of her contact there, but as she planned to do her fieldwork in the north of the country, she decided it was more ethical to approach a local committee. Although the administrator there was helpful, the process was quite opaque. There was uncertainty about whether Rachel would need to go and present her research in person, which she couldn't afford to do, because if they had asked for changes she would have had to wait another month, and she had neither the time nor the money. There was apparently a system of expedited review, but nobody could tell Rachel what the criteria were to qualify for that system. Then they said that her work could qualify if she had her materials translated into the local languages, and offered to arrange that, which she accepted; however, there were a number of delays due to difficulties in communicating by e-mail, with messages failing to arrive in both directions. As a result, Rachel's extension was used up and so were two more months, and she reached the point where she simply didn't have time to travel for fieldwork if she was to complete her PhD.

Ethics interactions

The story of Rachel's attempts to do fieldwork in sub-Saharan Africa has a lot to teach us about how research ethics can interact with political, professional, social, institutional and individual ethics.

Sub-Saharan Africa is a highly politicised region, and the impact of colonisation by various countries is still strongly and widely felt. Rachel was aware of how this interacted with her plans and her work in South Sudan and Liberia. Her proposed research initially found political favour in both countries, but civil wars and health crises are political situations that cause political change. The UK government, too, directly affected Rachel's research by changing its guidance on South Sudan, and later Liberia, from green to red, in response to the civil war and the Ebola outbreak, respectively. These changes were ethical decisions on the part of the UK government, designed to help protect the safety and welfare of UK citizens.

Social ethics, too, came into play here. Rachel was keenly aware of how the civil war in South Sudan and the Ebola outbreak in Liberia were affecting those societies. In particular, even if there had not been barriers due to threats to life or institutional ethics, Rachel was clear that it would have been inappropriate to try to do her fieldwork in those countries when they were in crisis. Research questions that people regard as important in times of peace and health are not regarded as important in times of war or sickness. As Rachel put it, "People didn't need some white girl coming round asking questions that had nothing to do with their current crisis" (personal communication, 1 February 2017).

In terms of professional ethics, Rachel worked within the 2009 National Occupational Standards for Community Development. These are underpinned by five key values that were developed through extensive consultation: equality and anti-discrimination, social justice, collective action, community empowerment and working and learning together (Lifelong Learning UK, 2009: 5–7). The case study above shows that these values are a close fit with Rachel's approach to her work, particularly in South Sudan.

Institutional ethics also played its part, particularly when the University of Southampton was unable to insure Rachel to travel, first to South Sudan and then to Liberia, for her fieldwork. Most insurance companies are profit-making private sector institutions, for which ethical practice involves making enough money to compensate the shareholders who support the business. Therefore insurers will not offer insurance when the risk is too great. For the University of Southampton, it would be unethical to allow a doctoral student to travel abroad for fieldwork without insurance, because providing insurance cover is part of the University's duty of care to its students.

Rachel's individual ethical stance of wanting to redress injustice and inequality attracted her to working with communities in the UK and overseas. Her work with such communities sharpened her focus on issues of trust in post-conflict zones. While she was a doctoral student, she made the ethical decision to suspend her studies for some weeks, despite deadline pressures, to concentrate on fundraising to help people in West Africa caught up in the Ebola crisis. Rachel's own ethical position has led her to feel indebted to people who offered to help her in South Sudan and in Liberia, and to feel strongly, still, that she needs to fulfil the commitments she made to them as soon as she is able to do so.

Ethics and methods

Some researchers argue that ethics is method and method is ethics. It seems to me that, for the purposes of discussion and consideration, it is more useful to think of ethics and method separately. Having said that, there are areas of overlap. For example, some methods are more ethical than others – and some are positively unethical. For example, coercing or forcing people to take part in research is, technically, a recruitment method. However, you won't find it in any research methods textbook, because it is unethical – although, sadly, it does happen (Cox and McDonald, 2013: 227). In other cases, a method that is ethical in one context may not be ethical in another. For example, it might be perfectly ethical to use a paper-based survey to investigate satisfaction levels among users of a tennis club, but unethical to use the same method to investigate satisfaction levels among users of a club for people with visual impairments. Conversely, in some situations there are methodical ways to approach research ethics, such as when planning a research project and trying to think through the ethical issues you might encounter at each stage of the process (see Chapter 6 for more on this). So, rather than saying 'ethics is method and method is ethics', I'd say 'ethics supports method, and method should be ethical'. It's not as glib, but, for me, it's more useful.

Another argument I take issue with is that ethics is more relevant, necessary or important for qualitative than for quantitative researchers. Some argue that qualitative research ethics is unique (Tolich, 2016: 33), although this is in fact a reaction to research ethics committees/institutional review boards trying to impose regulation designed for quantitative research onto qualitative research, where it does not fit. Quantitative researchers, just as much as qualitative researchers, need to think through the ethical issues associated with planning research, setting it in context, gathering and analysing data, reporting, presenting and disseminating their findings. So I would argue that quantitative researchers have as much to learn from this book as qualitative researchers – and I am not alone in thinking this way. For example, there is a move among both some Euro-Western and some Indigenous quantitative researchers to promote reflexivity in their work (Shimp, 2007: 154; Walter and Andersen, 2016: 50; Cluver et al, 2014: 53), despite this being more commonly seen as an option for qualitative researchers to enhance their ethical approach. Reflexivity has been described by a Euro-Western researcher as 'critical analysis of the theoretical, methodological, disciplinary, personal or practical issues which affect the research process' (Dean, 2017: 147). One Indigenous view is that 'It is important to acknowledge one's personal subjectivity in the research one is undertaking ... Through the acknowledgement of one's bias, we are ensuring that our perspectives are not hidden' (Sherwood, 2013: 211). Reflexivity will be discussed in more detail in Chapters 6 and 9. The next section gives a reflexive account of my motivations for writing this book.

Reflexivity in practice

Most Indigenous researchers, and Euro-Western researchers who practise reflexivity, agree that the researcher needs to appear as an agent within research (Wilson, 2008: 32; Kovach, 2009: 49–50; Dean, 2017: 147). Indigenous and Euro-Western researchers go about this in different ways. For many Indigenous researchers, it is important to introduce and locate themselves so that their readers can locate them geographically, socially, conceptually and in other ways too (Wilson, 2008: 12; Kovach, 2009: 110–12; Lambert, 2014: 38). For Euro-Western researchers who practise reflexivity, it is important to put themselves into the research, or at least those bits of themselves that are relevant to the project (Dean, 2017: 147). As a Euro-Western researcher, this is the approach I will follow.

Initially I wanted to write this book because I felt frustrated by the way research ethics can be compartmentalised within the Euro-Western paradigm. This is usually demonstrated through the well-rehearsed example of formal ethical approval requirements leading to researchers 'ticking the ethics box' and then ignoring ethics until the next project. It is also evident in books on research methods and ethics, which often treat ethics (and, indeed, methods) as a discrete 'thing' that is somehow separate from other aspects of research and life. While part of this is the linguistic problem of the way words categorise and distinguish aspects of our world, that is not, I think, the whole story.

I am not writing this book because I am some kind of ethical paragon, or because I want to set myself up as an ethics guru. I am interested in and aware of ethics, in research and more widely, and I try to make ethical choices in my life.

I wonder whether my interest in ethics is partly because I'm privileged and not privileged. On the one hand, I am white, British, middle class and tall, all of which confer privilege. On the other hand, I am female, bisexual and disabled, which reduce privilege. (If you are interested in reflecting on your own dimensions of privilege, there is a link to a useful 'privilege calculator' online.) Embodying this complex terrain means I feel like an outsider in almost every situation. I think this is useful in helping me to value, observe and analyse the ethical dimensions of life in general and research in particular. I am aware of my own ethical failures, and I also know that, sometimes, there is no good ethical choice to make. Political, social and institutional structures, and individual attributes, can combine to create situations in which it may be impossible to act ethically.

Including the Indigenous paradigm in a Euro-Western book may be one of those situations. In using the work of Indigenous researchers and authors to benefit my own work, I risk recolonising research ethics (Land, 2015: 26) by absorbing the Indigenous paradigm within a Euro-Western work (Wilson, 2008: 17). Yet I am also responding to calls from some Indigenous scholars for Euro-Western researchers to share, rather than claim, the intellectual space (Smith, 2012: 202). And I am responding to my own interest in Indigenous research. My relationship with Indigenous research is that of a student, with Indigenous researchers as my teachers; mostly through their writings and occasionally through their talk.

Indigenous researchers use and write about theories and techniques from the Euro-Western paradigm. It is not the same when Euro-Western researchers use and write about Indigenous theories and techniques, because the balance of power is so asymmetrical (Castleden et al, 2015: 1). However, writing yet another book on research ethics that completely ignores the Indigenous paradigm does not seem ethical either.

The more I learned about Indigenous research and ethics, the more compelled I felt to include that learning in my work. Yet the question of how to do that ethically was always with me. My aim is to acknowledge and respect Indigenous literature by reading carefully and representing the points made as fully and fairly as I can. From my position between the rock of potential recolonisation and the hard place of continuing to ignore the Indigenous paradigm, I think this is the least unethical choice I can make.

Structure of this book

This book is divided into two parts. Broadly, Part I is intended to equip researchers with useful knowledge about research ethics and how it works in the world. Part II builds on this knowledge to help researchers develop ethical skills for use at all stages of the research process. So, to put it very simply, Part I is the 'what' and Part II is the 'how' of research ethics.

Part I of this book comprises the first five chapters. Chapter 2 looks at the ethics of Indigenous research, and Chapter 3 considers the ethics of Euro-Western research. The aim is to set these paradigms side by side, not in competition but for the purposes of learning from a wider knowledge base than either can provide alone.

Chapters 4 and 5 are case studies of arenas where individual, social, institutional, professional and political ethics interact with research ethics. Chapter 4 discusses research ethics governance and review, and Chapter 5 reviews evaluation research. This is a type of research that rarely requires formal ethical approval, and the points made in the chapter may be relevant for other types of research that are not subject to research ethics review.

Part II of this book begins with Chapter 6, which describes how to plan a research project ethically. The next six chapters show how to work ethically in context-setting and literature reviews, data gathering and analysis, reporting, presentation and dissemination of research.

Chapter 13 is about ethical aftercare, and Chapter 14 is about researcher well-being. These are facets of research that are rarely discussed, yet vital to take into consideration.

This book's companion website (http://policypress.co.uk/resources/kara-ethics) includes online resources for students and teachers, and scenario-based exercises to assist with learning and teaching ethics in practice.

Conclusion

Research ethics is a multi-faceted, endlessly fascinating subject. It is linked with how we make and use laws, how we care for others and how we earn and spend money. Ethics in general runs through our lives like blood through our bodies: mostly invisible, but constantly functioning and affecting everything we do. Although it may not always be obvious, there is an ethical dimension to most – perhaps all – of the decisions we make and the acts we perform. In research, ethics underpins every stage of the process, and permeates our relationships with participants, colleagues, commissioners, funders and others. Therefore researchers need to be aware of ethical theories and principles, and of our own blind spots and values. Also, we need to be skilled in applying ethics in our work. This applies to quantitative and mixed-methods researchers just as much as to qualitative researchers (Cluver et al, 2014: 53).

This is a small book to tackle such large issues, which inevitably means some topics receive only an overview while others are discussed in more depth. The book's companion website (http://policypress.co.uk/resources/kara-ethics) contains resources to help compensate for some of these imbalances.

REFLECTIVE QUESTIONS

1. What do you want to achieve by reading this book?
2. Think of an ethical difficulty you have faced in the past (whether in a research project or not), and consider how you dealt with the problem. Would you do the same again today, or something different? Why?
3. How does your own individual ethics interact with one or more of: social, professional, institutional or political ethics? What are the implications of this?
4. Do you think research ethics involves different principles from other forms of ethics, or do you think the same ethical principles underpin all actions and interactions? Why?
5. In what ways are you privileged, and in what ways are you not privileged? How does this affect your ethical position?

CHAPTER 2

Indigenous research and ethics

Introduction

Many Euro-Western researchers have not heard of Indigenous research. In my view, this needs to change, for two main reasons.

1. Indigenous research and researchers have been oppressed and marginalised from the birth of colonial history to the present day. Continuing to ignore the work of Indigenous researchers effectively colludes with this oppression and marginalisation.
2. Indigenous research is a long-standing system of thought and action which includes ideas that are unusual to most Euro-Western researchers. Reflecting on this system and its ideas can be educational for Euro-Western researchers.

This book is informed by Indigenous research literature, interviews with some Euro-Western researchers who work with Indigenous researchers and direct contact with a small number of Indigenous researchers. However, I am not an expert on Indigenous research; only Indigenous researchers can be experts in their field. I am a student of Indigenous research methods and ethics, and I find that Indigenous researchers have much to teach me through their written and spoken words.

When I assert that reflecting on Indigenous research can be educational for Euro-Western researchers, I do not mean that Euro-Western researchers can learn to *do* Indigenous research. I would never attempt to conduct, or claim to have conducted, Indigenous research. Euro-Western researchers can think about such things as:

- a holistic style of thought and life which is very different from our ways of segmenting and compartmentalising;
- a different ontological and epistemological mindset which may shed useful light on our own;
- egalitarian methods which might be transferable to some types of research such as participatory or activist research;
- an approach to research ethics based on the Indigenous way of life and mindset which provides nourishing food for thought.

Here are some of the words used by Indigenous researchers from around the world to describe their research.

The ways of Indigenous research are as old as the hills and the valleys, the mountains and the seas, and the deserts and the lakes that Indigenous people bind themselves to as their places of belonging. It is not that Indigenous people are anti-research. They have always conducted research. (Cram, Chilisa and Mertens, 2013: 11)

[R]egardless of the topic, Indigenous research is about some kind of recovery, renewal, and reawakening. (Meyer, 2013: 252)

Indigenous research … is the knowing and respectful reinforcement that all things are related and connected. It is the voice from our ancestors that tell us when it is right and when it is not. Indigenous research *is* a life-changing ceremony. (Wilson, 2008: 60–1, original emphasis)

Indigenous research methodologies differ from the Western approach because they flow from a place, an Indigenous place, a tribe, a community. They flow from place-based tribal knowledge. (Lambert, 2014: 18)

[T]here are different categories of Indigenous methodologies. These should not be conflated, but rather recognized for the strengths each brings and the specificity of the contexts in which they apply. Categorizing Indigenous methodologies as a homogeneous group risks essentializing Indigenous peoples even more than we do now. (Walter and Andersen, 2016: 62–3)

Indigenous methodologies … calls for the non-Indigenous scholar to adjourn disbelief and, in the pause, consider alternative possibilities. (Kovach, 2009: 29)

Where Euro-Western research literature acknowledges Indigenous research, it often concludes that Indigenous research stems from Euro-Western philosophy. In fact the Indigenous research paradigm pre-dates the Euro-Western paradigm by tens of thousands of years (Cram, Chilisa and Mertens, 2013: 11; Passingan, 2013: 361; Steere, 2013: 388–391; Wilson and Wilson, 2013: 333). Every Indigenous culture involves some form of research (Kouritzin and Nakagawa, 2018: 9). Mi'kmaw Elder Murdena Marshall says: 'prior to the arrival of Europeans, the Mi'kmaw people were the scientists of Atlantic Canada – they had rich and complex knowledge about the medicines, plants, and animals in their waters, lands, and skies and they transmitted and enriched this knowledge, generation to generation, via highly effective, traditional modes of teaching and learning within stories, ceremonies, and mentoring' (Bartlett et al, 2015: 291).

Talking about Indigenous methods and methodologies might pique the interest of Euro-Western researchers who are keen to find new tools for their methodological toolbox. However, Indigenous methods are not often applicable to Euro-Western research, and Indigenous methodologies can no more be separated from their context than a river from the land on which it flows. What is useful for Euro-Western researchers is to learn and think about Indigenous methods and methodologies for the light they shine upon our own. In my view this is particularly useful when it comes to ethics.

Indigenous ontology, epistemology, knowledge and theory

Ontology refers to people's knowledge and beliefs about our world, and epistemology is the study of the nature of knowledge. In the Indigenous paradigm, epistemology and ontology are seen as relational (Chilisa, 2012: 20), culturally based (Wilson, 2008: 91) and belonging to communities rather than individuals (Wilson, 2008: 38). While there is great diversity among Indigenous peoples, and a range of place-based epistemological positions, there are also claims in the literature that Indigenous peoples worldwide have a common ontology (Wilson, 2008: 73; Kovach, 2009: 37). This is a holistic worldview in which everything is connected and related to everything else (Lambert, 2014: 18–19). From an Indigenous perspective, focusing only on one aspect of the world, such as humans, can be described as 'not ontologically sound' (Kouritzin and Nakagawa, 2018: 11).

Indigenous epistemology can be viewed as having three elements: knowledge (which exists outside of people), knowing (which exists inside people and results from direct experience) and understanding (knowing translated into thought, which may also lead to action) (Meyer, 2013: 256). This is different from Euro-Western research, which does not value, and sometimes does not even recognise, knowing in the form of internal experiential 'inward knowledges' (Kovach, 2009: 126–7). Also, in Indigenous epistemology, spiritual knowledge is often viewed as being on a par with mental, physical, emotional and other kinds of knowledge (Wilson, 2008: 89; Chilisa, 2012: 114). This leads to 'ethical principles that nurture harmony among people and to a relational accountability that emphasizes responsibility of the researchers and the participants to each other and the rest of the community, reciprocity, and rights of the researched to knowledge produced' (Chilisa, 2012: 122).

Indigenous knowledge is rooted in local communities and is not underpinned by colonial or imperial power (Chilisa, 2012: 99). It stems from Indigenous standpoints, and is assessed against Indigenous standards (Gaudry, 2015: 249; Walter and Andersen, 2016: 85). Indigenous knowledge is holistic (Okalik, 2013: 243) and is passed on orally from one generation to the next (Koitsiwe, 2013: 264). Knowledge may reside within people, stories, songs, dances, rituals, the natural world and dreams, among other things (Chilisa, 2012: 99; Walker, 2013: 308). However, although knowledge may reside within people, it is not generally seen as belonging to individual people, but as belonging collectively to groups, tribes, communities or the cosmos of which all these are a part (Wilson, 2008: 38). There are many ways of gaining or developing knowledge, which may include participating in ceremonies or dances, fasting and dreaming (Kovach, 2009: 66–7). There is little debate about subjectivity and objectivity; most Indigenous scholars agree that subjectivity is fundamental to, and permeates, Indigenous knowledge (Kovach, 2009: 111).

Theory in the Indigenous literature is treated very differently from theory in the Euro-Western literature (see Chapter 3 for more on this). Umbrella terms such as 'Southern theory' (Connell, 2007) or 'postcolonial theory' (Chilisa, 2012: 49) are used to describe a range of theories. Unlike Euro-Western social theories, these theories all acknowledge and discuss the impact of colonialism and imperialism on people's systems and understandings of knowing (Chilisa, 2012: 48; Smith, 2012: 61). They also acknowledge the existence of Euro-Western theories, a courtesy that is rarely extended in reverse (Connell, 2007: 105). Yet social theories have been, and are being, developed by Indigenous peoples in 'the global periphery' (Connell 2007: viii), which includes countries and continents such as Australia, Africa, Iran, India and Latin America. Indigenous theories cannot necessarily be transplanted into other cultural contexts (Connell, 2007: 96). Like Euro-Western theories, they have arisen from the preoccupations of a particular time and place. Unlike many Euro-Western social theories, Indigenous theoretical perspectives do not generally address ethics directly. However, when applied to research, they prioritise the interests and voices of marginalised groups and relate to wider concerns of social justice (Tikly and Bond, 2013: 435).

Ethics and axiology

Much of the Indigenous research methods literature uses the term 'axiology' where the Euro-Western literature more commonly uses 'ethics'. Axiology is a wider term than ethics, describing 'the branch of philosophy that deals with the nature of ethics, aesthetics, and religion ... and their role in the construction of knowledge' (Chilisa, 2012: 21–2). For Chilisa, this puts axiology on a par with ontology and epistemology. Axiology privileges values such as relational accountability, respect and reciprocity (Wilson, 2008: 77; Chilisa, 2012: 22).

Some Euro-Western scholars of ethics see values as barely relevant. For example, virtue ethicists tend to regard values as an individual frame of reference whose use in research is optional, rather than something that can be shared between people or used to create an ethical framework for a group or community (Macfarlane, 2009: 32; Carpenter, 2018: 40). This offers an interesting contrast with some Indigenous scholars for whom 'research can never exist in a value free zone', while values are 'an unavoidable feature of research practice' (Walter and Andersen, 2016: 50). Of course some Euro-Western scholars, such as feminist researchers, take a similar view (Gillies and Alldred, 2012: 45; Hesse-Biber, 2014: 5). Other Euro-Western ethicists give more prominence to values, but define them differently, such as by distinguishing between 'intrinsic values', specific to the research process, and 'extrinsic values' that are not research-specific but nevertheless affect the ways in which research is, or can be, conducted (Hammersley and Traianou, 2012: 36–7). Alternatively, for the Indigenous researchers Walter and Andersen, extrinsic and intrinsic values are 'concepts that are palpably part of methodology, *all* methodology' (2013: 49; original emphasis). A tiny minority of Euro-Western researchers have begun to privilege values such as relationality and accountability (for example, Doucet and Mauthner, 2012: 132; Warren, 2014: 65; Kuntz, 2015: 75). (See Chapter 3 for more on Euro-Western ethics.)

In a seminal paper on the ethics of Aboriginal research, Marlene Brant-Castellano used a tree as a symbol to represent 'the relationships between individual behaviour, customs and community protocols, ethics, values, and world view' (2004: 100). The leaves represented individual behaviours. The upper branches represented protocols and customs, and the lower branches represented ethics and rules governing relationships. The trunk of the tree above ground represented values and deeply held beliefs about good and evil. The trunk below ground represented worldview or conception of reality, and the roots represented the earth that supports us and the unseen world of spirit. This is a useful depiction of a broad and holistic approach to axiology such as that taken by many Indigenous researchers.

Indigenous research ethics

Ethics in the Indigenous research paradigm is as pervasive as ethics in the Euro-Western paradigm, albeit with a rather different flavour. For example, Indigenous ethics tends to be place based, recognising the intimate relationship between Indigenous peoples and the lands in which they live (Coulthard, 2014: 72).

As well as a common ontology, there are significant commonalities in the ethical principles used by many Indigenous research communities around the world. Some of the literature suggests that four key ethical principles form the basis of much Indigenous ethical research practice (Chilisa, 2012: 22; Wilson and Wilson, 2013: 343). These principles are:

1. relational accountability
2. communality of knowledge
3. reciprocity
4. benefit sharing

Relational accountability acknowledges that 'research happens in relationships between people' (Potts and Brown, 2015: 33). Researchers are regarded as accountable to all who are in relationship with them and with the research. Those who are in relationship with researchers are not only other living humans, but may also be, for example, animals, ancestors, the land, the cosmos, the research itself, ideas and dreams (Chilisa, 2012: 20–1, 122). Not all Indigenous peoples have the same views of this; for example, the Plains Cree people of Canada have different traditional beliefs about dreams from the Māori people of New Zealand (Kovach, 2009: 58).

It seems to be generally accepted in Indigenous research that researchers will have relationships with research participants that were established long before the research takes place and will continue long after (Kovach, 2009: 51; Kouritzin and Nakagawa, 2018: 10) (see Chapter 13 for more on aftercare). The quality of these relationships is viewed as more important than the research. So, a researcher, working in accordance with the principle of relational accountability, has to ask themselves how their research work will help to maintain and develop the relationships on which that research is built (Wilson, 2008: 119).

Cora Weber-Pillwax (2001), cited by Chilisa (2012: 118), suggests that researchers working with relational accountability should consider questions such as the following.

1. Which research methods can be used that would help to build respectful relationships between the topic of study and the researcher?
2. Which research methods can be used that would help to build respectful relationships between the researcher and the research participants?
3. How can the researcher relate respectfully with participants so they can form strong relationships together?
4. To what extent is the researcher responsibly fulfilling their role and obligations to the participants, the topic and all of the Indigenous relations?

Communality of knowledge recognises that everyone has valuable knowledge to contribute to research. Chilisa (2012: 116) says: 'Knowers are seen as beings with connections to other beings, the spirits of the ancestors, and the world around them that inform what they know and how they can know it.' Knowledge generated from research is understood as belonging to everyone. For most Indigenous researchers, knowledge cannot be owned because it is part of the relationships between people (Wilson, 2008: 121) – and not only people, but also ancestors, the land, ideas – effectively everything (Chilisa, 2012: 116; Rix et al, 2018: 8). In summary, knowledge is relational (Gaudry, 2015: 255).

Reciprocity means that relationships and exchanges should be mutual. For many Indigenous researchers, this is an obligation that comes with relationships (Sherwood, 2013: 216). As always in the Indigenous paradigm, these relationships are not limited to those between people. They include, for example, relationships that people have with the environment. Within such relationships reciprocity involves never taking more than you need from the land and its animals for nourishment, shelter, entertainment, medication, clothing and so on, and giving back care and respect to the environment in return (Johnson, 2013: 201).

Benefit sharing means that participants and communities should benefit from research as much as researchers do. Giving back to communities and participants is a central principle of Indigenous research methods (Lambert, 2014: 65). This should be done in a way that is useful to communities and participants, which requires the researcher to be in relationship with those communities and participants so that they can find out what will be useful for them (Kovach, 2009: 82).

We can see that all of these principles of Indigenous axiology – relational accountability, communality of knowledge, reciprocity and benefit sharing – are linked with each other. This is a holistic, egalitarian ethical approach which recognises research as a key element of community building and social change, rather than as something that exists within time-limited projects (Potts and Brown, 2015: 37). For some Indigenous researchers, the journey is as important as the destination (Bowman, Francis and Tyndall, 2015: 344; Kovach, 2015: 52). However, although this is not currently acknowledged in any Indigenous research literature I have found, I understand that not all Indigenous researchers follow Indigenous or other ethical principles (McGregor, 2018). Also, although the literature is clear that these common principles exist, that doesn't mean all Indigenous people think or act in the same way. Even within a single community or tribe there may be disagreements or factions (Rodriguez-Lonebear, 2016: 255).

The Indigenous approach doesn't negate issues of power, but recognises that within a relationship of unequal power, ethical safety is more likely to be achieved by developing interdependence and trust (Gray et al, 2017: 24). However, Euro-Western researchers have found that reciprocity, in particular, can have negative and even dangerous results if attempted within a relationship of unequal power (Israel, 2015: 137–8). So, while Euro-Western researchers can learn from Indigenous principles, those principles cannot necessarily be transferred wholesale to Euro-Western research contexts.

Care for the land, the environment, the natural world and human communities is at the core of Indigenous ethics (Wilson and Wilson, 2013: 350). Unlike most Euro-Western researchers, the Indigenous literature suggests that Indigenous researchers do not differentiate between ethics for individuals or communities, work or leisure, regarding the same ethical principles as applicable throughout (Kouritzin and Nakagawa, 2018: 9). (Although of course individual Indigenous researchers and scholars have choices here, just as Euro-Westerners do.) Also in the Indigenous paradigm, with its holistic approach, different types of ethics, such as individual, social and institutional ethics, are not separated. This feeds into Indigenous research ethics, in that 'an Indigenous research framework must not solely be an intellectual construct, for it cannot be understood in the absence of its practical manifestations, which involve living life in a way that reflects goodness' (Kovach, 2009: 63).

In the Indigenous paradigm individual and social ethics are inextricably linked. Chilisa (2012: 194) explains the *ubuntu* worldview prevailing in her native Botswana: 'I am because we are, I am we, and we are because I am.' This has implications for research in communities who share that ontology. For example, one implication is that informed consent becomes a process rather than an event, and is multi-faceted, involving individual, community, group and collective consent (Chilisa, 2012: 196) (see Chapter 7 for more on this). Māori researchers in New Zealand take a similar approach, because consent there is relational, given by one person to another because of the trust between them, rather than for a specific project or set of questions (Smith, 2012: 137). There is an assumption within these approaches that consent will be negotiated and renegotiated as necessary. So, consent in much Indigenous research is a dynamic process rather than a static event (Potts and Brown, 2015: 27). (See Chapter 8 for more on consent.)

National censuses and Indigenous research

It is evident that the Euro-Western and Indigenous research paradigms are very different from each other. This can cause problems when the paradigms collide. National census research provides an example of such collision.

Most Indigenous researchers are keenly aware of the political nature of research (Kovach, 2009: 24; Potts and Brown, 2015: 25) and often link research explicitly with work for positive social change (Smith, 2013: 95). By contrast, some Euro-Western researchers reify the concepts of objectivity and impartiality in research. For example, the US, Australian and UK governments all claim that their census research will be objective and impartial (US Government, undated: 1–2; ABS, undated: 1; UK Statistics Authority, 2009: 3). Nevertheless, census questions are set or approved by government ministers for political reasons. Unlike many surveys, the operation of census research is not subject to Euro-Western ethical scrutiny. In some countries, such as Australia, people can be forced to participate in census research, and handed punitive fines if they refuse; something that no research ethics committee/institutional review board would countenance. (See Chapter 3 for more on this.)

The US, Australian and UK governments all expect their census research to be internationally comparable (Citro, Martin and Straf, 2009: 13; ABS, undated: 3; UK Statistics Authority, 2009: 8). However, Indigenous researchers have noted that 'the practice of comparison is itself deeply political' (Walter and Andersen, 2016: 38–9). Statistical comparison is particularly troublesome for Indigenous peoples. For example, in Australia the census form currently asks whether a person is Aboriginal, Torres Strait Islander or neither. This offers two categories of Indigeneity when in fact there are hundreds: from the Tiwi people of the north to the Wudjari people of the south, the Arrente of the centre and the Muralag people of the Torres Strait, to give just four examples. Aboriginal and Torres Strait Islander peoples speak around 150 different languages and have different histories and cultures from each other (Walter and Andersen, 2016: 38). Treating them as two homogeneous groups is reductive, erasing the richness of diversity within some of the oldest cultures on our planet. Also, this categorisation completely ignores at least one other Indigenous group that is not originally native to Australia. South Sea Islanders were forcibly taken from Fiji, Vanuatu and the Solomon Islands in the late 19th century to work on sugarcane plantations in northern Queensland (Lambert, 2014: 93). Many of their descendants still live in the area but they are not considered Indigenous people within Australia. As a result, they suffer even more marginalisation and hardship than Aboriginal or Torres Strait Islander peoples, because they are separated from their land and have no statutory protection or support (Lambert, 2014: 94; Mark Little Sun Warcon in Lambert, 2014: 101–4). Without recognition in a census category, they are unlikely ever to receive such protection or support.

I can imagine Euro-Western readers thinking, "But there's diversity within the settler community, too." Indeed there is, and there is also power: power to set the questions Indigenous peoples have to answer, power to force people to respond, power to interpret those responses and power to commission and disseminate national research without seeking any input into the design, collection, analysis or use of the findings from Indigenous peoples themselves (Walter and Andersen, 2016: 34). Within census research practice, as more widely, Indigenous peoples are viewed through a deficit model: poor, unhealthy, ill-educated and so on (Ball and Janyst, 2008: 37; Rix et al, 2018: 6). Census researchers are, broadly, well meaning, aiming to help reduce the deficits they perceive. Yet they operate from a specific and dominant position: middle-class and Euro-Western (Walter and Andersen, 2016: 35). If Indigenous peoples were involved in census research, they might suggest that it is less important to identify differences between categories of ethnicity, and more important to establish why those differences exist, which might involve asking some searching questions about 'the dimensions of white colonizer settler privilege to identify how social resources and opportunities can be shared more equally' (Walter and Andersen, 2016: 35). It seems likely that such an approach would be quite uncomfortable for Euro-Western census researchers, which may help to explain why Indigenous peoples are excluded from the production of census research in Australia.

Colonisation influences the kinds of questions researchers ask (Hornung, 2013: 135). Also, however scientific and rigorous an analysis, the nature of the questions used to collect data inevitably shapes the interpretations a researcher is able to make of their findings (Walter and Andersen, 2016: 27). The census is just one example of the way in which national research – by which I mean research conducted within the boundaries of countries recognised as such by Euro-Western peoples – does not marry well with Indigenous priorities (Scougall, 2006: 53). There are many others, and it is beyond the scope of this book to cover them all.

The census research described above displays a lack of cultural competence. Cultural competence involves understanding and respecting the customs and ways of life of others. We have seen that different Indigenous peoples have different customs and ways of life from each other. This suggests that an Indigenous researcher from one tribe or community, wishing to conduct research within a different tribe or community, would need to acquire the necessary cultural competence (Wehipeihana, 2008: 42; Lambert, 2014: 75). It is certain that a Euro-Western researcher would need to acquire a suitable level of cultural competence to engage Indigenous people successfully in research (Hernandez, 2013: 68). (See Chapter 5 for more on cultural competence.)

Data sovereignty

An important ethical principle for many Indigenous peoples is 'data sovereignty', that is, the concept that data is owned by, and subject to the laws of, the nation where that data is collected. This is connected with the wider concept of self-determination that is enshrined in the 2007 United Nations Declaration on the Rights of Indigenous Peoples. Claims to data sovereignty stem from the principle that Indigenous peoples have the right to self-determination (Kukutai and Taylor, 2016: 14).

The most advanced form of data sovereignty is encapsulated in the OCAP™ principles of the Canadian First Nations peoples (Kukutai and Taylor, 2016: 15). OCAP stands for Ownership, Control, Access and Possession. Work on data sovereignty is also underway in Australia, New Zealand and the US (Kukutai and Taylor, 2016: 15), and no doubt other countries too. The OCAP principles 'reflect First Nation commitments to use and share information in a way that brings benefit to the community while minimising harm' (First Nations IGC, 2014: 5). The idea that Indigenous communities have the right to determine the use of data that is gathered within their purview conflicts with Euro-Western concepts like intellectual property and academic freedom (Patterson et al, 2006: 52).

Data sovereignty is quite a new movement and the explosion of digital data can make data itself seem like a recent innovation. However, Indigenous peoples have gathered and used data in sophisticated empirical ways for centuries, probably millennia (Rodriguez-Lonebear, 2016: 254–5). Many Indigenous communities defined rights and responsibilities for use of data within their oral traditions (Kukutai and Taylor, 2016: 14–15). So, the data sovereignty movement is not so much new in itself as a new way of asserting an existing ethical approach.

Conclusion

On the whole, academia has not valued or shown respect for Indigenous research or Indigenous ways of knowing (Absolon in Kovach, 2009: 153; Chilisa, 2012: 76; Coombes, 2013: 73; Sherwood, 2013: 213), although there are some recent signs that this is beginning to change (Kovach, 2015: 44; Gentelet, Basile and Asselin, 2017: 5). This lack of respect is one effect of institutional and structural racism. Another effect is that Indigenous researchers often have great difficulty, or find they are unable, to access funding for research or evaluation (Koitsiwe, 2013: 273; Thomas, 2013: 52; Traore, 2013: 172, 185; Yantio, 2013: 129–30). Of course Indigenous researchers are not the only people of colour who are silenced and marginalised by racism in academia and research (Spates and Gichiru, 2015: 1922). However, the almost complete lack of acknowledgement of, let alone engagement with, the Indigenous research literature by Euro-Western research authors is a very particular kind of silencing. One of the aims of this book is to help to put an end to that oppressive silence.

This book does not aim to romanticise or reify Indigenous research or ethics. Nevertheless, the Indigenous paradigm mostly comes across as positive in the literature, which is likely to influence the tone of this book because most of my learning is from that literature. This is one similarity to Euro-Western research where writers and publishers also tend to focus on the positives. However, I have heard from an Indigenous source that unethical practice can be found in Indigenous research as well as in Euro-Western research (McGregor, 2018). I cannot point to external evidence of this in the same way that I can with Euro-Western research through bodies such as Retraction Watch. The Indigenous research literature is a comparatively young body of work and tends to locate unethical practices within Euro-Western research, which is perhaps not surprising, given the massive and continuing impact of colonialism.

I have learned that aspects of the life-ways of some Indigenous societies conflict with Euro-Western ethics and with my own ethical perspective. For example, some Indigenous societies are intensely patriarchal, such that women have no role in approving the research that may take place in those communities, and have to consult their husbands before they participate in research (Tindana, Kass and Akweongo, 2006: 2, 5). In other Indigenous societies, men and women have different roles and there may be rules prescribing the interactions between them (McNulty in Lambert, 2014: 80). As I come from a society where women's equality is enshrined in legislation (if not always, yet, in practice), these kinds of customs seem unethical to me. Perhaps the customs of my society seem unethical to others. Either way, it is important to note that not all Indigenous societies are patriarchal. There are some societies where women have taken on, and succeeded in, traditionally male roles (Toby in Lambert, 2014: 97), and others where women are leaders (Lambert, 2014: 172). These variations in gender roles offer a useful illustration of the differences between Indigenous peoples that the term 'Indigenous peoples' can unhelpfully obscure.

This chapter has offered a brief introduction to a very large and complex topic. If you would like to find out more, there is a reading list on the book's companion website (http://policypress.co.uk/resources/kara-ethics).

REFLECTIVE QUESTIONS

1. This chapter focuses on the Indigenous research paradigm and begins to contrast it with the Euro-Western research paradigm. What are the disadvantages of taking such a binary approach?
2. How can reflecting on different approaches to life and thought be useful for researchers?
3. What is your own ontological perspective or worldview?
4. Do you think ethics should be viewed holistically or broken down into, for example, individual, social, institutional, professional and political ethics? Why?
5. You have been asked to help make national censuses more ethical. What changes would you advise?

CHAPTER 3

Euro-Western research and ethics

Introduction

Euro-Western societies value some different principles and ideas from Indigenous societies (although of course there are also areas of overlap). For example, the principle of autonomy is highly valued in most Euro-Western societies, while the principle of collectivity is highly valued in many African societies (de Vries and Henley, 2014: 80). Also, there are a range of Euro-Western epistemologies and ontologies. Nevertheless, most Euro-Western ontologies are based on the idea that it is possible to separate wholes into parts: to differentiate, for example, spiritual from physical, and emotional from cerebral. And most Euro-Western epistemologies are based on the idea that knowledge is held by individuals.

This book highlights some of the ways in which Euro-Western research may not always be as ethical as its adherents would like to think. In this context, it is necessary to note that the oppression of Indigenous peoples through Euro-Western research is not confined to history (Moodie, 2010: 818; Rix et al, 2018: 5, 7). For example, American museums, universities and other institutions still hold the remains and burial offerings of around two million Indigenous people, even though legislation was passed to change this as long ago as 1990. Because Euro-Western researchers have labelled these materials as 'data', they have been able to avoid repatriating the human remains and burial offerings which are so important to Indigenous peoples (Dunbar-Ortiz, 2014: 231).

We know that Euro-Western research has been used in support of atrocities around the world, including within Euro-Western society, such as Nazi medical research on concentration camp prisoners during the Second World War. This led to the Nuremberg Code of 1948, the first international code of research ethics. Yet this did not prevent future atrocities such as the American Tuskegee Syphilis Study, in which hundreds of poor and illiterate African-American men were not told about, or given treatment for, diagnosed syphilis.

It is equally important to acknowledge that most Euro-Western researchers do a great deal to ensure that their research is as ethical as possible. Euro-Western research has achieved an enormous amount to benefit people all around the world. For example, the global eradication of smallpox in humans and rinderpest in cattle, the internet and the growth in renewable energy sources all owe their existence to Euro-Western research methods. However, there are still a huge number of problems for Euro-Western researchers to solve. One of those problems is how to ensure that all Euro-Western research is truly ethical. Ethics theory can help with this, as can codes and guidelines. None of these offers all the answers but they are a good place to start.

Ethics theory

There are four main theories of ethics that appear in the Euro-Western literature: deontology, consequentialism, virtue ethics and value ethics. Deontology is the most prescriptive. The word comes from the Greek word 'deon' meaning 'binding, dutiful, proper'. This theory holds that acts are good or bad in themselves, regardless of consequences. So, for example, telling a lie is held to be bad without exception, even if hearing that lie makes someone feel better. Consequentialism states that the outcome of an act – its consequence – is what matters. So, within this theoretical approach, telling a lie is fine if it makes someone feel better; it is bad only if it causes harm. Deontologists tend to want a universal set of rules to follow at all times, while consequentialists believe that it is important to take the context into account when making ethical decisions.

Virtue ethics suggests that ethical practice stems from the individual; that good people are ethical, and that trying to be a better person will help you become a more ethical researcher (Macfarlane, 2009: 165). However, there are many examples of good people doing bad things, and vice versa (Singer, 2016: 253), which seems to contradict those suggestions. Also, while it may be worth trying to live up to high moral standards, most people are not able to be truly virtuous at all times, as Macfarlane acknowledges (2009: 42). And even a virtuous act will not necessarily lead to good results (Chambers, 1992: 5–6). For example, Milgram and Zimbardo were demonstrably virtuous researchers, with noble motives, who nevertheless conducted highly unethical research (Recuber, 2016: 49).

Value ethics does not appear as a formal category in the philosophical literature, but it is regularly used as a basis for ethical research, evaluation and allied forms of social action in a range of fields (for example, Westall, 2009: 7; Edwards and Mauthner, 2012: 19–20; Chevalier and Buckles, 2013: 226; Christie and Alkin, 2013: 37–8). Some Euro-Western researchers consider that no research is value free (for example, Gillies and Alldred, 2012: 45; Hammersley and Traianou, 2012: 38; Hesse-Biber, 2014: 5). Therefore, value ethicists argue, one ethical approach worth taking is to make existing values 'visible and therefore contestable by all interested parties' through discussion (Palfrey, Thomas and Phillips, 2012: 122–3). Another option is for those involved to agree on a specific and shared value base that researchers and others can refer to in case of ethical difficulty. In some cases such a value base will already exist. For example, the Code of Occupational Ethics for the Youth Service in Wales contains such a value base, and states that 'The purpose of this code is to provide Youth Service workers with guidelines for making ethical choices in the conduct of their work' (ETS Wales and YMCA Wales, 2012: 1).

This is a useful illustration of a key difference between value and virtue ethics: in working with value-based ethics, the researcher is required only to take the prescribed ethical approach *in the conduct of their work*. This may make it easier to require higher standards than if the researcher were required to take the prescribed ethical approach at all times, as in virtue ethics. (There are occupations, such as the US judiciary and the UK civil service, which require staff to uphold the same occupational values in their personal as in their professional lives. Some virtue ethicists suggest that this should also apply to researchers (for example, Macfarlane, 2009: 45) but at present it does not.)

Another theoretical categorisation from the Euro-Western literature divides ethics into ethics of justice and ethics of care. Ethics of justice refers to treating everyone equally, as the law aspires to do. Ethics of care refers to making sure everyone is looked after and, as far as possible, their needs are met – which clearly can't be done by treating everyone equally. However, these approaches are not necessarily mutually exclusive. Drawing on the work of Sevenhuijsen (1998), Edwards and Mauthner (2012: 22) argue that if you use ethics of care to contextualise justice, you can see the two as part of a single process incorporating 'reconciliation, reciprocity, diversity and responsibility, and with an awareness of power'.

In practice, most researchers draw on a combination of theoretical perspectives for help, depending on the problem they are facing and its context (Morris and Morris, 2016: 203). Some of the people I interviewed for this book showed that they were aware of this.

> "For students, I would say they are trying to just follow the rules, and they think that's the most important thing, which may be fine, but then thinking about the virtue ethics position, what does it mean to me? I'm here as a researcher, there are things I'm going to do that are behind closed doors, what are my values and moral principles that are going to guide how I act as a researcher? There may be things where the rules would say it's fine, it's OK, but I don't think it is, then what choice am I going to make on that? And how am I going to describe that choice to people I meet? I think that the theories can help us to consider why we're doing what we're doing and how we can defend what we choose."

I agree with this interviewee that while each theory is in some sense deficient when taken in isolation, all are useful in helping Euro-Western researchers to think through how we should approach research ethics in general and address specific ethical issues.

This is a very swift skim across the surface of Euro-Western ethical theories. To discuss these theories in detail would take a whole book in itself. If you wish to delve more deeply, please see the reading list on this book's companion website (http://policypress.co.uk/resources/kara-ethics).

Ethical codes and guidelines

Many Euro–Western professions and institutions, and even some countries, cherish the idea of a universal research ethics that can be codified to cover all eventualities (Schrag, 2016: 319). There are innumerable codes, guidelines and statements of research ethics, drawn up by national and international bodies, institutions and professional societies and associations. The existence of such documents seems to support the idea of universalism, but it doesn't take a great deal of examination to demonstrate that very little in ethics is actually universal. For example, most people agree, in general terms, that killing other people is wrong. Yet many people are equally happy to agree that, in some contexts, killing people is right. Language helps here because we can create separate concepts by using different terms for different types of killing such as abortion, execution or euthanasia. This enables us to argue, for example, that euthanasia is ethically sound in some contexts while execution is not – or vice versa.

Even professional ethicists don't agree on whether there is scope for universal ethics – and, if there is, what kind (for example, dialogical universalism, intersubjective universalism or interactive universalism (Fitzpatrick, 2008: 24–5)). This is probably because, at least in Euro–Western terms, there is no universal way in which people think: 'the way we happen to organize the world in our minds is neither naturally nor logically inevitable' (Zerubavel, 1997: 12). Some Indigenous scholars view this differently, conceptualising 'the underlying systemic knowledge bases' of Indigenous peoples worldwide (Wilson, 2008: 54).

As we saw in Chapter 2, the literature suggests that there are commonalities between the ethical principles of many Indigenous peoples around the world. There are also commonalities between the ethical principles of many Euro–Western peoples. Yet, in research those principles are put into action by individuals, pairs or small groups of people influenced by many interacting factors such as their research topic and their own worldviews. This means that guidelines, codes or principles, made up (as they must inevitably be) of broad concepts, require those concepts to be interpreted in their application to specific situations. Codes or guidelines, however detailed and helpful, cannot cover every possible eventuality (Grinyer, 2009: 4) and will never be the only influence on a researcher's ethical decisions (Morris, 2008: 196). Also, guidelines and codes may lay out ethical considerations, but not rank them in order of priority (Posel, 2014: 160). This means that when a researcher encounters a situation where ethical considerations clash, they have to decide which should take precedence. (For examples of these, see the scenarios on this book's companion website: http://policypress.co.uk/resources/kara-ethics.) Different researchers will make different interpretations of ethical concepts (Morris, 2008: 11) and different decisions about how ethical considerations should be prioritised. Furthermore, a single researcher may make different interpretations of ethical concepts, or different decisions about prioritising, at different times or in different contexts (Ross and Grant, 2014:

170). Each separate interpretation or decision may be recognisable, and justifiable, as ethical (Ross and Grant, 2014: 178).

Given all of the above, it is perhaps not surprising that different guidelines and codes of research ethics include different requirements (de Vries and Henley, 2014: 78). For example, the RESPECT Code of Practice for Socio-Economic Research was developed by and for the European Union. The RESPECT Code is not mandatory. However, there is a clear expectation that professional researchers in the EU will uphold scientific standards, comply with local laws and avoid social or personal harm (RESPECT, 2004: 1).

The RESPECT Code is an impressively succinct four pages. By contrast, Canada's national *Tri-Council Policy Statement: Ethical Conduct for Research Involving Humans* ('the Statement') is 220 pages long. It is a cross-sector document, produced by three research funding agencies: the Canadian Institutes of Health Research, the Natural Sciences and Engineering Research Council of Canada and the Social Sciences and Humanities Research Council of Canada. The latest version of the Statement was published in 2014, and was under review at the time of writing. It was first developed by a panel of people in the 1990s, including Indigenous people and research participants, and its Chapter 9 (pages 109–37) covers work with Indigenous participants and researchers. This document is close to mandatory because researchers will not receive funding from the Canadian agencies who produced the Statement if they do not comply with the ethical principles set out therein (TCPS2, 2014: 3).

Like the Statement, the *Australian Code for the Responsible Conduct of Research* ('the Code') was developed by three statutory bodies: two research funding councils and Universities Australia (Australian Government, 2007: 1). However, the Code is very different in style and content from the Statement. Like the RESPECT Code, which describes itself as advisory rather than prescriptive, the Code takes a supportive rather than a quasi-mandatory approach, using phrases like 'guide institutions and researchers', 'promotes integrity' and 'providing advice' in its first paragraph. Also, rather than trying to include everything in one document, the Code makes explicit links with several other relevant documents such as the *Guidelines for Ethical Research in Australian Indigenous Studies* ('the Guidelines'), and states an expectation that researchers will also read and abide by those documents where relevant to their work.

It is interesting to note here that the Euro-Western system of producing ethics statements, codes and guidelines is being adopted by some Indigenous peoples at national, local and community level around the world (Kovach, 2015: 58). For example, the Guidelines are produced by the Australian Institute of Aboriginal and Torres Strait Islander Studies (AIATSIS). As with the Statement, the Guidelines are – and are clearly stated to be – mandatory for all researchers who receive funding from AIATSIS, and are designed to inform all other research with Australian Indigenous peoples. They are made up of 14 principles (AIATSIS, 2012), as follows.

1. Recognition of the diversity and uniqueness of peoples, as well as of individuals, is essential.
2. The rights of Indigenous peoples to self-determination must be recognised.
3. The rights of Indigenous peoples to their intangible heritage must be recognised.
4. Rights in the traditional knowledge and traditional cultural expressions of Indigenous peoples must be respected, protected and maintained.
5. Indigenous knowledge, practices and innovations must be respected, protected and maintained.
6. Consultation, negotiation and free, prior and informed consent are the foundations for research with or about Indigenous peoples.
7. Responsibility for consultation and negotiation is ongoing.
8. Consultation and negotiation should achieve mutual understanding about the proposed research.
9. Negotiation should result in a formal agreement for the conduct of a research project.
10. Indigenous people have the right to full participation appropriate to their skills and experiences in research projects and processes.
11. Indigenous people involved in research, or who may be affected by research, should benefit from, and not be disadvantaged by, the research project.
12. Research outcomes should include specific results that respond to the needs and interests of Indigenous people.
13. Plans should be agreed for managing the use of, and access to, research results.
14. Research projects should include appropriate mechanisms and procedures for reporting on ethical aspects of the research and complying with these guidelines.

In contrast, Chapter 9 of the Statement is based on three core principles: respect for persons, concern for welfare, and justice (TCPS2, 2014: 113). However, in the chapter as a whole, these core principles are unpacked to reveal that, broadly, they contain the same principles as the Guidelines.

None of these comparisons is intended to suggest that one country, people or document is somehow superior to, or more ethical than, another. In fact, although these kinds of ethics documents may be presented very differently, on close examination they tend to have many similarities. Several of the documents refer to the constantly evolving ethics landscape, and any differences between them may be due to the date of the latest review, as well as to differences in local customs and values. These comparisons help to demonstrate that there are few if any hard-and-fast rules when it comes to research ethics, whether at international or individual, national, local or project level. This again underlines the importance of researchers learning to think and act ethically.

Documents such as codes and guidelines are useful beyond research practice itself, for example for raising awareness (Desautels and Jacob, 2012: 445), for helping to maintain standards, and for teaching. However, one reason why individual ethics are always needed is that institutional codes of ethics cannot cover all possible eventualities (Williams, Guenther and Arnott, 2011: 1; Posel and Ross, 2014: 11). Codes and guidelines are limited in their applicability to specific situations and to all the nuances and complexity with which researchers have to contend (Morris, 2008: 14). A few institutions have recognised this, such as the Medical and the Human Sciences Research Councils of South Africa, which both have rights-based ethical guidelines that emphasise the need to take socio-cultural context into account when designing research (Posel and Ross, 2014: 12). Anecdotal evidence suggests that some research ethics committees/ institutional review boards are enabling researchers facing unexpected ethical dilemmas to return for further advice. Nevertheless, these kinds of flexibilities are unusual, and may not always be easy to manage in practice. Also, however flexible and enlightened the regulations may be, conforming to regulations does not always equate to acting ethically (de Vries and Henley, 2014: 83) and ethical guidelines cannot ensure ethical behaviour (Leone, Stame and Tagle, 2016: 162). Indeed, the uncritical application of Euro-Western ethics guidelines to research with Indigenous communities – even up-to-date guidelines that privilege diversity and collaboration – can cause harm and so be unethical (Brunger and Wall, 2016: 1863).

As a result, it seems to me that pluralism is more relevant here than universalism. Thinking is social (Zerubavel, 1997: 13). Knowing is material (Barad, 2007: 379). Humans want to find patterns, academics demand definitions, and governments require policy. In these contexts universalism has evident appeal, yet binaries are unhelpful and language is reductive. Ethics cannot be separated from ontology and epistemology (Barad, 2007: 381), that is, ways of knowing the world, and how those ways of knowing are learned. By pluralism I don't mean 'a collection of individualities'; I mean the interconnectedness of everything. The Euro-Western physicist and social theorist Karen Barad (2007: 393) expresses this well when she says 'Ethics is ... about responsibility and accountability for the lively relationalities of becoming of which we are a part.'

In January 2018 the World Economic Forum published a Young Scientists' Code of Ethics which espouses precisely this approach. The Code includes seven principles as follows.

1. Engage with the public
2. Pursue the truth
3. Minimize harm
4. Engage with decision-makers
5. Support diversity
6. Be a mentor
7. Be accountable. (WEF, 2018: 5–11)

Although 'the truth' might seem universalist, the document also speaks of 'truths' and acknowledges the potential of 'negative, undesired, inconvenient and inconsistent results' to lead to useful insights and learning (WEF, 2018: 6). 'Harm' is defined as something that can happen 'to science, to others, to the environment, to society, and to [researchers] themselves' (WEF, 2018: 7). And although the Code is essentially a Euro-Western product, it makes a strong statement on the importance of diversity, stating that diversity requires 'an environment in which the ideas of all are evaluated equally' and that 'The goal is to achieve a research environment in which diversity in all its forms is not a barrier' (WEF, 2018: 9). This is encouraging language; its impact in practice remains to be seen.

Euro-Western research and politics

Euro-Western positivist research of the 19th and 20th centuries was believed to be free of politics and of the values on which political actions are based. Research, it was thought, could be done in isolation, with the researcher as neutral observer and dispassionate analyst. That view is now being discredited and more Euro-Western people are becoming aware that research is not only inextricably entwined with the rest of life, but also a political act. Some argue that it is good research practice to take, and state, a politically informed position (Kuntz, 2015: 123). There have been calls from researchers around the world to link research explicitly with efforts to achieve positive social change (for example, Zuberi and Bonilla-Silva, 2008: 336; Gillies and Alldred, 2012: 57; Jolivétte, 2015: 8; Land, 2015: 28–9; Foster, 2016: 10).

As we saw in the previous chapter, one form of research that is unequivocally political is research conducted by Euro-Western national governments. Governments conduct a lot of research, from one-off local projects to national surveys that may be repeated at regular intervals, in some cases for centuries. For example, the Australian census dates back to 1788, the US holds individual census records going back to 1790 and the first full UK census was held in 1801. As we saw in Chapter 2, in some countries it is mandatory to complete all or part of the census and this is legally enforceable, with penalties for those who do not comply. For example, at the time of writing, Australian legislation allows the imposition of a fine per day of refusal, which in 2016 was A$180 per day, and a one-off fine of up to A$1,800 for giving misleading information. UK legislation allows for a one-off fine for non-completion of up to £1,000, plus a criminal record.

Governments justify this coercive method of research recruitment by saying they need accurate data to help plan public services, from transport to welfare. Yet there are tried and tested survey research techniques using sampling that enable accurate inferences about the whole population to be made. Indeed, some census research uses these, such as the American Community Survey, which forms part of US national census research. Again, though, the onus is on participants to respond or to face penalties, rather than on survey researchers to obtain a suitable sample. So, in a range of Euro-Western nations it seems that politics trumps ethics.

Conclusion

This chapter has shown that Euro–Western research ethics are contested, multiple and not always applied. It has also shown that a great deal of thought has gone into Euro–Western research ethics to date. We have reviewed some examples of unethical Euro–Western research, and also demonstrated that Euro–Western research has had some very positive impacts on the world. This is a complex picture. Adding in the quite different approach of Indigenous research ethics makes the picture more complicated still.

We saw in Chapter 2 that Indigenous research methods and methodologies do not necessarily translate into other cultural contexts. This also applies to Euro–Western research methods and methodologies (Gaudry, 2015: 246–7). Some may be useful at times in Indigenous cultural contexts, such as community-based participatory research, or the emancipatory methods and methodologies developed by Euro–Western people to address various forms of oppression within their own societies such as sexism, racism and ableism (Kovach, 2015: 46). But, on the whole, Euro–Western methods and methodologies are usually more appropriate for Euro–Western research in Euro–Western contexts, and Indigenous methods and methodologies are usually more appropriate for Indigenous research in Indigenous contexts.

And what of research ethics? My view is that Indigenous approaches to research ethics are useful for Euro–Western researchers to consider. It may be that Euro–Western research ethics are also useful for Indigenous researchers to consider, although that is not for me to say. In the rest of this book, I will set the two approaches side by side, to see what may be learned.

REFLECTIVE QUESTIONS

1. Which ethics theory or theories do you find most convincing or appealing? What are the implications of that for your research work?
2. What do you see as the factors that can lead a good person to act unethically, or vice versa?
3. If a new national census were based equally on ethics of justice and ethics of care, how would it differ from existing national census research?
4. Which are more important, thoughts or feelings? Why?
5. If ethics trumped politics in Euro-Western societies, what would be different in the world?

CHAPTER 4

Research ethics regulation

Introduction

Examination of the Euro-Western research literature shows that Euro-Western scholars seem happy to treat research ethics as though it exists in isolation, separate from other forms of ethics such as individual, social, professional, institutional or political ethics. A similar examination of the Indigenous research literature suggests that many Indigenous scholars do not make such a separation. I argue that this is one of the areas where Euro-Western researchers can learn from those Indigenous researchers. It seems to me that there are a number of nodes where individual, social, professional, institutional, political and research ethics coincide. Examples include research ethics regulation and evaluation research. In this chapter, I aim to explain and demonstrate these links with respect to research ethics regulation; in the next chapter I will perform a similar exercise with respect to evaluation research.

Research governance

In the Euro-Western paradigm, research governance is the system of overseeing the ethical conduct of academic and professional researchers. This is a regulatory system that exists at institutional level within universities, health authorities and other organisations with staff who do research with human (or animal) participants. The principles on which the system is based are largely drawn from biomedical research. This can make it difficult to apply those principles effectively to research in the social sciences, arts and humanities (Israel, 2015: 45; Dingwall, 2016: 25).

The research governance system is implemented by specific groups of people known as research ethics committees (RECs) in the UK, as institutional review boards (IRBs) in the US, and by other names elsewhere. RECs, IRBs and their equivalents are committees that have the power to approve – or withhold approval of – the ethical quality of proposed research projects. In one sense, this sounds like a great idea: independent expert scrutiny and feedback to ensure that all research is ethical. However, in practice, it doesn't necessarily work that way.

There is a strong vein of comment in the Euro-Western literature suggesting that RECs/IRBs are not helping researchers to conduct their work more ethically. This does not mean that individuals on those committees are unethical; most try hard to do a good job of advising researchers on ethical practice. However, the system of research governance that committee members have to work within may not always enable fully ethical actions. Some commentators assert that this system is itself unethical, because it is secretive, top-down and unaccountable. The decisions of different RECs/IRBs are often inconsistent (Schrag, 2011: 123; Stark, 2012: 6; Colnerud, 2014: 246). Also, RECs/IRBs are slow to respond to changes such as the advent of online social networks, for example, Facebook and Twitter, as data-gathering sites, even though these bring with them new ethical considerations (Walton and Hassreiter, 2014: 228). The literature does report occasions when RECs/IRBs have been helpfully accessible and flexible in their approach to unusual ethical difficulties (for example, González-López, 2011: 448; Colnerud, 2014: 246), but these seem to be the exception rather than the rule. Also, social research methods is a huge and fast-developing topic. Therefore it is not surprising that RECs/IRBs sometimes struggle when presented with applications for the use of methods with which their members are unfamiliar (Schrag, 2011: 124; Emmerich, 2013: 181; Howell et al, 2014: 211). This can also limit researchers' choices of methods (Dingwall, 2016: 33), as this interviewee explains.

> "The ethical approval processes in my university sometimes constrain how I design research. Sometimes because I know what the processes are, I pre-empt, so I won't choose particular types of research because I know it will be seen as a problem by the ethics committee. Some people don't understand social research and that's a problem. And actually, they don't understand ethics in a social research context. For master's students we've changed how we teach ethics as a result of this, which isn't necessarily a good thing; we're teaching them how to get stuff through an ethics committee, rather than teaching them how to manage ethics through the life of a research project."

There are suggestions in the Indigenous literature that Indigenous research ethics are sometimes linked with Indigenous research techniques, such as culturally appropriate holistic methodologies (Bull, 2016: 173). Perhaps this, too, may limit Indigenous researchers' choices of methods.

Euro-Western social researchers frequently complain that the existing system of research governance is drawn from a biomedical approach that cannot be applied in the same way to the humanities and social sciences. Some assert that the system grew up in response to abuse of biomedical research, and that no such record of abuse exists for research in the social sciences, arts and humanities (Schrag, 2011: 123). This is a perspective with which Indigenous researchers seem likely to disagree. For example, a number of Indigenous peoples are on record as feeling thoroughly abused by ethnographers (Kovach, 2009: 27; Smith, 2012: 70; Rix et al, 2018: 6). So, evidently, 'no such record of abuse' does not equate to 'no abuse'.

The biomedical ethics mantra is 'do no harm', and a key priority for Euro-Western research governance is to avoid harm to participants. Yet there is comparatively little thinking, in the Euro-Western paradigm, about how research might directly benefit its participants (Colvin, 2014: 62). By contrast, as we saw in Chapter 2, benefit to participating communities is one of the key tenets of Indigenous research ethics (Chilisa, 2012: 124; Smith, 2012: 130).

Some Euro-Western researchers want to take a participatory approach to their work, and in Indigenous research this seems almost universal. Ethical participatory research requires the involvement of participants from the very earliest stages. However, RECs/IRBs require researchers to gain formal ethical approval before making contact with potential participants. Some Indigenous consent systems have a similar requirement (Tindana, Kass and Akweongo, 2006: 2). This requirement can cause a range of difficulties for Euro-Western or Indigenous researchers in practice (van den Hoonaard and van den Hoonaard, 2013: 48; Gaudry, 2015: 252).

> "I didn't want my research to be only academically rigorous and theoretical and so on, but also of use to people. In the planning phase I consulted, engaged, chatted, discussed with practitioners, some of whom I'd made friends with during my work in the field and some new people. One supervisor was very supportive of this approach; the other, who is a more senior academic, was more hesitant. She wanted cool academic/theoretical challenges first and then later check whether they were of interest to the practitioners, but I said, 'No, let's see if we can find a match between practitioner questions and academic questions – that would be more meaningful.' So I went to workshops and conferences, did interviews etc., all before getting ethical clearance. I quickly realised there was a red flag there, because I was doing all of that without getting ethical clearance."

RECs/IRBs may require long and complex consent forms (de Vries and Henley, 2014: 79). Yet, overly bureaucratic consent procedures can cause anxiety and suspicion among participants and reduce trust in the research (Colnerud, 2014: 245). This can be a problem because it is trust, not bureaucracy, that leads people to take part in research. Yet trust, too, can skew research, such as through participants assuming that research will be beneficial to them without checking to make sure, or through researchers exploiting trusting participants (Tindana, Kass and Akweongo, 2006: 7).

There are differences between Euro-Western countries in how they approach research governance, with some taking a more relaxed approach than others. For example, Denmark decided in the mid-1990s that formal ethical approval was unnecessary for social science research (Israel, 2015: 60). At the other end of the spectrum, in some countries formal ethical approval is mandated by law. For example, in New Zealand it is a legal requirement for health and disability research, and for research conducted in universities (Israel, 2015: 56).

> "I've been studying in UK for some months. What was surprising for me is you are very sensitive about ethics. In Estonia we only have [to apply for formal approval for] topics that involve children or adults with some sensitivity, so I was very surprised that all PhD theses, even in economics, studying let's say people who are not paying taxes, they have to go through ethics committee.

> Here, social sciences, I would say not many topics go through ethics committee, just a few I would say."

Another aim of this book is to help researchers to act ethically in aspects of research that don't concern RECs/IRBs, or where the guidance of RECs/IRBs may be inadequate. This can include work across the Euro–Western/Indigenous paradigm boundary, as this interviewee explains.

> "Researchers 50 years ago worked in particular communities, recorded materials. We might want to find out what those were and use them. Then the question is, who do you ask for permission? So ethics boards would say, you need to go and ask the community leaders, or you need to ask the families of the people who were researchers in the past. But then sometimes that wouldn't be appropriate because what you potentially do is create divisions within families now. Also part of it is disrespectful to the people who took part in the research 50 years ago, because they've given freely of their time and their knowledge, and it could be perceived by some as if you go back, to their families, saying 'will you give us permission to use their material', you could be questioning their choice. You talk to people that you think will guide you in the best possible way, in the communities, then you make choices. You may get it wrong! You do it the best way you can. And you're also transparent about it, and you explain to people why you're doing what you're doing – are you OK with this? – you do a lot of asking, asking, asking. Then with the ethics board you explain what the issues are and how you're trying to deal with them and what the community context is, what you've been told by community members."

It is possible for Euro–Western RECs/IRBs to take a dialogic approach and support researchers in ethical practice (Bond, 2012: 108) but, on the whole, at present they don't. This means that researchers may be 'forced to adapt to the institutions' demands in terms of ethics' (Kouritzin and Nakagawa, 2018: 3). As a result, researchers are often left with a stark choice: comply with a REC/IRB directive that is in fact unethical, or find a way to resist or subvert the ethical regulation (see below for more on this). Also, researchers who serve on RECs/IRBs as well as conducting research in the field may experience significant role confusion from the differing views of ethics in the two different arenas (de Vries and Henley, 2014: 86).

As well as research governance and ethical review, some Euro–Western policy makers have begun to talk of 'research integrity'. This term can be confusing because it is not always clear whether the 'integrity' is that of the research or that of the researcher (Edwards, 2013: 4).

Some Indigenous researchers engage with or run RECs/IRBs, but the committee is not usually seen as taking precedence over the community and its culture (Chilisa, 2012: 295; Simpson, 2014: 106). Indeed, some Indigenous communities in Australia, Canada, New Zealand and most recently Africa have written their own codes of ethics for researchers to follow in researching them (Patterson et al, 2006: 53–4; Gray et al, 2017: 24–5, Nordling, 2017). The San people of southern Africa published their Code of Research Ethics in March 2017 (San, 2017). They use four headings: respect, honesty, justice and fairness, and care. It will be interesting to see how this operates in practice.

Formal ethics approval

RECs/IRBs are charged with the responsibility of granting or withholding formal approval for the ethical aspects of proposed research projects. They are also responsible, sometimes less overtly, for minimising any potential risk to their parent institution from proposed research (Dingwall, 2016: 27). This can cause ethical dilemmas for RECs/IRBs, such as if they are faced with a project that they judge to be ethical and worthwhile in itself, but which could cause problems for the reputation of their parent institution if it came to the attention of the mainstream or social media. Some have argued that RECs/IRBs can be seen as unethical if they put the interests of their parent institution before the possibility of knowledge advancement (Iphofen, 2011: 163; van den Hoonaard and van den Hoonaard, 2013: 116).

In early 2015 I analysed the ethics application forms then lodged online with The Research Ethics Application Database (TREAD). TREAD is hosted by Oxford University and contains application forms from all over the world that have received formal approval. I found that approval usually focuses closely on participant well-being. Data storage often features, and there is an occasional nod to researcher well-being. In all the forms I analysed, other aspects of research ethics, such as the ethical aspects of data analysis, writing or the presentation of findings, were ignored. Yet researchers experience ethical difficulties in many dimensions, including the conduct of colleagues, work with archival data and even ethical review systems themselves (Colnerud, 2014: 244). This seems to support the suggestions, mentioned above, that research regulation may be more about protecting institutions from litigation by disgruntled participants than about ensuring that research is truly ethical. I have found such suggestions in the literature (for example, Hamilton, 2016: 344), and they were also made by some of the people I interviewed for this book.

> "In my case, I think one of the issues is that the academics making up the committee are from law, and that brings a particular lens with it when it comes to ethics that can be quite black-and-white. It feels sometimes like it's more about risk to the university than about research ethics."

> "The ethical approval systems are not about ethics at all, they're about risk and they're about people interfering, to be honest. In terms of my own experience of ethical approval, it was a nonsense really, extremely bureaucratic, mainly about data storage. I don't have any issue at all about that being an ethical

issue, but once you've got [ethical approval], that's it. There was no sense of actually you'll come up against ethical issues all through your research, things you haven't thought of."

The Euro-Western system of seeking ethics approval involves filling in a long and complicated form. There are usually guidelines that can run to many pages. Some RECs/IRBs invite researchers to their meetings; others don't; but, either way, the final decision is usually taken behind closed doors (Stark, 2012). There are advantages to seeking formal ethics approval, because the process helps researchers to think through some of the ethical issues that might arise in data gathering before the event, and it may also help with debiasing (see Chapter 6 for more on this). However, there are also limitations to formal ethics approval. For example, it is not possible to foresee every ethical dilemma that may arise (Colnerud, 2014: 245). When researchers come up against an unforeseen ethical problem, they can't always go back to the REC/IRB. Some RECs/IRBs try to encourage and enable this, but, even so, there will almost certainly be times when they will need to use their own judgement (Moore, 2010: 39). Ethical work may be some of the most difficult work researchers do, and formal approval helps only up to a point. It is essential for researchers to obtain the knowledge, and develop the skills, to do good ethical work throughout their research practice (Colnerud, 2014: 249).

In the Indigenous paradigm, it may also be necessary to make a formal application to a REC/IRB. This may be a Euro-Western style REC/IRB, as these have been exported around the world (Israel, 2018: 98), or an Indigenous REC/IRB such as those mentioned above. In the latter, there is likely to be a more holistic approach to potential risks and hazards, and community members may take a continuing interest in the research and help to resolve any practical or ethical problems that arise. For example, the Māori researcher Cheryl Smith reports that problems in her *iwi* [tribe] began to jeopardise the successful completion of her doctoral studies. Four of her female relations decided to impose a *rahui* [restriction of access], which meant that nobody would talk to or visit Smith, or ask for her help, until she had finished her thesis. This was unpleasant for Smith, but effective; she completed her thesis within six months of the *rahui* being imposed (Smith, 2013: 92–3).

Not all research in either paradigm is subject to governance from a REC/IRB. For example, evaluation research is a particular type of research that is rarely scrutinised by RECs/IRBs, although in evaluation, as in all research, there are ethical considerations at each stage of the process (Morris, 2015: 33; Williams, 2016: 536). This will be considered in more detail in Chapter 5.

Research ethics and other types of ethics

The system of research regulation is one key arena in which research ethics interacts with individual, social, institutional, professional and political ethics. One example that highlights individual ethics is researchers' responses to the 'double bind' in which they may be put by a REC/IRB. This means 'either abandoning the methods and approaches in which one was trained; or holding on to them while filling out applications that misrepresent what one will be doing' (Lederman, 2016: 63). Some comply and submit, while others resist and subvert; no doubt the same researcher may do both at different times. Resistance and subversion may take a range of forms. Some people 'game the system' (Schrag, 2011: 125) by being economical with the truth. Furthermore, there is a growing body of evidence that researchers tell outright lies to RECs/IRBs, for both ethical (Keith-Spiegel and Koocher, 2005: 347) and unethical (Dreger, 2015: 237) reasons. This interviewee has a contribution to make.

> "Most of the people I know lied on their ethics form, about things that were quite instrumental, like whether your password was encrypted and where their laptop was stored, that kind of thing, because it was convenient."

Dreger cites the case of a biomedical researcher who made a deliberate error on an ethics application, every year for 16 years, which went unnoticed by the IRB. Although there is evidence of unethical behaviour by researchers, including those in the social sciences, arts and humanities, we have no idea how much unethical behaviour really occurs, nor how much harm results (Jennings, 2012: 89–90). Also, there is little evidence of the quality or effectiveness of ethical review (Nicholls, Brehaut and Saginur, 2012: 76).

Compliance with REC/IRB requirements does not, in itself, represent a high level of ethical commitment (Bond, 2012: 108). Even in terms of participant welfare, it is not REC/IRB requirements that protect people; it is people who protect people (Hamilton, 2016: 337). Some interviewees were aware of their individual responsibilities.

> "I think that's where we have professional codes of ethics, like for example research ethics, and then we come into that with our own ethical codes that we develop as individuals. Where the two intersect is where we express ourselves ethically or not ethically. There are some things in ethical principles from universities that intuitively will fit with my own ethical codes, and other things that won't, so they intersect in the way we actually behave."

Individual and institutional ethics can collide in various ways, as this interviewee shows.

> "For me there's always a tension/conflict between my ethics and the institution's ethics and the school's ethics. You wouldn't think there would be a problem, but those three layers interact and conflict all the time. For example, retention, I'm looking for quality, so is the school and so is the institution, but quality looks different to each of those three, so it's about integrity, landscapes of integrity

> collide. I sometimes feel my integrity is being challenged because something systemic is forcing me in some way."

Another place where individual and institutional ethics collide is in the conflict between institutional pressures to rank highly and to publish, and individual desires to do good-quality research (Castleden et al, 2015: 2).

> "I think overall one of the main barriers is the management arrangements, the managerialism that privileges numbers, league tables, statistics, over everything else. I think that drives people, and me, to cross a line sometimes. I try not to, but I'm aware that I might do one day, and I'm aware that other people do."

> "Everybody's over-evaluated, the KPIs [key performance indicators], the pressure to publish in the right places and get stuff done and the pressure to get funding, I think that puts a squeeze on ethics. I think that's created an atmosphere where it's very hard for people to make a space to act ethically, to listen to ethical review advice – it's really hard for people to make that space because they're so squeezed from so many other directions."

As this interviewee suggests, even research institutions are not inherently ethical. Another interviewee has a similar view.

> "The point for unis is to get grants, to do research, to publish and to be seen, and ethics is not part of that. It's something that has to be gone through but it's not viewed as inherent to the project. If anything, it's a barrier to what unis want to do."

Euro-Western institutional structures such as research governance, and the expectations and values they enshrine, can also conflict with the social ethics of communities (Castleden et al, 2015: 2). So, ultimately ethical research, in any paradigm, depends on the actions and interactions of individual people. This means that it is enormously important for researchers to understand what ethics are and how they operate in the world.

Professional ethics is another type of ethics that intersects with research ethics. Different sets of professional ethics are in play in the public, private and charitable sectors. Public sector institutions are organisations primarily funded from taxes paid by citizens, and their work is mandated in law, so that they are accountable to the government (which means political ethics are also in play here). As well as the universities and health authorities where research regulation applies, public sector organisations include state-funded education, social care, the emergency services and the armed forces. The key priority of public sector institutions is to deliver good-quality universal and (where necessary) specialist public services at a reasonable cost, to ensure citizens' needs are met and to give taxpayers good value for their money. These institutions are accountable to politicians who represent the public.

Private and charitable sector institutions are not usually subject to research regulation unless they are involved in conducting research in a public sector organisation where the regulatory system applies. Private sector organisations are businesses for profit, whose key priority is to achieve a financial surplus. These organisations are accountable to their owners and/or shareholders.

> "If you were to look at the behaviour of profit-making institutions like drug companies, institutionalised greed, or just a profit motive, is actually what drug companies are for; that's certainly a barrier to acting ethically."

Charitable sector organisations are not for profit and their aims are very varied. They may be grant-giving or service-providing charities, working across a wide range of areas including sports, animal welfare, the arts and the environment, among many others. They are mainly funded by donations, grants and legacies, and their key priority will be to meet their specific charitable aims. These institutions are accountable to their governing bodies, their funders and their recipients or service users.

These differing priorities mean that, broadly, the three sectors have different positions on professional ethics. Public sector ethics prioritises service to the public. Business ethics focuses on issues such as globalisation, sustainability and corporate social responsibility (Crane and Matten, 2016: 538). Charitable sector ethics centres on doing good works and maintaining public trust.

In each of these sectors, institutions 'depend on people persuading one another to follow particular courses of action, by drawing on resources that sometimes include coercive power, or self-regulation based on acceptance of differences in power and status, or using elements of desire as tools of persuasion. All of these resources operate at the level of *people* doing the persuading, choosing and self-regulation – within structural constraints' (Jones, 2015: 6). Therefore ethics within institutions exists at the individual level, where people are 'doing the persuading, choosing, and self-regulation'; and at the institutional level, within the 'structural constraints'. Structural constraints can promote ethical behaviour, such as through policies requiring the careful conservation of finite resources, or obstruct it, such as through institutional racism.

Institutional racism operates within professions such as the police, within societies and no doubt in other arenas too. It is enshrined in 'practices, policies, norms, rules, laws, traditions, and regulations' (Sensoy and DiAngelo, 2012: 128). This is usually covert rather than overt, so it is often easier to identify the effects rather than the direct causes of institutional racism. For example, it leads to: children of colour doing less well in school than their white counterparts (Hernandez, 2013: 64); more children of colour ending up in government care; a disproportionate number of people of colour being convicted of crimes; more crimes against people of colour than against white people going unsolved; people of colour having less access to wealth than white people – and these are only some of its effects. (Racism is not only perpetrated by white people, and people of colour are not its only victims. For example, in the UK alone, there is a long history of racism by English people against Irish people (Judd, 1996), and by British Asian people against British African-Caribbean people (Sawlani, 2013). However, I am focusing on white racism against people of colour because it reflects the major global ethical fault-line of racism based on colonialism and its legacy.)

Institutional racism is only one of the ethical fault-lines in institutions. Trying to give a comprehensive picture of them all would take a book in itself. The existence and impact of these ethical fault-lines vary between institutions. Researchers need to be aware of these fault-lines and, in our ethical practice, we should take into account how they affect our research projects and the people connected with those projects. To identify the fault-lines in an institution, look for the power imbalances and follow the trails they lay down. For example, this interviewee explains how some of the power imbalances work between their Euro-Western institution and the local Indigenous communities.

> "People are always trying to get around, trying to find ways to make it easier to deal with the ethics requirements of the ethics board for the communities – speaking very much as someone who works in and with Indigenous communities. So what I find in my work is that we want to work ethically, we want to be good partners; again I'm speaking as a non-Indigenous person here, but it's difficult to negotiate the really important ethical guidelines and protocols. Community expectations, there's just this mismatch between those and what is expected institutionally. Part of it is simply timelines, somebody has a research project, it needs to be done in a certain period of time, but it's impossible to do it in that period of time if one follows the protocol. And so then how does one negotiate that?"

As this interviewee suggests, there is a role for individual ethics here too. Last time I took an application to a REC, it had five members. The committee was chaired by a white man who did almost all the talking. There were three white women, each of whom was invited to speak once. There was one woman of colour wearing a hijab who did not speak at all. I should have challenged that. I wish I had. There is no good reason why I did not point out the evident impact of structural racism and sexism within that REC.

We saw in Chapter 3 that in Euro-Western societies government-level politics can trump research ethics. Research ethics also interacts with 'small p' politics, such as the politics of the academy. Some research ethics scholars have become involved in academic activism, largely as a result of frustration with the reductive and bureaucratic systems of research regulation. For example, a small invitation-only conference on ethics was held in October 2012 in Fredericton, New Brunswick, Canada. This was funded by the Social Sciences and Humanities Research Council of Canada and attended by 33 research ethics specialists from around the world (Gontcharov, 2013: 154; van den Hoonaard and Tolich, 2014). The conference was provocatively named the Ethics Rupture Summit and was explicitly intended to consider alternatives to formal ethical review. The outcome was the New Brunswick Declaration, dated 4 February 2013, which aimed to set out a new direction for social research ethics (van den Hoonaard, 2013: 104). The Declaration is concise, so I will share it here in full.

Signatories of the New Brunswick Declaration:
- **affirm that the practice of research should respect persons and collectivities and privilege the possibility of benefit over risk**. We champion constructive relationships among research participants, researchers, funders, publishers, research institutions, research ethics regulators and the wider community that aim to develop better understandings of ethical principles and practices;
- **believe researchers must be held to professional standards of competence, integrity and trust**, which include expectations that they will act reflexively and responsibly when new ethical challenges arise before, during, and long after the completion of research projects. Standards should be based on professional codes of ethical practice espoused by the full diversity of professional associations to which those who study human experience belong, which include the behavioural, health and social sciences, arts and humanities;
- **encourage a variety of means of regulating ethical conduct involving a broad range of parties** in promoting and ensuring ethical conduct, such as participant communities, academic journals, professional associations, state and non-state funding agencies, academic departments and institutions, and oversight ethics committees;
- **encourage regulators and administrators to nurture a regulatory culture that grants researchers the same level of respect that researchers should offer research participants**;
- **seek to promote the social reproduction of ethical communities of practice**. Effective ethics education works in socially-embedded settings and from the ground up: it depends on strong mentoring, experiential learning and nurturance when engaging students and novice researchers with ethics in research settings;
- **are committed to ongoing critical analysis of new and revised ethics regulations** by: highlighting exemplary and innovative research ethics review processes; identifying tensions and contradictions among various elements of research ethics governance; and seeing that every venue devoted to discussing proposed ethics guidelines includes critical analysis and research about research ethics governance; and
- **shall work together to bring new experience, insights and expertise to bear on these principles, goals, and mechanisms.**

It is evident that the Declaration did not seek a complete rupture from ethical review, but sought to try to humanise the process (van den Hoonaard and Tolich, 2014: 93). It is interesting to see the links with the Indigenous paradigm in the Declaration's emphasis on relationships, accountability and collaboration. The Declaration has made some impact in the years since its creation (Tolich and

Ferguson, 2014: 185–6), although that impact seems mostly to have been made through promotion by one or more of the Declaration's 33 signatories.

Some Indigenous researchers have little or no choice about whether to be activists, as the academic system forces them to work within the alien Euro-Western paradigm. This means that they face 'the inevitability of being accountable to culturally and epistemologically divergent communities' (Kovach, 2009: 164), such as RECs/IRBs and tribal elders. There seems to be no equivalent inevitability of non-Indigenous researchers being accountable to Indigenous communities, although some may choose to take this path. Perhaps this is one of the reasons why academia has been described as 'a crucial site for Indigenous activism' (Coombes, 2013: 81). As Chilisa (2012: 16) puts it:

> Researchers become political activists demonstrating commitment to addressing the challenge of including the voices of the colonized Other in all the stages of the research process and conducting research that translates into changes in the material conditions of the local peoples as well as their control over produced knowledge.

REC/IRB members also have activist potential (Hunter, 2017: 3), although there is, as yet, little evidence of actual activism. One exception is in New Zealand, spearheaded by Martin Tolich from the University of Otago. As we have seen, ethics review in New Zealand is a legal requirement only for health and disability research, and for research conducted in universities (Israel, 2015: 56). In 2012 Tolich was instrumental in setting up the New Zealand Ethics Committee (NZEC), which is unusual in not being affiliated to an institution (Marlowe and Tolich, 2015: 180). This meant that instead of having to protect an institution from risk, NZEC was able to focus entirely on the ethical attributes of the research designs presented by its applicants. NZEC was designed to offer free ethical review to all researchers who are unable to access institutional RECs/IRBs (Marlowe and Tolich, 2015: 182). These are mostly researchers conducting community-based participatory research (CBPR), some of which is in the area of health and disability. Nevertheless, because of their context, these researchers are unable to access the RECs/IRBs in New Zealand (Marlowe and Tolich, 2015: 184), although this may be no bad thing, as RECs/IRBs often find it hard to make accurate assessments of CBPR (Marlowe and Tolich, 2015: 181).

In its first year of operation, NZEC received 14 applications; in its second year, it received 51. Unsurprisingly, as Tolich is one of the 33 signatories, NZEC supports the New Brunswick Declaration. In line with the Declaration, NZEC has sought feedback from its applicants about their experience of working with NZEC. This is not common practice among RECs/IRBs (Tolich and Marlowe, 2017: 45).

Use of NZEC, and acceptance of its recommendations, were intended to be optional. However, the feedback showed that within a short period government agencies and funders began requiring contracted researchers, including market researchers, to use NZEC (Tolich and Marlowe, 2017: 43). Some applicants also sought ethical review to give their work more credence with academic publishers. It is notable that NZEC's aspiration to remain optional for researchers was eroded by the ethics and politics of other institutions and sectors.

Conclusion

Research ethics regulation is a flawed system when applied beyond biomedical science (Stark, 2012: 8; Dingwall, 2016: 25). We have seen that there are times when it operates creatively and flexibly. But evidence shows that in most cases the system's emphasis on institutional protection leads it to focus almost exclusively on the data–gathering phase of research at the expense of all other phases. Also, the onerous process of applying for and gaining formal ethical approval can lead some researchers to conclude that once approval is received they have 'done ethics' and need give it no more attention. The second part of this book is written in an attempt to counteract these tendencies. But, first, we will consider another node where individual, social, professional, institutional, political and research ethics coincide: evaluation research.

REFLECTIVE QUESTIONS

1. How could the Euro-Western system of research regulation be changed to make it more ethical?
2. Think of a situation where your own personal ethics have clashed with the ethics of an institution or a profession. How did you handle that situation? Would you now deal with it the same way, or differently?
3. What would help people to work together ethically in research teams involving members from different social, organisational and professional cultures?
4. Think of an institution you are familiar with, such as a university, school or hospital. What do you think is unethical about how that institution operates? What would need to change so as to make it, in your view, ethical?
5. Which matters more to you: the approval of your superiors, or the approval of your research participants? Why? What are the implications of this?[1]

Note
[1] Inspired by Kouritzin and Nakagawa (2018: 7).

CHAPTER 5

Evaluation research ethics

Introduction

Evaluation is a particular form of research that is designed to assess the value of something: perhaps a service, an intervention or a policy. Evaluation research is often discussed and written about as though it is a single unified approach. In fact there are a number of different theoretical bases for evaluation research, such as realist evaluation, utilisation-focused evaluation, feminist evaluation, empowerment evaluation and Indigenous evaluation. Yet, whatever the theoretical underpinnings, the key questions asked by evaluation research are likely to be similar, such as:

1. What is working well?
2. Where and how could improvements be made?

Evaluation itself is, arguably, an everyday human activity, and indeed ethical judgements are a kind of evaluation (Hammersley and Traianou, 2012: 19). Evaluation research is more specific and systematic than everyday evaluation. It is often commissioned research, purchased by one or more institutions, usually from one other institution or, sometimes, an individual. Perhaps because it is often purchased by and/or conducted within institutions, institutional ethics have a particularly strong influence on evaluation research (Leone, Stame and Tagle, 2016: 163). Professional associations of evaluators around the world have produced ethical codes and guidelines for evaluation research (Desautels and Jacob, 2012: 437). Evaluation research very often has a political agenda (Palfrey, Thomas and Phillips, 2012: 29), such as to support future funding bids or a planned change in policy, and may be explicitly linked with work for social justice (Johnson, 2013: 197; Mertens, 2013: 233). As a result, it offers another useful case study, because evaluation research acts as a node where individual, professional, institutional, social and political ethics come together and interact with research ethics.

It may, then, seem surprising that much evaluation research takes place beyond the purview of RECs/IRBs (Tolich and Marlowe, 2017: 44). In general, only evaluation research conducted within health authorities or universities is subject to formal ethical approval. And not always then, as this university-based interviewee revealed:

> "There is a view that personally identifiable information and data around researchers and students can be used for all sorts of things, so assessing teaching

> quality, making research more efficient, but not necessarily with buy-in from the people you're using the information about. There's quite a bit of that going on at the moment. Another area of our organisation is looking at that, exploring the ethics and the buy-in from students – to me it looks a little bit dodgy. So in the organisation there is a prevailing thing of grab all the data, stick it in a warehouse, see what we can do with it to evaluate the organisation more efficiently, reduce the burden on people by reusing data, help the organisation work more efficiently. That's been done without too much in the way of ethical concern."

General research ethics codes and guidelines rarely include provision for the ethical needs of evaluation research (Williams, Guenther and Arnott, 2011: 3; Williams, 2016: 538), although there are some ethical guidelines that refer specifically to evaluation (Williams, 2016: 541). Yet evaluation research can be highly unethical, right from the level of its topic (Marlowe and Tolich, 2015: 187; Morris, 2015: 33). Alarmingly, a sizeable minority of Euro-Western evaluators have repeatedly been found to think that ethical considerations don't apply to evaluation research, or that they have never encountered any ethical dilemmas in their work (Morris, 2015: 32; Williams, 2016: 545). Yet, as with other forms of research, evaluation research has a history of intrusion, invasion and extractive exploitation of Indigenous peoples by Euro-Western researchers (Scougall, 2006: 50; LaFrance and Nichols, 2010: 14). Individual evaluators have been shown to have varying levels of ethical sensitivity (Desautels and Jacob, 2012: 438) that, as with other types of researchers, are affected by personal, social, professional, institutional and political ethics (Leone, Stame and Tagle, 2016: 163). There is a lack of shared understanding among evaluation stakeholders about where the responsibility lies for the management of ethics within evaluation (Williams, 2016: 541). Also, when it does come within the purview of a REC/IRB, the committee may not understand the differences between evaluation and other kinds of research (Israel, 2015: 131–2, citing Williams et al, 2011). Perhaps as a result, some commentators have asserted that it is not a good idea for evaluators to delegate their ethical responsibilities to a REC/IRB or its equivalent (Palfrey, Thomas and Phillips, 2012: 122).

Maybe it is because most evaluation research is conducted without reference to RECs/IRBs that most books on evaluation research don't say much, if anything, about ethics. The literature that does exist is out of date, partial and inadequate (Morris, 2015: 38). There is rarely an entry for ethics in the index of an evaluation text. Yet evaluators are very concerned with closely related concepts such as equity and social justice, values and empowerment. Also, in recent years ethics has been a topic of discussion at the annual conferences of professional evaluators' associations around the world (Desautels and Jacob, 2012: 437), and some government departments, too, have become increasingly concerned about the ethics of evaluation (Williams, 2016: 535).

There is a sizeable academic community around evaluation research, with university departments around the world, professors of evaluation, specialist academic journals and so on. Yet evaluation is one of the most 'real world' types of research, as it is almost impossible to do evaluation research without taking its context into account (Chouinard and Cousins, 2007: 40; Alkin, 2013: 284). Indeed, there is a symbiotic relationship between evaluation research and its context, as the context shapes the evaluation research, while the evaluation research will reconstitute the context (Greene, 2013: 215). Perhaps as a result of this relationship, some evaluation scholars suggest that the ethical responsibilities of evaluation researchers 'extend beyond the boundaries defined by their study's immediate stakeholders' (Morris, 2008: 12). As with other forms of research, there are advocates of reflexivity as a method of assisting evaluation researchers to practise more effectively (MacDonald and Bourke, 2017: 150) and therefore more ethically. (See Chapters 1, 6 and 9 for more on reflexivity.)

There are a number of key ethical fault-lines around evaluation research to do with money, methods and publication.

Money

It is sometimes said that evaluation research 'follows the money'. This means that evaluation research happens when there is money to pay for it, and so what needs evaluating isn't always what gets evaluated. Also, in some areas, evaluation budgets are set to suit the grant-giver rather than to pay for evaluation research to be done thoroughly and well. This is particularly problematic in Indigenous evaluation research, where the relational approach is time intensive and therefore costly, which means that budgets are often inadequate (Johnson, 2013: 196; Israel, 2015: 131, citing Williams et al, 2011). The gentle pace of progress in Indigenous community affairs can be frustrating to Euro-Western evaluators who are used to working swiftly to finish projects by agreed deadlines (Scougall, 2006: 53). The knock-on effect of this is that evaluation research is often done 'to' Indigenous peoples using the Euro-Western paradigm, rather than being done 'with' or 'by' Indigenous peoples (Scougall, 2006: 53). This is effectively an extension of colonisation rather than 'the decolonising type of evaluation that has the potential to bring real healing to our communities' (Johnson, 2013: 196; Paipa in Wehipeihana et al, 2013: 292). There are exceptions, such as in New Zealand where relationship building and relationship management are planned and budgeted for in evaluation research (Pipi in Wehipeihana et al, 2013: 286), but this seems to be unusual.

Budget holders often have a great deal of input into evaluation research questions, methods and dissemination (Mathison, 2016: 96). Also, there is often pressure on evaluators to find positive results and so support future funding applications, which means that the vast majority of published evaluation reports are mostly or wholly positive.

> "I also think there may be an issue that the intent, particularly in evaluation studies, is to show the arts company or the social welfare thing is having a benefit; it's amazing to find that they always do. And maybe they always do. Is doing something better than doing nothing?"

This pressure may be direct and explicit, or indirect and implicit. Evidence suggests that, in general, pressure is greater on insider than on outsider researchers (Desautels and Jacob, 2012: 447). At times the pressure can be hard to resist, such as when the evaluator is in sympathy with the aims of the project being evaluated, or when the evaluator's income depends on payment for the evaluation research.

There is a worldwide community of evaluators looking for work, both individuals and organisations, who may be desperate for the funding that an evaluation contract would bring. Some people who conduct evaluation research are trained professional evaluators with support networks through professional associations and the like. Others are academic researchers who also have professional networks to draw on for support. Then there's a third category of evaluators: people whose professions do not include evaluation, and who are required to conduct evaluation research on top of their main job, often with little or no training or support (Kara, 2017: 10). This is a form of 'insider research', which can in itself be a major challenge, potentially leading to suspicion from colleagues about motives and methods (Markless and Streatfield, 2013: 197). I regard it as unethical to expect people to do evaluation research in these circumstances. The design and outputs may be of poor quality, and yet may still be used in seeking funding or developing services or policy, rather than more weight being given to evaluation research with better methods. This too, in my view, is unethical.

It is interesting to note that, of the 32 chapter authors contributing to *Indigenous Pathways into Social Research: Voices of a New Generation* (Mertens, Cram and Chilisa, 2013), 10 are evaluators. For some, this may have been a positive choice, but certainly not for all. For example, Issaka Traore from Burkina Faso was able to complete undergraduate studies in Ireland and was accepted for postgraduate study at several UK universities (the University of East Anglia, the London School of Economics and Swansea University), but was unable to secure the necessary funding. As a result he now works in Burkina Faso as an evaluator of development programs (Traore, 2013: 180). Traore's is not an unusual story. This doesn't mean that evaluation research is a soft option (Johnson, 2013: 193), but it is more accessible as a profession for researchers who don't have postgraduate qualifications. Increasingly, this may also apply to Euro-Western researchers as university tuition fees rise and economic uncertainties bite. Also, while some Indigenous researchers are able to find work as evaluators, the number and proportion of Indigenous evaluators overall is not high (Bowman, Francis and Tyndall, 2015: 343).

Methods

Evaluation research often uses a mixed-methods design. Any quantitative or qualitative method may be used in the service of evaluation, and many theoretical stances too. The ethical aspects of method that are relevant in research more widely are also relevant in evaluation research. However, there is one aspect of method that features more strongly in Euro-Western evaluation research than in other types of Euro-Western research (although it may also appear there), and that is stakeholder involvement.

Evaluation research often focuses on marginalised groups: those with disabilities, or living in poverty, or in poor health, or with low levels of educational attainment. Euro-Western evaluators often frame their projects in a 'deficit model', seeing potential participants as having problems to be solved by interventions or policies. This ignores the very real possibility that potential participants – disabilities, poverty and so on notwithstanding – may have great strengths, qualities and resilience (Mertens, 2013: 234). One view of service or programme evaluation holds that involving service users, other stakeholders and/or the wider public in evaluation research can help to address this ethical difficulty. Such involvement, in theory, leads to the production of more robust and useful findings (Millett, 2013: 327; CDC, 2014: 5).

While this may sound like a good idea – and sometimes it is – it can also raise as many problems as it solves. For example, however much commissioners or evaluation researchers may like the idea, service users, other stakeholders and/or the wider public may not choose to be involved in evaluation research (Cartland, Ruch-Ross and Mason, 2012: 171). Then, if they are involved, people may want or need to be paid for their contribution. However, there may be barriers to this, such as an insufficient evaluation research budget, or people receiving essential welfare benefits that would be compromised if they were paid from a different source. (See Chapter 8 for more on paying participants.) The prospect of payment also raises new ethical questions, such as: if the budget is insufficient, is it better to involve service users or the wider public a little bit, or not at all? In either case, why? (Hamilton, 2009: 214–15).

Another question this raises is: what are stakeholders' views and understandings of evaluation ethics? There is a small but growing discussion of participants' views of research ethics in the Euro-Western literature, led by health researchers. I have not found anything focusing on evaluation participants or about the views of other stakeholders. The literature suggests that potential participants are well able to weigh up the likely risks and benefits of participating in research (Dresser, 2015: 312; Pickering, 2018: 423). Participants often perceive risk and benefit differently from people on RECs/IRBs (Bell and Salmon, 2011: 92; Dresser, 2015: 306–11; Pickering, 2018: 423), but then they are in a different position, so that is probably not surprising. The literature also suggests that participants are highly sensitive to RECs/IRBs' paternalistic and patronising assumptions that ordinary people don't think about ethics (Cox and McDonald, 2013: 230;

Pickering, 2018: 423). People have a variety of motivations for taking part in research and one of these is that participating can be an ethical act in itself (Bell and Salmon, 2011: 89; Cox and McDonald, 2013: 228). People feel strongly that they are able, and should be enabled, to make their own decisions about how and when they engage with research and researchers, just as they make their own decisions about how and when to engage with anybody else (Bell and Salmon, 2011: 91). As Kouritzin and Nakagawa (2018: 8) put it, people should 'have the right to practice the ethics that they know', rather than being forced to act 'within ethics that they do not know'.

I asked my interviewees what they thought about participants' views of ethics. Sixteen (of a total of 18) of them answered, and there was a high level of agreement. They thought that participants wanted to feel safe within the research process, were irritated and frustrated by regulatory bureaucracy such as consent forms to be signed, and generally weren't nearly as knowledgeable or bothered about research ethics as researchers are.

> "Sometimes I think they think we're over-protective patronising twits! They know when something doesn't feel right, they know when people are genuine, they know when people are misconstruing things they say to fit."

> "I think that the humanity of ethics has completely gone, so if you and me are having a conversation, I develop a small sense of trust in you, in this short hour of our lives. If you ask me to sign a form, that value is completely not there. When we started the conversation, you smiled at me and told me some stuff, that was all I wanted. There was no need to sign a form. There is no recognition of that – I find that frustrating."

Where participants were well informed about research ethics, this caused different problems.

> "When I'm doing education research in a health setting, you're often working with participants who do have experience of NHS ethics procedures, and they can be quite tricky to work with as participants because they can be quite demanding in what they consider to be ethical. Sometimes that can make me feel as if I'm being quite slapdash, and I don't think I am, but it's a different approach. It can be the same if you're dealing with academics – they have a heightened awareness of ethics."

There was some divergence around the topic of anonymity and confidentiality, with some interviewees thinking that this should be ensured for all participants, while others thought that participants should be able to decide whether or not they would prefer anonymity (see Chapter 8 for more on this). Another area of divergence was that some interviewees thought the ethics procedures they needed to go through with participants helped to build rapport and trust. However, others mentioned that those procedures could have the opposite effect, particularly if a writing-based system of regulatory management was imposed on people with an oral tradition.

> "People have developed ways of getting consent verbally, keeping track of consent verbally, documenting so that it's more comfortable for the participants."

Even within the Euro-Western paradigm the introduction of bureaucracy, combined with the researcher's perceived authority, can cause misunderstandings.

> "Often people think we're the government."

> "Some of our difficulty is to try to be honestly as ethical as possible in the context of people who are still understanding ethics as something connected with power and authority."

There are accounts in the literature from people who have been involved in evaluation research as participants; these do not focus on ethics, but the variance is interesting. Some can identify personal benefit (for example, Beckett, 2009: 154); some find that, working with others, they can have a positive impact (for example, Goddard, 2009: 161–2); and others find that their involvement makes no difference to existing power imbalances and unethical practices (e.g. Sands, 2009: 156–7). It is also very difficult to tell whether involving service users or the wider public has had a positive impact on the quality of evaluation research (Morrow et al, 2012: 158).

None of this is to say that service users, other stakeholders or the wider public should *not* be involved in evaluation research. The point I wish to make is that involving such people, while often worthwhile, is complicated, resource intensive and not guaranteed to be beneficial for those involved or for the evaluation research. If such involvement is to stand a chance of being beneficial, it needs to be managed with considerable thought and care. Tokenism is definitely unethical.

Indigenous evaluation, of course, involves all stakeholders by definition. It also requires clarity about who owns and controls which parts of the knowledges that are used in, and produced by, the evaluation research (Williams, Guenther and Arnott, 2011: 4). Indigenous evaluation frameworks have been developed in some areas and these will be discussed in more detail below.

Publication

In Euro-Western evaluation negative findings are often buried, so publication bias is greater in evaluation than in most, perhaps all, other forms of research (Slavin, 2008: 7). This unwillingness to share learning increases the already high incidence of duplication (Fiennes, 2015: 36). Much Euro-Western evaluation is funded from the public purse, so it is unethical that there are many, many local government departments and non-profit organisations all doing small evaluations of very similar work. As Fiennes suggests, these evaluations are likely to be methodologically inconsistent, and not high quality, because each has a tiny amount of resource. If, for example, the 124 non-profit organisations in England offering housing/accommodation services to people with disabilities[1] could pool their evaluation priorities and resources, they should be able to commission some robust and rigorous evaluation research that would benefit them all.

That being said, there may at times be pragmatic reasons not to publish. For example, publication of an unfavourable service evaluation could lead to withdrawal of funding, closure of the service and job losses, causing harm to beneficiaries and staff. Instead, a decision not to publish could leave room for an opportunity to make improvements to the service. Also, a favourable evaluation isn't necessarily the end of the story. Circumstances will change, and the service, intervention or policy may change in response. And even publication of a favourable evaluation can cause harm, such as by making stakeholders complacent so they neglect to maintain high standards. On balance, though, as with all research, publication is likely to be more ethical than not publishing. (See Chapter 12 for more on this.)

In the Indigenous paradigm, some of the above may also apply, or it may be a community's decision whether or not to publish. Indigenous communities might have different – although equally pragmatic – reasons not to publish evaluation findings.

Ethical solutions

Some possible solutions to evaluation's problems have been proposed. One is to expand evaluator resources. If time-lines were more relaxed they would be more ethical (Williams, Guenther and Arnott, 2011: 7–8). Also, participants could have more control over at least part of the evaluation research budget. This could potentially be achieved using unconventional means of fundraising, such as crowd-funding, social investment bonds or community currency (Datta, 2016: 164–5), although fundraising using any technique is resource intensive in itself.

Another possible solution is to help Euro-Western evaluators to understand that they need to acquire a certain level of cultural competence before trying to engage Indigenous people in evaluation research (Hernandez, 2013: 68). As we saw in Chapter 2, cultural competence involves understanding and respecting the customs and ways of life of Indigenous peoples. It seems that, on the whole, culturally competent evaluation is likely to be 'grounded in the community context, in indigenous [sic] ways of knowing, and in a participatory approach' (Chouinard and Cousins, 2007: 51). An alternative way of working with this is the Central Australian system known as 'malparrara', in which a local Indigenous person works alongside a qualified non-Indigenous person to combine their cultural and professional knowledges (Scougall, 2006: 51). It is also possible that, at times, an independent evaluator with no prior knowledge of the community may be best placed to work on an Indigenous evaluation, just as external evaluators may be most helpful in any situation, although even without cultural competence any evaluator would need to display considerable cultural sensitivity (Scougall, 2006: 53). It is also essential to ensure that evaluation findings have cultural relevance (CDC, 2014: 2). Cultural incompetence can result in findings that are inaccurate and may even be harmful (Bowman, Francis and Tyndall, 2015: 343).

A third possible solution is to develop Indigenous evaluation methods wherever there are Indigenous peoples. Some work has been done on this. For example, in 2003, the Australasian Evaluation Society (AES) Board set Indigenous evaluation as one of the AES's strategic objectives (Wehipeihana, 2008: 40). In the US, the American Indian Higher Education Consortium, which is made up of over 30 colleges and universities controlled by American Indian tribes, has developed an Indigenous Evaluation Framework which brings together Euro-Western methods and Indigenous ways of knowing (LaFrance and Nichols, 2010: 13). 'The goal of this project is to develop evaluation processes that are robust enough to accommodate and value different "ways of knowing" within Indigenous epistemologies, build ownership and a sense of community within groups of Indian educators and evaluators, and effectively contribute to the development of high quality and sustainable science and mathematics education programs'"(LaFrance and Nichols, 2010: 14).

These kinds of structural advances, while clearly progressive and worthwhile, don't solve all the problems. The AES's leadership did not eradicate tensions in Australia, such as those between the expectations of agencies commissioning evaluations and of Indigenous evaluation participants, or between pressures to complete evaluation research on time and under budget while also offering appropriate benefit to the Indigenous communities involved (Scougall, 2006: 49). Similarly, Indigenous evaluation practices in the US were not able to overcome the tensions between government grant evaluation requirements and Indigenous communities' requirements (Grover, 2010: 33).

A fourth possible solution may be more effective because it is multi-faceted. This solution involves:

- improving ethical guidelines such that all guidelines for research also cover evaluation research, including Indigenous evaluation research where appropriate;
- making the commissioners, purchasers and managers of Indigenous evaluation subject to the improved ethical guidelines, and providing training, monitoring and support to ensure that this is implemented;
- either setting up specialist RECs/IRBs for evaluation research or ensuring that existing RECs/IRBs have a good understanding of the issues;
- moving towards a new paradigm of evaluation research with full involvement of stakeholders, including Indigenous communities where appropriate, in initiating and designing projects, collecting and analysing data, in culturally appropriate ways. (Williams, Guenther and Arnott, 2011: 9)

Given the complexity of evaluation in context, this kind of multi-faceted approach to increasing its ethicality seems more likely to be effective than any single approach. However, this is not to say that all single solutions are worthless; they may well be useful within a multi-faceted approach.

Conclusion

There have been calls for evaluation research to take a more explicitly ethical stance. However, there are differing views about how this should be done. Michael Scrivens, from the US, describes ethics as evaluation's 'last frontier' and sees 'applied ethics as a key discipline within evaluation' (Scrivens, 2016: 11–12). His view is that evaluators should make what he calls 'the ethical shift' towards altruism (Scrivens, 2016: 42–3), which is essentially a virtue ethics position (see Chapter 3 for more on virtue ethics). Chris Barnett and Laura Camfield, from the UK, by contrast, propose a more value-based system. They argue that evaluation research should take a different ethical approach from research more widely, by focusing on the well-being of all stakeholders (rather than just participants) and taking into account the duties of evaluation research to society as a whole (Barnett and Camfield, 2016: 528). Michael Morris, from the US, points out that some evaluators already link their work explicitly with a social justice agenda. He stops short of suggesting that all evaluators should do this, but he does make the point that if they did, it would 'greatly expand the range of issues regarded as ethical in nature by evaluators' (Morris, 2008: 12). Ricardo Millett, from Panama, and Leslie Williams, from the UK, do suggest that all evaluators should focus on social justice rather than 'do no harm', although Williams acknowledges that one barrier to this is the consequent increased resource requirement (Millett, 2013: 327; Williams, 2016: 545).

Sandra Mathison, from Canada, takes an even wider and more structural approach. She suggests that evaluators have a role in redressing inequality, and can do this by operating in a sociological style with a three-pronged approach. First, she suggests that evaluations should be independently funded; second, that publicly available evaluation frameworks and resources should themselves be evaluated for effectiveness; and, third, that an international academy of distinguished evaluators should be established to evaluate wide issues of social inequality (Mathison, 2016: 99–103).

Evaluators, like other researchers, need to be taught, and supported, to think and act ethically. This could be done, as Williams, Guenther and Arnott (2011: 9) suggest, by improving ethical guidelines for evaluators and linking them with training, monitoring and support, for purchasers, managers, and commissioners of evaluation as well as for evaluators themselves. This should apply to Indigenous and Euro-Western evaluation research. Further, I think that evaluation research needs to address ethics at every level – individual evaluator; evaluation methods; commissioning; and more widely in terms of its impact in society – if it is to become truly ethical.

REFLECTIVE QUESTIONS

1. Would evaluation research be more ethical if it was governed by RECs/IRBs? If so – or if not – why?
2. To what extent is bureaucracy an ethical practice?
3. If you are involving community members in evaluation research, with an adequate budget, should they be paid the same as professionals or not? Why?
4. Are there any circumstances in which you think it would be unethical to publish evaluation findings? If so, what might they be?
5. What, in your view, would need to change for evaluation research to become truly ethical?

Note

[1] Number generated by searching the Charity Commission register on 28 April 2017.

Part II
Doing research ethically

CHAPTER 6

Planning research ethically

Introduction

Ethical work begins as soon as you think of a possible research question (Ball and Janyst, 2008: 33). Will that question lead to good-quality research with beneficial results? Could those results be misused by people with different agendas? There is an argument that, when planning research, it is ethically important to consider the potential impact of that research on more than just the participants (Alldred and Gillies, 2012: 141). What could the impact of research be on a community? A culture? On the 'non-consenting others' who are named and discussed in research encounters without their knowledge or consent (Mannay, 2016: 123)?

> "One of the things about planning research is planning all the other stages and seeing what might lie ahead."

Of course it is impossible to foresee every eventuality. The chapters that come later are intended to help researchers develop the necessary skills to manage the unforeseen ethical difficulties that can arise in even the best-planned research projects. It is worth reading the whole of Part II of this book, to sensitise yourself to potential pitfalls and help you to plan effectively. This chapter will give an overview by introducing you to the planning process and the key ethical considerations.

Good planning for research is itself an ethical imperative because it will help to prevent many ethical problems in the course of the project. This involves thinking through, as far as possible, every stage of the research.

> "The planning phase is crucial because if you fail there the next steps are quite loose. I would say it is the most important; if the first plans are bad ones the next ones won't be good either."

> "There are a lot of things to think about at the planning stage that can help with problems later on."

For example, there are good ethical reasons for making a dissemination plan at the outset, because then that plan cannot be skewed by the research findings, subsequent political or personal clashes or other such factors that may come into play. Also, this enables you to inform potential participants of your plans, which equips them more fully to give (or withhold) consent (see below for more on this).

Choosing a research question

Most RECs/IRBs focus more on whether research will be done ethically than on whether it is ethical to do that research in the first place (Marlowe and Tolich, 2015: 187). However, the research and evaluation methods literature, from both the Euro-Western and Indigenous paradigms, suggests that ethical considerations should begin as soon as you think of a topic (Schwandt and Gates, 2016: 67; Walter and Andersen, 2016: 50; Leavy, 2017: 24). Is it a topic worth studying? Could it lead to social, economic or environmental improvement? Why might you want to do this piece of work? I would argue that all researchers should ask these kinds of questions at the outset of their research.

> "I think carefully about why I'm doing it: are any of my intentions ethically incorrect?"

Contract researchers may not have the freedom to choose their research topic, but in theory they have the freedom to choose whether or not to take on a project (Morris, 2008: 16). However, in practice, there may be barriers to this. For example, an employed contract researcher, whose boss tells them to work on a project they think is unethical, may face a choice between doing that research or losing their job. Similarly, an independent researcher may need the money a contract offers, which may tempt them to accept work on an unethical topic.

> "You do need to start thinking about what I think I'm going to be able to achieve in this setting, what's the point, and to what extent is it a worthwhile point?"

Research funders, too, may dictate research topics. When industry funds research, it has the potential to introduce bias from the outset. I am not saying that all industry-funded research is biased. Also, there are many ways in which bias can be introduced into research, so if a piece of industry-funded research is biased, that is not necessarily due to the source of its funding (Rowe et al, 2009: 268). However, when I read a literature review that concluded it is safe to eat soya products, and then discovered that the research had been funded by the United Soybean Board (Munro et al, 2003: 21), I read it again, more carefully. The second time, I noticed that the authors didn't outline the search or inclusion strategy they had used to select literature on which to base their argument. Also, they didn't mention the issue of potential bias, or say anything about how they had worked to counteract bias. These factors led me to treat the findings with some scepticism. The research may not be biased, but I don't have enough evidence to make a firm conclusion one way or the other.

Charitable and government research funders may also introduce bias by favouring some topics and so restricting the funding available for others. In particular, it is rare for such bodies to offer funding for research into topics that are meaningful for Indigenous peoples (Yantio, 2013: 129). So, funded researchers, too – and those seeking funding – need to consider whether their topic is ethical and, if not, whether they should take on the project (Morris, 2008: 16).

> "Before you even go into all the detail of what's involved, is it worth doing? Does it have merit? Who will benefit, and how, if this research goes ahead? Just because you've been funded to do it, that doesn't mean it necessarily has merit or integrity in and of itself."

One other thing to consider at this stage is whether your research question is based on a deficit approach. Euro-Western research is generally designed to solve problems, and so it often focuses on people's difficulties while ignoring their strengths and the contributions they do, or could, make to society (Lambert, 2014: 67; Walter and Andersen, 2016: 22). This can have the unintentional effect of further stigmatising people from groups that are already stigmatised, which is clearly unethical. There are methodological frameworks that can help to avoid this, such as appreciative inquiry (Whitney and Trosten-Bloom, 2010), although they are not widely known or understood.

Designing your research

Once you are confident that you have an ethical topic and research question or questions, you need to create an ethical research design.

> "There's obviously all the practical aspects of the ethics around the framing of the research project. It's needing to tread a line so you're honest with your participants in what you're doing. Even if you use different language, the sentiment has to be the same, otherwise it's unethical."

One of the difficulties here can be that if you are passionate about your topic and research question (and it's best if you are), it can be hard to step back and take a broader view. But it is *essential* that you are willing to find, and use, evidence that contradicts your convictions. The way to do this is to look at your topic and question(s) from all sides.

> "I had a master's student working in an FE [further education] college. She wanted to do research on class sizes, but she basically wanted to 'prove' that smaller class sizes were better. So her first draft of questions, that was going to generate the data that she would be writing her research on, was all skewed to find that smaller class sizes are more effective for learning. When I first saw them, my point was, you haven't asked any questions about the positive sides of large class sizes."

This example shows how well-intentioned and passionate researchers can completely miss important ethical dimensions in their planning (Jennings,

2012: 91). It also shows how useful it can be to have a less passionate and more experienced pair of eyes on your proposal.

Cultural competence is also essential (see Chapter 5 for more on cultural competence). Proposal assessors in Australia have found that at least 90% of Euro-Western researchers who want to do research with Indigenous peoples have not learned about the ways of life or cultural sensitivities of those peoples and do not know how to work with them (Hornung, 2013: 140). Research methods that may be effective in Euro-Western societies may not be effective when used with Indigenous peoples (Wilson, 2008: 110–16; Traore, 2013: 176).

> "I do want to see there's been some consumer engagement in the design. We have in Australia a consumer participation statement; it's a really good statement around why consumers should be involved in research, why they can be. I think it's an area people pay lip service to really whereas I see it as one of the key components of research."

This is an important point for Euro-Western researchers, as a form of cultural competence may be needed for any research where participants are from different social groups to the researcher. In these cases, involving potential participants in research design can help to hone a researcher's ethical sensitivity.

Research design is not the only area where you may want to consider involving participants. Some Euro-Western methodologies, such as participatory and community-based research, and most if not all Indigenous methodologies, require the involvement of participants throughout. Other forms of Euro-Western research can benefit from participant involvement at any or all stages of the research (Sinha and Back, 2014: 485). However, participant involvement requires significant resources of time, money and support, so this needs careful thinking through at the planning stage.

If you are recruiting staff to work on your research project, you have to think carefully about the skills and qualities they will need. If you are in the Euro-Western paradigm, you are likely to think of research skills and associated qualities first. However, these may not be the only, or even the primary, skills they need. Lucie Cluver led research to gather an evidence base about social work intervention for families in South Africa whose children were affected by AIDS. She consciously recruited researchers who had high levels of empathy and experience in working with children affected by AIDS, and found that this had unforeseen consequences. Specifically, when faced with very sick or traumatised children, the researchers sometimes chose to make interventions rather than simply gathering data. Cluver asks whether her team would ever have prioritised 'scientific over humanitarian principles' (Cluver et al, 2014: 46). I wonder how ethical it would be, in doing research with such families, to pay no attention to those qualities in recruiting researchers.

Planning your context setting

The key to ethical context setting is to think widely: beyond your field, discipline or community. There are three key questions to answer here.

1. What are the sources you need to cite to set your own work into context?
2. How and where can you find those sources?
3. How much time will you need to gather and absorb them?

You are likely to need to scope out the context-setting work at the planning stage, which will involve figuring out and documenting your search strategy and doing the initial searching, so that you can answer these questions effectively. Don't forget to include work you disagree with or dislike.

Planning your data gathering

Interviewees for this book had quite a lot to say about planning data gathering (which again suggests that this is a higher-profile stage of the research process than others when it comes to ethical considerations). Both data and participants need to be treated with care. A key ethical issue in planning your data gathering is to consider whether you need to gather primary data or whether you can use secondary data, that is, data that has already been gathered by others. In the Euro-Western paradigm there are good ethical reasons for using secondary data if you can, although as always this raises new ethical problems (see Chapter 7 for more on this).

Some of the ethical difficulties you may encounter with data gathering will be beyond the powers of any individual researcher to overcome.

> "If you're doing systematic reviews of data, then there is a problem of drug companies hiding stuff, or of academics who don't want to share their data, and that is an ethical issue and has to be addressed at policy level."

Whatever kind(s) of data you gather, and however you gather your data, aim to gather only as much as you need to answer your research question. Novice researchers often believe that more data leads to better research, but this is not so. Gathering too much data places an unnecessary burden on both participants and researcher, causing extra work at both the gathering and analysis stages of research.

Planning your data analysis

Failing to plan your data analysis is unethical because it will adversely affect your well-being (see Chapter 14 for more on researcher well-being).

> "It's really interesting how often people leave out any information about what form of data analysis. I find that extraordinary: somehow they'll get it and then, what then? They say 'we'll think about that when we've gathered the data', but how you gather the data is centrally linked with how you're going to analyse it."

As this interviewee says, the type(s) and nature of your data have implications for your data analysis. You need to think through, as best you can, the methods you will use for analysis, and the time and other resources you will need. Analysis includes data preparation, coding and description, as well as the core interpretative work of analysis itself. You also need to plan how you will store your data securely.

Planning your reporting

The first step in planning how you will report your research findings is to identify your audience(s). Then consider what kinds of reporting will best meet their needs. In practice, most Euro–Western research is reported in writing, but there are augmentations (such as visual methods) and alternatives (such as oral reports) that will be appropriate for certain audiences. Conversely, much Indigenous research is reported orally, although writing is increasingly being used and valued by Indigenous researchers. You will need to plan the resource requirements for the production – and, where necessary, translation – of your intended research outputs.

Planning your presentation

Presentation of research processes and findings, to live audiences (whether in person or using technological means), needs to be considered at the planning stage of research.

> "Sometimes it's when you think about how to present the findings you can identify a problem at the planning stage."

Key questions include the following.

- To whom will you want to present your work?
- What are their needs?
- How can you best meet those needs?
- Do you envisage involving participants or other stakeholders in your presentations?
- If so, what are the resource implications?

It is galling to arrive at the presentation stage of a research project, think of a wonderful way to present your research and then realise that you don't have the time or the money to use that method. Therefore it is important to think about presentation during the planning process, with the aim of allocating enough time and funds to present your process and findings effectively to as many people as you would like to reach.

Planning dissemination

Even the very end stages of research should be carefully planned at the earliest opportunity. This is an ethical imperative because it helps to guard against the risk of findings that prove unpopular being withheld from publication, unused or misused – although of course there are no absolute guarantees (Morris, 2008: 21).

Dissemination may have considerable implications for participants, so it is important to be able to outline your dissemination plans to them if they are to be able to give fully informed consent to take part in your research. For example, if you want to disseminate your findings through the mainstream media, you need to be aware of journalistic ethics. These are closer to the Indigenous than the Euro-Western paradigm in one respect: journalists do not like to use pseudonyms for their participants, although there are occasionally exceptions, such as where revealing the identity of a participant could put them in danger (see Chapter 8 for more on pseudonyms). However, when you pass on your findings to a journalist, you relinquish editorial control. This is covered in more detail in Chapter 12 and you need to be aware of possible implications at the planning stage.

Planning aftercare

Conventional Euro-Western research requires planning all the way to the end of the project. However, these days, ethical researchers plan beyond the last publication or presentation. Aftercare has been shown to be necessary for participants and communities, data and findings, and for researchers themselves. As we saw in Chapter 2, in the Indigenous paradigm, where researchers usually belong to the communities in which they conduct research, aftercare is a given, part of the holistic approach to life, work, relationships and accountability. In the Euro-Western paradigm, understanding of the need for aftercare is quite recent, and many RECs/IRBs, research commissioners and funders have not caught up with this ethical imperative. That puts the onus on researchers to plan and implement aftercare, as necessary, depending on the nature of their project.

Planning for researcher well-being

Advance preparation is a good safeguard for researcher well-being (Moncur, 2013: 1885). Think about the project you propose. Does it present physical risks to the researcher(s)? Or emotional, mental or spiritual risks? Are there relational risks, such as the potential for being discriminated against, bullied or harassed? If you can answer 'yes' to any of these questions, think first about whether you can redesign the research to avoid those risks without losing quality. If that is not possible, then think about what you can do to mitigate the risks to yourself and your colleagues.

The ethics of collaboration

At the start of the planning process it is an ethical imperative to do everything possible to make your research inclusive for, and accessible to, all potential participants and stakeholders. In this context, research can be a collaborative effort from the planning stage onwards. Collaboration in research is common in Euro-Western research, and almost inevitable in Indigenous research. Collaborators may include participants, other researchers, people with relevant professional expertise and other stakeholders.

Indigenous researchers report some very unethical 'collaborations', in which Euro-Western researchers position themselves as principal investigators (PIs) or team leaders and impose Euro-Western methods. They use Indigenous colleagues to do the routine work while they take the credit for the research and their Euro-Western institutions hold the copyright to all the work produced (Chilisa, 2012: 89; Sherwood, 2013: 213). Euro-Western PIs have also used Indigenous 'collaborators' so as to be able to access Indigenous-specific research funding (McGregor, 2018). This kind of abusive 'collaboration' perpetuates colonial dominance (Castleden et al, 2015: 16).

At the other end of the spectrum, there are examples of highly ethical collaborations, such as research done with Roma, Europe's Indigenous nomadic peoples, using critical communicative methodology (CCM). This is a particularly ethical framework that (among other things) involves participants from the very start of the process in planning and designing, as well as conducting, the research (Munté, Serradell and Sordé, 2011: 260). The use of CCM demonstrates that collaborations between Indigenous participants and Euro-Western researchers can 'resist domination and promote and respect human rights, social justice, democracy and healing' (Chilisa, 2012: 296).

The ethical aspects of working collaboratively in research are not often considered. Mutual respect and effective communication are key, as are clear shared expectations. Spend time articulating, and learning to understand, each other's worldviews (Chilisa, 2012: 296). Do what you say you're going to do, when you say you're going to do it – or explain why you can't, at the earliest opportunity.

Formal ethical review

You may need to apply for formal ethical review, as previously discussed in Chapters 1 and 4. Planning for ethical review involves building in enough time for your REC/IRB to go through its process. However, it is not ethical to take the view that formal ethical review *is* ethics, and that, once you receive approval of your project from your REC/IRB, you have 'done ethics'.

> "Planning of ethics is a first stage and needs to be a continual process across the project. You have to be quite open about where the project might take you."

As this book amply demonstrates, ethical difficulties can arise at any stage of your research project, before, during and after formal ethical approval.

> "Formally, in terms of ethics, one ought to start doing that balancing around, are the burdens I'm going to place on participants justified by what I'm going to find out here? I'm not sure any of us formally do that equation."

RECs/IRBs do not usually consider whether or not research topics are, in themselves, ethical. Nevertheless, it is important for researchers to do so (Marlowe and Tolich, 2015: 187). Some commentators go further: 'An ethical project and ethical methods must flow from an ethical research question whose proposer is critically aware of his or her subject position' (London and Macdonald, 2014: 101). Also, it is not only the topic and the methods that the ethical researcher needs to consider, but also the operation of the research throughout the project.

> "It's something I really focus on when I'm reviewing applications: who's included, who's excluded? Most annoying when it goes 18–65, as if people over 65 have nothing to contribute! I really advocate more imaginative and creative thinking about research methodologies that are relevant and appropriate to the group. Ways to get data that are not just standard. I think technologies are making it more and more possible; more people are using mobile phone technology and other things to really engage with e.g. young people or people with disabilities who are normally seen as too hard."

If you are planning a project where you will not need to apply for formal ethical approval, it will help if you can take the time to agree with relevant colleagues the ethical principles or values, or an ethical protocol, on which your research or evaluation will be based (Williams, 2016: 544). This will prepare you for the unforeseen ethical difficulties that can arise in any research project.

Obtaining formal ethical approval is part of the reality of many researchers' lives. This book does not attempt to offer a step-by-step route to successfully obtaining ethical approval, because there are so many variables among research projects, RECs/IRBs and approaches to research ethics in different communities and disciplines. The book is designed to equip you with the knowledge and skills to help you navigate any system of ethical regulation that you may encounter.

Individual barriers to ethical action

As you can see from the list in Appendix 1, I interviewed a range of people for this book, from doctoral students to professors, from generalists to ethics specialists, and from several countries on five continents. One of the questions I asked was, 'Do you think there are any internal barriers to acting ethically, i.e. within individual people? If so, how would you describe these?' People mentioned things like habit, pressure to succeed, self-interest, ambition and lack of knowledge. Some people said they didn't understand the question, and/or that it wasn't something they had thought about. To my surprise, not a single person mentioned cognitive biases.

Cognitive biases are automatic and replicable errors in thinking that have been studied extensively by psychologists. They are features of our automatic cognition or 'fast thinking' (Kahneman, 2011: 12–13). This is based on the schemata we develop to help us make inferences about the world around us (Cerulo, 2010: 117). Over 100 cognitive biases have been defined by Euro-Western scholars, and some are highly relevant to researchers. These include:

- attentional bias: a tendency to pay more attention to some features of a situation than others, which may impair judgement;
- belief bias: prioritising beliefs over data, findings or facts;
- Berkson's paradox: a counter-intuitive statistical result where two values may appear to have a positive correlation when in fact they are negatively correlated;
- bizarreness effect: the unusual is easier to remember than the more common;
- choice-supportive bias: remembering your decisions as better quality and/or more fully informed than they actually were;
- confirmation bias: a tendency to give more credence to data or findings that confirm existing beliefs;
- conservatism: the inability to change one's beliefs even when presented with new evidence supporting that change;
- empathy gap: under-estimating the strength of feeling, and/or the influence of emotion, in oneself or others;
- expectation bias: giving more credence to data and findings that agree with expectations for research, and less to those that don't;
- framing effect: presenting information in a way that can affect the conclusions drawn from it, such that different presentations of the same information can lead to different conclusions;
- fundamental attribution error: over-estimating the role of personality, and under-estimating the role of context, on a phenomenon;
- group attribution error: believing that links between individuals and groups they belong to are stronger than they really are, even in the face of evidence;
- hindsight bias: seeing something in the past as having been predictable, even though it wasn't at the time;
- illusion of truth: believing something is true when in fact it is only familiar;
- ingroup bias: the urge to give preferential treatment to people in groups you belong to;
- negativity bias: higher awareness of negative than positive experiences;
- stereotyping: expecting a person to have certain qualities because of one or more characteristics of that person.

Indigenous researchers have identified other cognitive biases. For example, Chilisa has defined the 'sameness error', that is, thinking things are the same when they're not. This can operate very widely, for example through universalist assumptions that ignore and disadvantage less powerful people, or more narrowly, for example believing that men and women have the same ability to negotiate in intimate relationships (Chilisa, 2012: 81, 84).

These kinds of biases adversely affect decision making (Croskerry, Singhal and Mamede, 2013a: ii58), although bias is not the only thing that affects decision making. Contextual factors, such as whom we are with, and individual factors, such as blood sugar levels or tiredness, can also have an impact. Yet researchers are expected to make good methodological decisions when necessary, and constantly need to make good ethical decisions. Learning to debias is part of this process.

Debiasing

Debiasing is not a straightforward skill like learning to type or to milk a cow. First you have to accept that biases exist and that you have them and want to change. Then you need to develop the ability to detect your own biases (or enlist the help of others), figure out how to change those biases and implement the changes successfully (Croskerry, Singhal and Mamede 2013b: ii65). Ironically, some cognitive biases themselves, such as conservatism or the status quo bias (where the status quo is preferred over change), can act as impediments to debiasing.

In recent decades there has been a growing fashion for institutions, including universities, to offer their staff 'unconscious bias training', usually delivered online or in a short group session. This may be helpful in raising awareness for some people, but is unlikely to effect significant behaviour change in the majority (Noon, 2018: 204).

Some researchers are trying to create a taxonomy of cognitive biases and the debiasing strategies that are most effective in each case. Whether or not this is even possible, we're certainly not there yet. However, Croskerry, Singhal and Mamede (2013b: ii67–8) have gathered information about some strategies that can help. These include:

- getting more information, because biases have more room to operate where information is insufficient;
- using structures, such as checklists, to ensure rigorous thinking – some people find that completing ethics approval forms can help with this (Colnerud, 2014: 248);
- being aware of emotions and taking steps to mitigate their influence on decisions;
- valuing scepticism: remembering that if it looks too good to be true, it probably is;
- seeking the opinions of others, particularly in complex situations;

- thinking about whom you are accountable to and considering how they might regard the decision you are making;
- being mindful: using deliberate slow thinking to help overcome the biases caused by automatic fast thinking.

This leads us to another debiasing strategy that is increasingly being used by researchers of all kinds: reflexivity. This involves slow thinking and mindfulness: taking a step back to consider what you know about the situation at hand, and how you know that (Taylor and White, 2000: 201). In doing reflexive work, you need to draw on emotional as well as cognitive resources. Ethical reflexivity in research requires the consideration of many interrelated questions, such as the following.

- What do I think about this situation? Why do I think that?
- How do I feel about this situation? Why do I feel that way?
- Have I taken into account my thoughts and feelings about all relevant theoretical, methodological, disciplinary, personal or practical issues affecting the situation?
- What impact could my thoughts and feelings have on my decision making in this situation?
- Who else is implicated in this situation? What might they think? How might they feel? What impact could my decision making have on them?
- Should I make this decision alone, or consult other people? If others, then whom? Why?
- Which of my biases might be in operation here? What impact could that have on my decision making? What can I do to minimise that impact?
- How can I use the information gathered from this exercise to make my research more ethical?

Reflexivity can help researchers to understand how to work ethically in practice (Guillemin and Gillam, 2004: 263). There is more information about reflexivity in Chapter 9.

Conclusion

A highly valued word in Euro-Western research is 'rigour'. This usually refers to the alleged quality markers of post-positivist research such as reliability, validity and auditability (LoBiondo-Wood, Haber and Singh, 2014: 307). It is interesting to note that 'rigour' is a synonym for 'inflexibility'. Yet there is scope for conducting rigorous research in more flexible ways, as these Indigenous researchers write:

> ... rather than the goals of validity and reliability, research from an Indigenous paradigm should aim to be authentic or credible. By that I mean that the research must accurately reflect and build upon the

relationships between the ideas and participants. The analysis must be true to the voices of all the participants and reflect an understanding of the topic that is shared by researcher and participants alike. (Wilson, 2008: 101)

Rigor comes from the voices and feedback of our own people; it comes from testing the results with our communities; it comes from multiple cross-checks with our colleagues; and it comes from a methodology that requires compulsory self-disclosure of where you are from, whose family you belong to, and what interests you have in the research. (Smith, 2013: 95)

When it comes to planning research, I take 'rigour' to mean 'thoroughness'. Ethical planning means planning the whole research project as thoroughly as you can at the outset. And not only the nuts and bolts such as what data to gather and how much, but also topics such as communication, establishing a value base and managing the inevitable unforeseen problems, as this interviewee suggests:

> "The most important thing in planning, that allows one to do research in an ethical way, is to figure out how communication is going to take place and who is going to communicate with whom. Having a clear plan for transparency, for dialogue, for resolution of issues where people don't agree. So that means that when ethical issues arise, when problems arise, there's a framework within which they can be discussed."

Indigenous researcher Wilson takes this further, suggesting that researchers take a strategic approach to their process (2008: 39). 'Strategies of inquiry' (Wilson, 2008: 40) allow for any changes of methodology that may become desirable as the research develops. Indigenous researchers have existing frameworks within their societies for discussing problems that arise, such as palabre or sharing circles (see Chapter 8 for more on these). Euro-Western researchers, and cross-cultural research teams involving Indigenous and Euro-Western people, would probably find it helpful to agree on a suitable framework or system to use for this purpose.

REFLECTIVE QUESTIONS

1. What do you think are the most important ethical considerations when planning research?
2. How do you know when you have a good research design?
3. To what extent do you agree with the maxim that 'if you fail to plan, you plan to fail', and why?
4. How important do you think knowledge and understanding of context is in research? Why?
5. The conclusion to this chapter put forward some different ways of thinking about rigour. What does rigour in research mean to you?

CHAPTER 7

Ethical context setting and literature review

Introduction

All research needs to be contextualised. Whether in the Euro–Western or the Indigenous paradigm, any piece of research is part of the worldwide exchange and development of knowledge that has gone on – and will go on – throughout human history. Some people think of this as a conversation. As with face-to-face conversations, there are ethical considerations: it's important to take turns to speak, listen attentively and be polite and respectful to your fellow discussants. In research, the metaphor of the conversation includes the whole process, not only the parts involving actual speech.

> "With my recent study, I had good intentions, but I had to be careful that my intentions didn't trample on the intentions of previous people who have informed this body of knowledge."

This interviewee is aware of the conversation between their intentions and those of others, which they needed to listen to and respect in their own work. This chapter will show you what this means in practice when you are contextualising your research.

There are different ways to contextualise different kinds of research. Academic research is usually contextualised through a literature review. Evaluation research will probably be contextualised through a document analysis. Participatory or community-based research may be contextualised through face-to-face conversations between people. There are no hard-and-fast rules about how research should be contextualised. It is, though, important that it should be set in context.

There are two main reasons for this. First, the work involved in contextualising research helps to clarify ideas about *what* to investigate and *why*; perhaps also *how* to make that investigation. Second, this clarification helps to *locate* work within the wider conversation. It shows where work fits into communities such as the academic community around the discipline, or a community of practice, or, for an Indigenous researcher, their Indigenous community. However, this does not mean that all context setting is done at the start of an investigation. There is often a chunk of work around contextualisation that is worth doing early in the process, but context setting can also be ongoing, particularly in some disciplines.

> "Literature review in the arts and humanities is ongoing. A lot of the data is often books, other people's work; you're creating a new argument with those as data. It's not necessarily literature review, then results. New issues can arise throughout the process. Sometimes you write your literature review at the end."

It is really important to do this contextualisation ethically. When I teach or discuss research ethics with Euro-Western scholars and research practitioners, they regularly shock me by asserting that there are no ethical considerations to take into account in contextualising research. Some of the people I interviewed for this book expressed similar views, even though I had asked them a direct question about ethical issues in setting research into context.

> "On first being asked that question, my gut reaction is: I often don't consider there to be ethical issues, and I think that's not just me, I think a lot of people would think that the literature review process is ethics free."

> "Until I saw that question, I think I would have thought it was pretty ethics free, and I'm not sure I can articulate an answer to this, but I thought no it's not, how can it be? Everything has an ethical dimension. There would be ethical issues in terms of my practice, how I do it in an ethical way. It was a really challenging question: I hadn't thought about it before."

There are ethical issues around:

- how to define 'literature' and its equivalents;
- searching thoroughly;
- keeping and using records in your work;
- reading effectively;
- citation and plagiarism;
- communicating and publishing research.

This chapter will discuss each of these issues in detail.

What is 'literature' anyway?

'Literature' is a Euro-Western term meaning 'information that is written and published'. This is too narrow a definition for the research being conducted by many people around the world. Of course there are some research projects, particularly in the Euro-Western tradition, that can be contextualised using formally published written literature alone. However, much research in the Indigenous paradigm does not use such literature at all, and even some research in the Euro-Western paradigm may use very little.

> "Our ethical framework allows for research where there is little or no literature to support the merit but you can make a case. Generally, I want to see an engagement in the argument of why there's merit by looking at the context: we know this, but we don't know that. So this research will answer questions the literature currently doesn't answer, or will support an area of literature that isn't strong."

Sources of information for Indigenous research include metaphors and proverbs, stories and songs, poems and dances, legends and tattoos (Chilisa, 2012: 16, 60). Indigenous researchers can contextualise their work through social interaction such as dialogue and ceremony (Wilson, 2008: 60–1). Also, even in the Euro-Western tradition, the definition of 'literature' used to contextualise research is widening, and may now include 'grey' and self-published literature, novels, poems, ephemera such as leaflets or event programmes, zines and so on (Kara, 2015: 59).

> "I generally like to see some addressing of grey literature, not just peer-reviewed. That's where you more often find the real world, the voices of concern of communities that have come up through community research."

As a result, rather than following the Euro–Western tradition by referring to 'literature', I will use the term 'sources' in this chapter to acknowledge and include all of these possible bases for contextualisation, except where I am referring only to formally published material.

Searching thoroughly

Whatever kind of contextualisation you use, you need to search your sources thoroughly. Figuring out your search strategy takes time, imagination and thought. How and where you search will depend on your topic and your resources, as well as the amount of available information.

> "I think that's about inclusion and exclusion, what you include and what you don't include. You can't capture it all. It's about being fair to other people and what they've done, and being respectful."

Most searching will be done on the internet these days. It is important to understand the scope of the search tools you use, as this interviewee explains:

> "One thing I encourage my doctoral students to use is DOAJ [Directory of Open Access Journals] because a lot of peer-reviewed journals in the developing world are published as open access. I think students are sometimes surprised to look at – for example, go into our own online library, you have all these individual databases, collections from the publishers that live within that universe, and then there are search engines that are multi-database search engines but they still

don't include everything. The DOAJ includes materials that would not otherwise appear. If the topic is global, then I encourage people to, say, don't look only at Western scholars who are studying Latin America or Australia or somewhere; [look at] remote areas of the world – what are the scholars saying who are coming from that culture? Not just the Western scholars publishing in Western journals, what is the scholarship coming out of that place? You can't read every possible thing in the world or you'd never get anything done, but it's thinking about how to be more inclusive and having a rationale that makes sense."

This book's companion website (http://policypress.co.uk/resources/kara-ethics) includes more information about how to find journal articles from non-English-speaking countries.

Sadly, these days it is also necessary to search the internet to find out whether an author you are planning to cite is bona fide. The website Retraction Watch was set up in 2010 by the American medical reporters and writers Ivan Oransky and Adam Marcus to publicise articles that are retracted, or de-published, from academic journals. Some articles are retracted because of serious mistakes that are discovered after publication, while others are retracted because of fraud, such as the fabrication of data. (Non-serious mistakes, such as typographical errors, can be dealt with through the publication of a correction.) There is also the option of a partial retraction, where a section of an article is retracted, rather than the whole (Gawrylewski, 2007). Oransky and Marcus founded their website partly because retractions are not well publicised (Oransky and Marcus, 2010). As I write, eight years later, academic search engines still index works that have been retracted, so they are usually available to download from the internet. This means that there is no way to know that a work has been retracted without searching elsewhere to find out, which adds a time burden to research work.

"I was surprised, reading materials for my course, I found many, many articles about how top scientists are not citing – actually for me it was most surprising when you see databases because some years after publication somebody found out that they have cheated, so blacklists exist in terms of literature. They have a blacklist in economics for example. So for me I was really shocked, when I do a literature review and I'm citing somebody, I don't know whether these people, in three years' time, five years' time, it comes out that they have been cheating also. Somebody was cheating, all the system goes – academic literature is very fragile in that sense; you never know when some publications might not be correct at all, and what does it say about your work? For me the system is very very thin in that sense."

Most of the retractions logged by Retraction Watch are in the life sciences, probably because the site's founders are both medical writers. However, there are a few from the social sciences and allied disciplines such as geography and theology. One implication of this is the need to read very carefully, with awareness that publication in an academic journal does not necessarily mean an article is accurate or truthful. (See below for more on ethical reading.) Even when journal editors have high levels of integrity they can be hoodwinked by fraudulent authors. This has been playfully demonstrated through the publication of spoof or ironic articles in journals from a variety of disciplines, which indicates that all readers need to be on their guard, both for these and for the non-playful equivalents (Ronagh and Souder, 2015: 1545).

Keeping and using records

In the Euro-Western paradigm, when you are contextualising your work, it is important to keep records of what you did, when and why, that are linked to your search strategy design. This is good research practice, as it will help you to keep track of your sources and spot any gaps that you might need to fill. The ethical dimension is that doing this will enable you to describe your search strategy accurately when you report on or write up your research.

Many people use a grid for record keeping: either on paper or electronically. If you're working electronically, spreadsheet software is helpful because it enables you to sort your records, which can make spotting gaps much easier. Column headings could include such things as the following:

Written	**In person**
Date of search	Date of encounter
Search term used	Conversation with
Date of source	Brief summary of relevant points
Author	Any other information
Title	
Brief summary of relevant points	
Any other information	

In the Indigenous paradigm, the concept of keeping records can be alien and linked with traumatic experiences or memories of oppression and disempowerment (McKemmish et al, 2010: 34; Russell, 2005: 165). Some Indigenous peoples view all records that relate to them as belonging to them, while the Euro-Western institutions that hold such records espouse values of individual/organisational rather than collective/community ownership, and so they may not even disclose the existence of such records (McKemmish et al, 2010: 33).

There is some recognition in the Indigenous literature of the importance of record keeping for research, although it is expressed very differently than in the Euro-Western literature. For example:

> One thing that I might do differently a second time around is to write more as I go along. Not only would I keep more notes, which as I review seem a bit incomplete ... but also I would do more journaling

and recording my feelings along with the process. I would have to be careful though that the writing doesn't interfere with the process. It was only by being completely engaged in the process that ideas and relationships became clear to me. (Wilson, 2008: 135–6)

From a Euro-Western perspective, the idea that writing could interfere with the research process is unusual. Euro-Western researchers might benefit from considering the implications of this idea.

Ethical reading

Choosing what to read has ethical dimensions, particularly if your potential field of sources is very large.

> "I think that there are ethical issues about framing or bounding, about the way researchers frame the issues they work on, pick and choose issues to focus on and leave out other issues. The literature review is one of the first places to do that: the bias is an ethical issue."

There may also be unexpected issues in cross-cultural research, which has been described as a 'potential minefield of possibilities for cultural offense' (González and Lincoln, 2006).

> "I've begun to see this issue differently since moving here. New Zealanders are very easily offended – they take things personally even when they are clearly articulated as issues on a social level. This means that I need to build in a further level of trying to think very carefully about potential sensitivities that in my own culture I would not have considered at all."

When contextualising research with a cross-cultural dimension, it is ethically advisable to read material from any applicable language, to ensure that all the relevant work is taken into account (González and Lincoln, 2006). Of course this is not always possible, but every effort should be made, including looking for, or working to create, translations where necessary. (See Chapter 9 for more on the ethics of translation.)

In practice, ethical reading means taking the time to understand what you're reading, the argument being presented and where that is located in the wider conversation. It means not just skim-reading the abstract of a journal article, or the introduction and conclusion of a chapter or book, and then making assumptions about the rest. Of course it's fine to skim an abstract or an introduction and conclusion as an initial assessment, to help you figure out whether you want or need to read the whole text. But, for example, it is not truly ethical to read an abstract, and then cite the article on the basis of the key 'take-away' point, without reading and digesting the rest of the author's words and ideas. There are two main reasons for this. First, you risk misunderstanding the author's point because you won't understand the basis for the argument they are making. Second, you won't be able to assess the quality of their work, so you won't know how much weight to give it within your own research.

> "Not taking things out of context, or picking and choosing things to support your findings when those sentiments weren't meant in the documents or literature you're talking about."

Whatever form of contextualisation you use, it is important to read work coming from different standpoints than your own. Most people do research because they care about the topic they are investigating, sometimes very deeply. This can make it difficult to find and read work that could contradict your views. Yet that is exactly where you need to make most effort: to read work that you know you disagree with or that you may disagree with. Giving such work due consideration will help you to strengthen your own argument and might enable you to change your mind. As researchers, we do need to be open to changing our views if we find new evidence, which may come in the form of a compelling written or spoken argument.

> "We'd still be trundling about in wooden wheels if we hadn't challenged that as the best way to travel."

Ethical reading is also effective reading. It helps you towards more ethical research in other ways, such as by enabling you to: cite other people's work more effectively; acknowledge other researchers more accurately and appropriately; and understand more fully where your work fits within the wider academic conversation.

Citation, plagiarism and respect

At the start of this chapter I mentioned the need to be respectful to others. One of the ways this is done in the Euro-Western paradigm is through citing accurately and avoiding plagiarism. Citing accurately involves giving information about the sources for the ideas you have presented in your work. These sources could be academic literature, 'grey' literature, mainstream media, social media, personal communication and so on. Wherever possible, the information you provide about your source should give enough detail for a reader to find it for themselves if they wish to investigate further. Avoiding plagiarism means not passing off other people's work as your own, whether accidentally or deliberately. Something that is hard for many people to understand is that it is also deemed unethical, in the Euro-Western paradigm, to plagiarise your own work. This isn't always easy to avoid, particularly if you write a lot.

> "Avoiding self-plagiarism. For people who are writing multiple kinds of materials, that can be a bit challenging."

Avoiding self-plagiarism shows respect to publishers, who expect to be publishing original material. Citing accurately and avoiding plagiarism shows respect in two other directions. First, it shows respect for the people whose work or views you are citing, by acknowledging the contribution they have made to your work. Second, it shows respect to your readers, by enabling them to follow and understand, as far as possible, your thought processes. But, again, making this clear is not always easy.

> "Adequately acknowledging your sources is certainly an important issue: can be tricky at times – APA or MLA. There are things we think, 'Well where do I distinguish between my interpretation of this and what I've got from someone else?' How can you adequately show that, demonstrate that?"

There have been cases of inaccurate and even fraudulent citation. Dreger gives an example of following a citation back to the source, only to find that there was no mention of the topic cited anywhere in that source (Dreger, 2015: 158). Given the huge number of books and articles published each year in the Euro–Western paradigm, many of which have a small readership, there are probably many more inaccurate and fraudulent citations than we realise. No doubt this also applies to plagiarism.

The literature suggests that this is unlikely to be the case in the Indigenous paradigm because dishonesty is less common (Kovach, 2009: 103). Victoria Steere, an Indigenous woman from the land some call Alaska, writes:

> In our world, until the late 1970s and early 1980s, lying almost never occurred. It was a horrible insult to be called a liar. Lying violated all our society's social mores and norms, whether Iñupiat, Yupiit, Athabaskan, and so on. Trusting others to be truthful and attorneys to honestly work for our people created a lot of long-term problems for us. (Steere, 2013: 386)

Also, historically, writing was not highly valued by Indigenous peoples, and indeed some Indigenous authors faced hostility from their communities for writing about Indigenous matters (Bussidor in Lambert, 2014: 177). However, in more recent years, I understand that writing has become more valued and dishonesty has increased, to come closer to Euro–Western levels (McGregor, 2018). Perhaps these are some of the newer impacts of colonialism and imperialism on Indigenous peoples.

In the Indigenous paradigm, respect is viewed in a more complex and holistic way. Respect for other people is an integral and essential part, but it is not the whole. In the Indigenous paradigm, respect also includes respect for communities, tribal knowledge, the land, the cosmos, ideas and ancestors, among other things (Wilson, 2008: 86–96; Kovach, 2009: 19, 99, 164; Chilisa, 2012: 118). Respect is part of the relational ethical imperative. It can be shown to Indigenous people by others through cultural sensitivity and competence (see Chapters 2 and 5 for more on cultural competence).

Publishing and communicating research

There are ethical dimensions to publishing that will affect the choices some researchers make about what and how to draw on as they contextualise their research. For example, Euro-Western academia privileges publication of academic articles in highly ranked journals, which publish in English or European languages (González and Lincoln, 2006). Many of these journals are behind paywalls and so are available only to those affiliated with universities or other institutions that enable access. Researchers working in some universities have little or no choice about where to publish because of institutional imperatives based on the need to rank as highly as possible in league tables. However, researchers who are not affiliated with universities or other institutions that enable access are unable to read and use paywalled work.

The cost of open access (OA) publishing can be a barrier to publication. This applies to some university-based researchers, particularly more junior staff who don't have access to institutional budgets, and to non-university-based researchers who don't have any kind of budget. It seems ironic that scholars working outside universities may be able to afford to publish only in paywalled academic journals that they are unable to read. That being said, some OA journals will waive fees for non-salaried scholars. OA publishing has made more research available to more people, but it is not universal, and much high-quality research is still published in paywalled journals.

Barriers to research access mean that it is not always possible to make a simple ethical choice about the literature you want to use to contextualise your own work. It can be helpful to record any literature you would have liked to use but were unable to access.

Conclusion

This chapter has demonstrated that, contrary to the beliefs of many Euro-Western scholars, there are a wide range of ethical issues to consider when setting research into context. This is important for our own research and for those who, in the future, may read and use our research. Careless contextualising can lead to errors being replicated (Ronagh and Souder, 2015: 1538). It is every researcher's responsibility to ensure, as far as possible, that we give an accurate and balanced context for our work.

REFLECTIVE QUESTIONS

1. Do you always read background material attentively? Why?
2. Do you draw on a narrow or a wide range of sources? Why?
3. Is there anything you could do to make your reading practices more ethical?
4. Can you think of any sources of information that should not be used to contextualise research? If so, what are they, and why shouldn't they be used?
5. Are there any barriers, for you, to OA publishing? If so, how could you overcome them?

CHAPTER 8

Ethical data gathering

Introduction

Data gathering is the phase of research that receives most ethical scrutiny within the Euro-Western paradigm. This is partly because it carries most risk to institutions: if participants are unhappy with the way they are treated by researchers, they may take legal or social action against the institution concerned. Therefore, most ethical scrutiny focuses on participant well-being. It is of course an ethical imperative for researchers to do all they can to ensure the health, happiness and safety of people who are participating in their research. And not only individual people, as this interviewee recognised:

> "I've been doing a project in a school; it reflects what's going on in the school, but how do I protect the school?"

For some laboratory-based researchers, there is a straightforward way to manage this:

> "Ethically, I'm participant #1 in all my studies because I would never ask someone to do something I wouldn't do, and I need to see it works properly."

But those who work in more naturalistic settings can't use this approach. Also, there are many other ethical dimensions to consider when planning and carrying out your data gathering. Many are not covered by formal ethical approval systems, and (as we saw in Chapter 4) some may even be caused by those systems.

> "There's a real danger of research suffering because of ethics. It's a fine balance. It's ethically problematic if the research is failing. Anonymisation doesn't necessarily make the research stronger, it makes it more ethical, and that is an interesting balance to be struck."

This is very much a Euro-Western perspective and is based on the premise that researchers have no relationship with participants except through the research (Ellis, 2007: 5). The Indigenous perspective is quite different. Most Indigenous peoples understand and accept that researchers and participants will already be in a relationship that predates and will outlive the research (Kovach, 2009: 51). This can happen in Euro-Western or cross-cultural research, where it is called 'insider research' (Liamputtong, 2010: 109), but there it is the exception rather than the rule.

Even the terminology used to discuss this stage of the process has ethical dimensions. The conventional Euro-Western term is 'data collection', but this import from STEM (science, technology, engineering and mathematics) disciplines sits oddly with research whose participants are human, as if people are containers of data for researchers to download on request. Some researchers prefer the term 'data construction', to demonstrate that data is created by participants in response to, or with, researchers. I use 'data gathering' with the aim of covering all perspectives, because there are other terms too, as this interviewee demonstrates:

> "I do talk about data generation; I don't talk about data collection. When you're working with people to develop data that is not just existing, I consciously use that word 'data generation' to acknowledge that it's not just me as a researcher revealing things; it's co-produced with other people."

Fieldwork is the stage of research at which you are most likely to encounter ethical dilemmas – or trilemmas, or quadrilemmas – that have to be resolved very quickly. There are any number of reasons why researchers can find themselves under time pressure, from external time-scales imposed by funders, to participants at imminent risk of death (Posel, 2014: 156–7). This chapter is designed to help you think through and resolve ethical difficulties that you may encounter at the data-gathering stage. The chapter will cover topics such as: the ethics of sampling, the use of secondary data, Indigenous methods, paying participants, naming participants, researcher–participant friendships, consent beyond the form, gathering data online, recording, working with gatekeepers and sharing data. This is by no means a complete list of issues that you may need to consider when gathering data, but it does serve to illustrate that there are a wide range of topics to think through, and not all are directly concerned with participant well-being.

Sampling

Your first step in data gathering is to decide who will participate in the research. In conventional Euro-Western research, the researcher decides which categories of people they want as participants, then seeks consent. In the Indigenous paradigm, with its emphasis on relationality, the decision is often more mutual (Kovach, 2009: 126). In either paradigm, though, it is important to think through who you are planning to include – and who, therefore, you are planning to exclude – and why.

It is also important to work out how big your sample should be. There are no hard-and-fast rules for this, whether you're doing quantitative, qualitative or mixed-methods research, but there are some relevant ethical considerations. The ideal is to gather just enough data to enable you to answer your research question. If you gather too much, you are placing an unnecessary burden on some of your participants – and on yourself. If you don't gather enough, your project will fail.

It is also good ethical practice to do all you can to avoid sampling errors (Leavy, 2017: 111). Euro-Western research defines various sampling errors, such as selection error (where only people who are interested in the topic take part in the research) and non-response error (where participants have different characteristics from those who do not respond). These errors are based on the principle that if a sample is chosen according to the rules of Euro-Western research, it will be representative of an entire population, and so the findings from the research can be generalised to the population concerned. This principle does not always apply in Indigenous research, which is often specific to its context (Kovach, 2009: 37; Lambert, 2014: 18). Euro-Western approaches to sampling, such as probability, purposive or snowball sampling, are used within some Indigenous research, although usually within the overarching ethical principles of respect and relationality (Kovach, 2009: 126).

Secondary data

Euro-Western researchers increasingly regard the use of secondary data as ethical for a number of reasons. First, gathering primary data places a burden on participants and researchers, so should be undertaken only when absolutely necessary.

> "Something I feel is very often unappreciated is research fatigue, the fact that, especially with interviews, focus groups, workshops, questionnaires, all those kinds of tools, we as researchers do not take sufficient responsibility for the fatigue and over-research of people."

Second, the use of secondary data enables that data to be set more clearly in its time and historical contexts than the use of primary data (Coltart, Henwood and Shirani, 2013: 16). Third, if data gathering is resourced from public funds, that data should be seen as a public resource, to be shared and reused for public benefit (Coltart, Henwood and Shirani, 2013: 16).

The corollary of this is that if you're gathering primary data, you should take whatever steps you can to make it available for reuse. One common method is to include an option for participants to give permission for this in your consent procedure.

> "Secondary data lives on and should be used. If you're publishing it, you need to set out the description of your data, how you've come to create that dataset, laying out your methodology for users to pick up on to allow them to use it correctly. Basically the onus is on you to try to make sure that anyone else that discovers your data further along down the line can use it."

However, some commentators are suggesting that this kind of consent is not fully informed, and reuse of data requires renewed consent (Grinyer, 2009: 1). This presents practical difficulties for researchers and an increased burden on participants or their representatives, who may become irritated or even traumatised by repeated requests for consent (Grinyer, 2009: 2). The solution to this is, when participants first consent, to talk with them about how they want their data to be used and whether they want to be involved in future consent processes (Grinyer, 2009: 3–4).

More and more secondary data is available to researchers, including government data, open data, historical and archival data. Much of this is online, which makes it a great deal easier to find and use. However, using secondary data also has ethical aspects. For example, the use of historical or archival data might seem ethics free to some Euro-Western researchers, particularly if all the participants are now deceased. However, even in the Euro-Western paradigm, disclosure of sensitive topics such as criminal behaviour could cause distress to the person's descendants by changing their memory of their ancestor and therefore the landscape of their family (Crossen-White, 2015: 115–16). Some Indigenous scholars are clear that they want personal archival data to be released only to family members until many hundreds of years have passed (Russell, 2005: 164). People who create online databases of historical data do not always recognise the potential risks those databases may create, which means that researchers using those databases need to be keenly aware of the potential for harm to living beings (Crossen-White, 2015: 114). Of course it is impossible to know exactly what will cause harm, because different people have different views, thoughts and feelings. But for this reason, maintaining the anonymity even of those long dead may be important when using secondary data (Crossen-White, 2015: 117).

Some commentators regard it as unethical for Euro-Western researchers to use archival or other secondary data to research questions to do with Indigenous peoples unless they do so within a collaborative, community-based framework with the full involvement of those Indigenous peoples (McKemmish et al, 2010: 41; Lambert, 2014: 13). Others recognise different approaches to collaboration, such as those based on cross-cultural dialogue (McGregor, 2014: 348–9). (See Chapter 6 for more on the ethics of collaboration.)

Indigenous methods

Methods of gathering data in the Indigenous paradigm often privilege listening and talking in groups. These are not like Euro-Western focus groups held specifically for research purposes (Lambert, 2014: 32). They are established ways of sharing information that have different names in different societies but seem to have common elements. For example, these methods are called 'kgotla' in Botswana, 'palabre' in Burkina Faso, 'talking circles' and 'sharing circles' in the US and Canada, and other names in other places. The elements that these groups have in common seem to be: everyone is allowed to have their say; nobody may interrupt when someone is speaking; decisions are reached by consensus; and discussions are given as long as they need, which may be several hours. If a consensus decision cannot be reached, plans are made to reconvene after more thinking time and perhaps the gathering of further information from other people.

Some Indigenous researchers also have different ideas from Euro-Western researchers about what constitutes data. For Euro-Western researchers, data is primarily numbers and/or words, with a growing minority also regarding visual materials, audio and video as data. In the Indigenous paradigm, stories may be highly prized as ways of communicating and sharing information, messages and teachings, and can also be regarded as data (Kovach, 2009: 99; Lambert, 2014: 29). Other forms of data include dreams, metaphors, proverbs, songs, myths, taboos and jokes (Chilisa, 2012: 16, 61, 131; Walker, 2013: 304).

Some Euro-Western researchers have also used some of these methods. However, they are not the same, even if they have the same names. They are different because they are used within different epistemological frameworks. A Euro-Western psychologist may analyse participants' dreams; a Euro-Western sociologist may gather and analyse metaphors from a body of literature. These researchers are not using Indigenous methods, because a method used by a Euro-Western researcher cannot be Indigenous unless it is being used within a fully Indigenous research framework led by Indigenous people (Kovach, 2009: 35).

Naming participants

The Euro-Western system of research governance usually requires researchers to take responsibility for their participants' anonymity before participants can be consulted. This approach can be seen as paternalistic in its implication that participants are unable to weigh the risks and benefits of anonymity versus disclosure for themselves, when in fact they may be better able to do this than researchers (Gerver, 2013: 135). The literature suggests that there are situations where imposing, or even offering, anonymity to participants can do more harm than good. For example, American researcher Kristen Perry conducted educational research with Sudanese refugees. The IRB required her to use pseudonyms for participants to ensure their anonymity. To Perry's surprise, her participants were upset by this, and it caused at least one participant to refuse to take part in her research. On investigation, she found out that 'forced name-changing was a common tactic of repression by the Sudanese majority' (Perry, 2011: 911). Other researchers from both paradigms have found that some or all participants want to be known by their own names for a wide range of reasons (for example, Ellis, 2007: 14; Kovach, 2009: 148; Chilisa, 2012: 119; Matebeni, 2014: 120).

For many Indigenous researchers, it is an ethical imperative to name any participant who wishes to be named (Wilson, 2008: 10). This is acknowledged in some ethical codes and guidelines. For example, Chapter 9 of the Canadian Statement states explicitly that there may be occasions where 'individual attribution, with consent, is appropriate' (TCPS2, 2014: 132). The Statement also acknowledges that the protection of participants' privacy is an evolving area of research ethics (TCPS2, 2014: 132).

In Euro–Western research, some areas of interest require participants whose anonymity may be difficult or impossible to maintain.

> "Anonymisation and consent need to be dealt with carefully and iteratively. If you're interviewing authors who are fairly well known, can it even be done?"

Where possible, you should talk to participants about anonymity, and give them the level of anonymity they prefer.

Paying participants

Different stakeholders have different views on paying participants. For example, some researchers take the view that payments adversely affect the quality of data, change the relationship between researcher and researched and make life difficult for other researchers who can't pay participants to do research (Colvin, 2014: 62; van Wyk, 2014: 208; Weeks, 2014: 144). Participants, however, may take the view that research organisations are wealthy, research is a professional activity and if their contribution is desired they should be paid for their time and input (Hamilton, 2009: 214; Colvin, 2014: 59–60; Pickering, 2018: 420). Different disciplines also have different views: for example, in general, anthropologists and lawyers don't approve of paying participants, while medical researchers and psychologists do (Colvin, 2014: 61; Back, 2015: 66). Payment to participants doesn't necessarily have to be financial; it can be payment in kind (Hamilton, 2009: 215; Colvin, 2014: 65), although to be ethical it does need to be something participants value and see as fair reward for their involvement. One thing many participants seem to appreciate is feedback on researchers' work and findings (Colvin, 2014: 66; Lambert, 2014: 215) (see Chapter 12 for more on this), although this is probably insufficient in itself.

You should certainly reimburse participants for any out-of-pocket expenses they have incurred for their participation (Hamilton, 2009: 220). Beyond this, where money is seen as the most ethical form of payment, it can be difficult to figure out how much participants should earn for their contribution (Hamilton, 2009: 214; Colvin, 2014: 70). In particular, it can be hard to find the right balance between fair compensation for involvement and, in effect, coercion to take part, especially if potential participants are in poverty (Colvin, 2014: 71).

> "Some say there must be no inducement to take part, but I often think there should be a voucher. Some projects I've been involved we've given actual cash. They've given an hour of their time; they should have their travel refunded. I've got experience where some funders are very happy to provide that and some aren't. So in some cases, the project I was talking about where we gave money was with young adults who were out of work; it didn't feel right to be inviting

> participant after participant in – thanks very much now we've got this shiny project report we can write. In other cases, if it was interviewing head teachers at their place of work, it's probably not going to be cash, but it might be, you write them a nice thank you card afterwards, it's just that valuing."

Where participant payment could be an issue, you need to work out how to manage this at the planning stage of research (Hamilton, 2009: 224; Colvin, 2014: 74) (see Chapter 6 for more on planning research).

Researcher–participant friendships

One of the implicit ethical principles that pervades the Indigenous research literature is that communities may have secret knowledge and/or sacred knowledge, that they will not, and should not be expected or even asked to, share with outsiders (Kovach, 2009: 73; McKemmish et al, 2010: 35; Koitsiwe, 2013: 273; Bowman, Francis and Tyndall, 2015: 345). This is possible in the Indigenous paradigm because of the principle that knowledge is collectively held. In the Euro-Western paradigm, the corresponding principle is that knowledge is individually held, and that secrets and spirituality are, on the whole, private and individual matters. Yet Euro-Western institutions also hold secret knowledge, such as knowledge that is commercially, politically or personally sensitive. Knowledge is kept secret from some people within institutions by what is known as 'Chinese walls' (internal information barriers to prevent conflicts of interest) or other methods of upholding confidentiality. And Euro-Western institutions, such as faith organisations, also hold sacred knowledge that they do not readily, perhaps ever, share with outsiders. Some Euro-Western communities, too, hold secret knowledge, such as communities of interest (surfers, online gamers and so on) or marginalised communities (rural homeless people, immigrants with a shared background and so on). The type of secrecy here is more permeable: if you become part of one of these communities, by choice or circumstance, it is likely that other members will share secret knowledge with you.

You need to be aware of the potential for secret and/or sacred knowledges to be present, and to understand that in any research, however full the informed consent that has been given, you may reach a boundary beyond which a participant will not answer. Researchers may not even be conscious of such boundaries in practice, as knowledge sharing and its boundaries are a part of life that most people are familiar with and skilled in negotiating. Yet we do need to be aware of these issues, as this interviewee explains:

> "There are ethical considerations about how much you do or don't push, what else you ask, how you debrief them. Things to think about in terms of the questions I ask and how that impacts on them and shapes or reshapes them. Does it cause any damage? How will I even know?"

Indigenous researchers often face an ethical dilemma about how much information to share with Euro-Western people in case it is misused (Kovach, 2009: 73; McGregor, 2014: 348). Some Euro-Western researchers are aware that their participants may face a similar dilemma. This makes some researchers uneasy about building too much rapport with participants (Duncombe and Jessop, 2012: 118), particularly if they are vulnerable and so perhaps more easily swayed.

> "If you are really skilled at qualitative research you can take people to places where they might not have anticipated that they would be going, and I think there's a real tension there. That's what you want to be doing to get depth into your research objectives, yet however much you've prepared people, it's unlikely they will have taken part in an interview like this before, thinking about things in a way they haven't done before. There's a real power issue that needs to be addressed in qualitative ethics."

The 'commodification of rapport' (Duncombe and Jessop, 2012: 110) can seem quite cold-hearted.

> "I find the whole research relationship thing, in terms of building relationships, really hard. It's the kind of thing I battle with the most. I'm a vivacious, engaged, friendly person; people think 'oh she's great she's my friend now' and I'm not your friend, I've just done an interview and I'm not going to see you again. I want to have a warm friendly interview with people, but then I don't want them to feel bad because I've gone and I'm never going to see them again. I find that very difficult to deal with."

Making friends with participants is an integral part of some Euro-Western researchers' methods, particularly ethnographers and feminist researchers (Ellis, 2007: 98; Duncombe and Jessop, 2012: 109; Mfecane, 2014: 126). In fact, the use of friendship as a means to an end is widespread in society (Goffman 1959, cited by Mfecane, 2014: 128). However, becoming friends with participants, particularly in ethnographic or longitudinal research, raises a range of context-specific and complex ethical dilemmas for Euro-Western researchers (Ellis, 2007: 10). These can 'emerge, overlap, and change unpredictably', within both formal research encounters (Duncombe and Jessop, 2012: 109) and informal encounters (Mfecane, 2014: 130). As a result, a researcher whose participants are also their friends will need to be ethically fleet of foot. Yet if you are in this situation, managing ethical difficulties is not your responsibility alone. Friendship is a mutual affair in which both parties have power and agency (Duncombe and Jessop, 2012: 119; Mfecane, 2014: 129). This also has implications for aftercare, which is covered in more detail in Chapter 13. What is relevant here is that you have a responsibility, towards the end of any research encounter, whether for qualitative or quantitative research, to check how participants are feeling.

"I do definitely think there's an issue with aftercare in the immediate aftermath of an interview. I was quite taken aback with the amount of personal information people told me about distress and fear and things like that. I felt I needed to – even in quite a small way – make sure they were OK."

If a participant reports any problems, you should give whatever help you can, which may include putting them in touch with other support mechanisms where appropriate (Ila Bussidor in Lambert, 2014: 173–4).

Consent beyond the form

Much research these days relies on written consent forms. This treats consent as though it is an event rather than a process. However, even obtaining consent in the first place is a process, and after that consent-related dilemmas can arise at any stage.

The usual system of informed consent in Euro-Western research is to give people who are willing to participate a form to sign (or, if online, a box to click) to state that they have given their consent. An underlying assumption of this system is that one researcher will have a defined number of encounters with a certain number of participants, or with participants from a specific group or groups. Also, in this system, the obtaining of informed consent is viewed as an event. However, there are some factors that this system does not take into account. For example, some participants, such as participants in longitudinal research or those with cognitive impairment, may need consent to be sought at various times during the research (Robinson et al, 2011: 331). Ethnographers may work with participants for years, so may need to renegotiate consent as their research progresses. At other times, they may have too many 'participants' to seek consent from, for example, everyone at a sporting event or working in an organisation (Grugulis and Stoyanova, 2011: 343; Fleming, 2013: 36–7). Fleming (2013: 38) suggests that if this applies to your research design, you should go back to first principles and confirm that your research is worth doing. If your findings will not be useful, then the research should be abandoned. Fleming further suggests that if the research is worth doing, you should consider whether there are other research methods you could use, which would allow for informed consent within a good-quality design. If not, then you may have a good case for doing research without obtaining informed consent across the board – or even at all (Fleming, 2013: 38).

In Indigenous research, several types of consent may be needed. Chilisa (2012: 196) identifies four types of consent: individual, community, group and collective. For example, in Botswana a researcher may need consent from a REC/IRB, from a village chief (who in turn will seek consent from the village council) and from participants (Chilisa, 2012: 195–6). Consent from participants may involve individuals and groups, such as families, because some Indigenous people are aware of the issue of 'non-consenting others' (Mannay, 2016: 122), and so will refuse to speak for family members (Chilisa, 2012: 196).

There is a convention in Euro-Western research that if someone is deemed incapable of giving informed consent to participate, say on the grounds of learning disability or youth, then consent may be sought from their carer or parent acting on their behalf. However, this assumes that the carer or parent is more able than the potential participant, which may not be the case, for example, if the carer or parent experiences poor mental health or addiction to alcohol or drugs (Bray, 2014: 32).

> "We might have this lovely articulate letter about the study. Doesn't mean that people understand it."

Revising or refining the consent form may help, but this is not guaranteed. It may be that lack of understanding is not so much the issue as lack of attention (de Vries and Henley, 2014: 82). Some people are beleaguered by bureaucracy, or used to ticking 'I agree' boxes without reading what they are agreeing to. Others work from an oral tradition where written information is rarely used, even by those who are able to read and write (Czymoniewicz-Klippel, Brijnath and Crockett, 2010: 335–6).

Most processes of informed consent include details of circumstances in which researchers will need to break confidentiality and contact the relevant authorities, such as if they are made aware of the risk of significant harm to a person. However, when such circumstances do arise in the course of a research or evaluation project, it can be difficult to know how to act (Morris, 2008: 19; Cluver et al, 2014: 44) because this in itself can create new ethical dilemmas. Is it right to follow the instruction to contact the relevant authorities if those authorities are so overstretched that they're unlikely to be able to help (Cluver et al, 2014: 45), or if the authorities themselves are corrupt (Weeks, 2014: 148)?

Euro-Western researchers also need to recognise that the vast majority of participants have negotiating skills that they may use to set their own terms for involvement in research (Matebeni, 2014: 115). One interviewee for this book felt strongly that involvement in research shouldn't be on a 'yes or no' basis.

> "In a research agreement we should be able to either provide more explanation or just say 'OK, well if you're not comfortable with this part of it, you can still be a participant in my study'. We can negotiate, come up with options."

Truly ethical consent, in any paradigm, may or may not include a written element but will always be based in authentic and respectful dialogue (de Vries and Henley, 2014: 89–90). This isn't always easy to achieve, as it requires good interpersonal skills and time. Nevertheless, it is the standard we should all be aiming for.

Gatekeepers

As we saw in Chapter 6, consent may be needed from several people in Indigenous research. In Botswana, a village chief seems to act a little like a Euro-Western 'gatekeeper', that is, someone who has the power to put researchers in contact with potential participants. The big difference is that a Botswanan village chief will not take a decision alone, but will work with their community to create a consensual decision (Chilisa, 2012: 195). Euro-Western gatekeepers may consult one or more other people, but they are not generally obliged to do so, and they may make their own decision about whether or not to help a researcher contact potential participants.

In a parallel to the different layers of consent that may be needed within Indigenous research, there can be different layers of gatekeeping in some types of Euro-Western research. For example, someone doing research in a school may need initial consent from the head teacher, then consent from different departmental heads and/or class teachers, and may even encounter 'peer gatekeepers' who influence their friends to consent or refuse to take part in research (Agbebiyi, 2013: 537).

In some Indigenous societies it is inappropriate to refuse a direct request for help. In these societies, rather than gatekeepers, Indigenous researchers may use friends or relatives as intermediaries. This is an ethical approach because it provides space for the potential participant to say 'no' if they wish (Wilson, 2000, cited in Wilson, 2008: 130).

Being refused access by a gatekeeper can be a frustrating experience, particularly if you care deeply about your work. One ethical approach to help minimise this is to involve gatekeepers in designing research, which may increase their sense of ownership and so lead them to be more supportive (Agbebiyi, 2013: 538). In general, you need to treat gatekeepers as ethically as anyone else.

Gathering data online

In the southern hemisphere gathering data online, especially through Facebook, is particularly appealing to researchers (Walton and Hassreiter, 2014: 238). There are a range of reasons for this, such as: geographic distances, mobile populations and the ease of accessing Facebook through public computers or someone else's device, for those who don't have their own. Euro-Western researchers, too, are showing considerable interest in using social media for data gathering (Bryman, 2016: 558–60). This raises a number of ethical difficulties. For example: should you 'follow' or 'friend' your participants? Should you comment on, share/retweet or 'like'/'favourite' your participants' posts? Is 'lurking' (looking without interacting) a form of covert research and therefore unethical, even if you have permission to conduct research on the platform concerned and lurking is a known feature of social media? Do all these issues, and others, need to be negotiated separately with each participant? If so, could that affect or skew the research findings? And so on. The ethical dimensions of conducting research through social media could easily fill a book by themselves.

> "Sometimes I'll be the researcher who is taking data from an online forum without seeking consent. In other cases I will ask individual informed consent for every fragment of data I'm going to be quoting. Where I think there's a significant reputational issue for the individual concerned, or if it's going to be identifiable. That's not just good ethical practice it's good research practice as well, because you get more understanding about the meaning of the data to the person concerned."

> "Things such as Twitter, Facebook, internet data; there's a whole society now dedicated to that sort of work. Just because it's freely available doesn't mean you get free use of it. Permission should still be sought if you want to be ethical because they're not expecting their tweets to be mined for research data. The results of your analysis could potentially cause harm."

Also, it is difficult to fully inform potential participants about what they are consenting to if you are planning to present or disseminate data online. Once text and images are placed online, it is not possible to control completely how they may be used, shared or downloaded (Mannay, 2016: 113). It is very difficult for researchers or participants to think through the implications of research outputs being easy to find online in 10 or 20 years' time (Brady and Brown, 2013: 105). This interviewee recognised that what might feel empowering today might feel quite the opposite in the future:

> "If you're looking at social media analysis, you're having a duty to protect people because although it's out there publicly it's not something they might want highlighted in five or ten years' time."

This has implications for aftercare, which is covered in more detail in Chapter 13.

Recording

The standard procedure in Euro-Western research is to record research encounters, often with an audio recorder, sometimes using video to gather more information and/or taking some photographs along the way. Participants may be given the opportunity to say 'no' to this, as recording can be intrusive, although in practice few refuse (Bryman, 2016: 480). For some Indigenous communities, in some circumstances, recording may be unwelcome.

> "A lot of it has to do with making sure that whatever [the] materials we record are, it's OK to record them. We're not violating restrictions of some kind, of use of the materials or that we are asking the right people, so if there are certain

> kinds of ceremonial protocols, for instance, that will sometimes depend – different people have ownership of those, or storage of them, and we need to make sure that we're not offending when we're asking. So again a lot of communication is needed, beforehand and also while we're doing it."

This does not only apply to audio recordings. Photography and video, and even writing, can make some Indigenous participants feel uncomfortable (Traore, 2013: 175).

> "For Indigenous or native peoples there are issues of respect for cultures which may not agree with recordings – visual or otherwise."

However, other Indigenous people are keen to be recorded, depending on the purpose and nature of the research (McGregor, 2018).

Written records may be helpful if other forms of recording cannot be used, although the writing may have to be done after, rather than during, each research encounter (Traore, 2013: 174).

Sharing data

There is a strong argument within both the Indigenous and Euro-Western paradigms that it is ethical to give participants, for checking, copies of any data you have taken from them. This applies to all kinds of data, but particularly to written data generated from verbal input. Grammar is used differently in speech and in writing (Biber, Conrad and Leech, 2002: 3), which means that the same words in the same order can give a very different impression to a reader than to a listener. This has caused problems for both Euro-Western and Indigenous researchers (Bannister, 1996: 55; Wilson, 2008: 71). Giving copies of this kind of data to participants enables them to check and amend the information if they feel the need, which will improve the quality of your research (Kovach, 2009: 99–100).

One key difference between Indigenous and Euro-Western research is that in Indigenous research participants are generally thought to own the data (McKemmish et al, 2010: 33; Lambert, 2014: 214 – see Chapter 2 for more on this). By contrast, in Euro-Western research, data is owned by the researchers or by the commissioners or funders of research. Also in Euro-Western research, as we have seen, it is considered ethical for researchers to make primary data available for others to use as secondary data, although of course it needs to be suitably anonymised. In the Indigenous paradigm, with its greater emphasis on context and participant ownership, this may not be so appropriate.

Conclusion

This chapter has covered a considerable amount of ground, but it has not addressed all dimensions of ethical data gathering. Nor could it do so, because new ethical issues arise all the time as researchers develop new methods and spaces for gathering data. However, the more ethically you gather your data, the higher quality that data is likely to be, which should raise the quality of your research as a whole.

REFLECTIVE QUESTIONS

1. How can you guard against choosing methods of data gathering that appeal to you, rather than methods that are most likely to help you answer your research question?
2. Have you experienced any conflict between friendship and research? If so, how did you resolve it? Would you take the same path if a similar situation arose in future, or would you act differently another time? Why?
3. What makes a method ethical or unethical, and why?
4. Under what circumstances would you breach a participant's confidentiality? Why?
5. Think about your current research project, or a research project you would like to undertake. What are the most ethically troublesome aspects of the data-gathering process? How could you best address these?

CHAPTER 9

Ethical data analysis

Introduction

Researchers sometimes invent data to make their results look better. A notorious example from the 21st century is that of the Korean stem cell researcher Hwang Woo-suk, who reported that he had been able to create human stem cells by cloning. It was later found that his data had been fabricated, although he claimed that he was deceived by other members of his research team. He lost his job at Seoul National University and received a suspended prison sentence for embezzlement of research funding and other ethical violations, although he was cleared of fraud. Sadly, he is not unusual. A meta-analysis of surveys of scientific misconduct found that around one in 50 scientists admitted fabrication, falsification or modification of data or results, and up to one in three admitted various other unethical practices such as making changes to research in response to pressure from funders (Fanelli, 2009: 8).

Data manipulation is subtly different from data fabrication because, rather than being invented, real data is presented inaccurately. This could be done, for example, by combining interesting factors from several otherwise uninteresting cases to create one interesting case for presentation. (In some forms of research, it is acceptable to create a composite case, if that composite case is authentic and recognisable as representative of the individual cases and the researcher makes it clear that the case is a composite.) Another way data could be manipulated is by using software to change the presentation of visual data. There is nothing wrong with using software to improve a visual image, such as by adjusting the brightness or contrast of a whole picture to make it easier to view. But erasing or changing part of a picture is a form of data manipulation (Winston, 1998: 60), and therefore unethical and unacceptable.

I think it would be a rare researcher who has never been tempted to manipulate their data. Some of the people I interviewed for this book were keenly aware of the risk, and most linked it with institutional pressure to conduct and publish research that breaks new ground.

> "This pressure gives people a kind of feeling that you have to have positive and surprising results. Negative is not good enough; they don't provide anything very surprising, so people might have an urge to leave out some data or some interview or some answers in [a] questionnaire that would make things look better than they are."

Recent research suggests that although this is a common hypothesis, it may be inaccurate. Looking at examples of unethical uses of images, Fanelli and his colleagues found that 'academic culture, peer control, cash-based publication incentives and national misconduct policies' (or the lack of them) were the factors affecting scientific integrity (Fanelli et al, 2017: 1). They further found a lower risk of unethical use of images in countries where incentives to publish are related to career advancement and institutional prestige (Fanelli et al, 2017: 5). This is only one study, so it's not conclusive. However, the results do support the prevailing hypothesis, in as much as they point to structural factors, rather than individual lack of virtue, as the primary causes of misconduct.

Data analysis is a process with several stages, each of which comes with ethical considerations. The key stages are: data management, preparation, coding, description and interpretation. As always, though, these stages are not discrete. Researchers and evaluators are likely to move back and forth between different stages rather than proceeding through them in a linear way. Nevertheless, the distinctions facilitate discussion, and discussion is important, because Euro-Western research practices mean that data analysis is often conducted by researchers – sometimes just one researcher – without oversight or scrutiny. This makes the analytic phase of research particularly susceptible to ethical problems, from bias to fraud.

> "We have had some bad cases. Sometimes in your team is some member who is not that good in ethics – they will make data look more positive than it is."

On 29 May 2017 Retraction Watch listed 3,087 academic articles that had been retracted due to ethical breaches, of which 433 (14% or one in seven) were retracted as a result of fake data. Of course this does not mean that one academic article in seven includes fake data – but the very possibility that someone might draw such a conclusion demonstrates the need to take great care when describing and interpreting data.

Indigenous research practices are often more collaborative, which can help to ensure ethical practice (Wilson, 2008: 121–2). Yet the Indigenous literature on research methods, like the Euro-Western methods literature, says much more about methods of gathering than methods of analysing data. Therefore the two paradigms may have parallel difficulties in describing, explaining and discussing analytic processes. This applies to the analysis of both quantitative and qualitative data.

> "People say it's more of an issue for qualitative research, but it's completely an issue for quant[itative analysis], because how you look at your data, how you analyse it are key questions when you're looking at survey results as much as interview or observational data."

The Euro-Western literature on research ethics rarely mentions data analysis, focusing instead on the ethics governance priorities of consent and confidentiality. This may partially explain the problem with many REC/IRB applications that say *what* they will do to analyse data, such as use a specific theoretical perspective or a particular software package, but not *how* they will analyse the data (Iphofen, 2011: 42). Yet data analysis is a crucial part of every research project, and there are a wide range of ethical considerations. For example, if you gather data directly from people who are giving their time purely to participate in your research, it is important to analyse all that data, or you have wasted some of their time (and your own). Then analysis should be thorough and rigorous, to give you the best chance of finding answers to your research questions.

For some Indigenous researchers, when doing research in general, and analytic work in particular, they are in a relationship with ideas. Their relationships with ideas are seen as needing to be built, respectfully, in the same way as any other relationship (Wilson, 2008: 114). Also, they need to interrogate other relationships, such as those between existing ideas, and relationships with other people or phenomena that may be built further as a result of the research (Wilson, 2008: 119). This is a more holistic and experiential way of knowing than the Euro-Western approach (Wilson, 2008: 123).

Data management

Data, whether hard copy or electronic, should be securely stored. In Euro-Western research, data is seen as belonging to the researcher(s) or the research funders. As a result, data storage protocols are usually produced by institutions, funders or clients. They generally refer to such things as locked filing cabinets for hard copy, encryption of electronic data and clarity about who is able to access the data. If you have promised your participants confidentiality and anonymity, you need to ensure that this is maintained when you store their data. That being said, data management is another ethical imperative for researchers which is often rather less of a priority for participants.

> "There was a case recently reported to an ethics committee where a researcher was interviewing people in the back of a van using a laptop. They were people sleeping on the street, just out of prison and so on, and one of the participants stole the laptop. We went into conniptions because loads of people's data was on that laptop, till we realised it would probably take Bill Gates to crack the code. We said to that researcher, 'You must go back to all those participants and tell them the laptop has been stolen and their data is in someone else's hands' and the participants weren't that bothered, they just said 'yeah, OK'."

It is good ethical practice to offer participants the opportunity to withdraw their data from your project, at any time, up to the point where analysis has progressed so far that it would be difficult or impossible to disentangle their data from the rest (see Chapter 13 for more on this). However, even if someone withdraws their data during or soon after data gathering, the input they gave will inevitably have influenced your thinking and analysis.

Conversely, there may be times when you need to return data to participants, such as if they have lent you documents or artefacts that they gathered or created for your research. In these cases, data should be returned as soon as you can and in the condition in which it was given to you.

In the Indigenous paradigm, data is seen as the property of the communities who provided it (McKemmish et al, 2010: 33; Croft-Warcon in Lambert, 2014: 78). In this paradigm, data should be stored in accordance with community or cultural protocols.

Data preparation

Depending on the type(s) of data you use, and how your data was gathered, preparing it for analysis may include various tasks such as: checking the level of accuracy and completeness of your dataset(s), data entry and transcription. Data preparation often involves laborious work requiring meticulous care, which can be time consuming even if you're using secondary data (Coltart, Henwood and Shirani, 2013: 14). It can also be very boring – but ethical data preparation means taking care to prepare your data as well as you can. Carelessness can lead to errors, and errors at the initial preparation stage could be magnified when you formulate your findings.

Checking datasets for accuracy and completeness is a more or less onerous task, depending on the size and complexity of the dataset. You may need to do this more than once. For example, if you have video data to transcribe, you will need to start by ensuring that all the data is viewable and noting the length of each section. Then, particularly if you have outsourced transcription, you will need to check that each transcript accurately represents the data.

If you gather data online, you can probably side-step the tedious chore of data entry. Manually gathered data, though, will need to be entered into a computer to facilitate analysis. Whether you outsource this or do it yourself, you need to establish a protocol for the task so that data can be entered in a consistent way. The protocol should say how each record will be identified and linked back to the primary data, usually through a unique identifier given to the electronic record and written on the hard copy. The other details of the protocol will depend on the nature of your data. Also, whether you outsource the task or do your own data entry, you should spot-check some records to ensure accuracy and completeness. If you find any errors, keep looking; if you find many errors, you will need to go through the whole dataset again. This is even more laborious and annoying than doing it in the first place, especially if you have paid someone else to do it for you.

With much data, the selection of what to include is made before or during the gathering process. With some large or complex datasets, this has to be done as part of preparation. For example, video data can be prepared through the creation of a 'content log', that is, a brief description of each video as a whole, or of segments of each video of equal length (Derry et al, 2010: 18). The content log provides an overview of the data and so enables the researcher to select relevant parts for detailed transcription.

Transcription itself has a number of ethical dimensions. A protocol should be used for transcribing audio data, to ensure consistency. Such protocols can be simple or detailed, in some cases running to several pages (for example, McLellan, MacQueen and Neidig, 2003: 74–81). Audio data transcription is fairly straightforward, and can take place before coding and analysis begins. Video data, however, is much more complex. While a protocol is still likely to be helpful to begin with, transcripts may be iteratively revised during video analysis until the researchers are sure they have a consistent record of the aspects of their video data that are most likely to help them answer their research questions (Derry et al, 2010: 19–20).

Transcribing your own data is a good way to begin familiarising yourself with its content, and transcribing other people's data is a worthwhile occupation for some. However, transcribing sensitive or traumatic material can lead to negative emotional and physical effects (Wilkes, Cummings and Haigh, 2014: 299–300).

> "I think something that again is often overlooked is if people are transcribing interviews. That can be very tough on them if they're listening to really distressing things. I don't think that's very often addressed by researchers."

This indicates the need for good self-care if you're transcribing your own data (see Chapter 14 for more on this). It also indicates the need for recognition of potential harm to external transcribers; something that is often overlooked in the consideration of research ethics.

Data coding

Whether data is qualitative or quantitative, you need to code it to facilitate analysis. Quantitative coding is generally more straightforward than qualitative coding: some responses can be autocoded as themselves, such as points on a rating scale, while most others simply need a numbered or lettered code. You may also need one or more codes for missing data, which should be codes that are not used for anything else, such as XYZ or 999. With quantitative data coding, therefore, the ethical imperatives are consistency and accuracy.

These also apply with qualitative data, although here the situation is not so straightforward. A code, or label, can be applied to a chunk of data of any size from a single letter or pixel to an entire document, image or audio or video file. Clearly, then, there is a great deal of researcher choice, even with the application of a predetermined coding frame; more, if emergent coding is used. So there are further ethical imperatives around rigour and avoidance of bias. Also, qualitative coding in particular is an arduous and time-consuming task. Yet coding needs to be done carefully and thoroughly if the analysis is to be robust.

Data description

When data has been coded, it needs to be described. This can be done using descriptive statistics (frequency, range, averages and so on) for quantitative data, and descriptive language for any kind of data. For some people, description is neutral; you simply say what is there and don't say what isn't there. But, again, there is such a lot of choice, particularly for those who write in English or in other languages that are similarly rich in synonyms. The ethical imperative at this stage, then, is to describe data as clearly and usefully as possible.

An echo of Indigenous research ethical principles can be found in Euro-Western researchers Doucet and Mauthner's writing on the ethical aspects of data analysis (2012). These feminist researchers focus on relationships and accountability, although from a Euro-Western perspective: they emphasise relationships with research respondents and non-human subjects, and talk about accountability in terms of transparency. They go further, though, and, like Mannay's (2016: 123) identification of 'non-consenting others' at the data-gathering stage, they discuss hidden relationships that we need to consider at the analytic stage, such as with the readers and users of research (Doucet and Mauthner, 2012: 123). One way in which researchers can describe data effectively is by knowing what will be of use to their readers and users.

Description is an essential step in the analytic process, but it is not the whole of that process.

> "This notion that you just do a few interviews and write them up and that's that, I don't think that's ethical, I think you have an ethical responsibility to do proper analysis."

And proper analysis involves interpretation.

Data interpretation

Interpreting data is at the core of our work as researchers, and it is one of the areas where researchers have most power. Euro-Western researchers have done great damage to Indigenous peoples by mis-interpreting their opinions and stories (Sherwood, 2013: 207; Tatow in Lambert, 2014: 86–7). Some Euro-Western researchers still refute the importance of interpretation in research, but Indigenous researchers have always acknowledged its role in analysis (Kovach, 2009: 34).

The ethical imperative here is to stay true to your data and to your participants. Working collaboratively can be helpful, for researchers in any paradigm, with colleagues, participants or other interested parties. In fact, several Indigenous researchers assert that data interpretation is better done collaboratively rather than alone (Walker, 2013: 303–4, citing Begay and Maryboy, 1998: 50–55; Smith, 2012: 130). However, collaborative working can bring new ethical difficulties, depending on who your collaborators are and what power imbalances may be in play. This was discussed in Chapter 6, and there are some further issues specifically around data analysis, as this interviewee suggests:

> "If you involve participants in analysis, it's about how much power in terms of the research findings you give over, and again there's no rule on that, is there? Especially as a more experienced researcher now, somebody who is engaged theoretically as well, there may be things you can see that other people can't see and that may be really challenging. If you involve people, you're taking on a lot of extra responsibility for guiding people through that. You've got to take that really seriously and you can't under-estimate the time."

This interviewee is talking about what Euro-Western researcher Annette Markham calls 'interpretive authority'. Markham (2012: 15) suggests that researchers develop their interpretative authority through 'rigorous and constant practice'. Then interpretative authority becomes 'a tool of analysis' (Markham, 2012: 7). This raises the question of how participatory analysis can really be. Some researchers solve this problem by concluding that everyone brings different knowledges and skills to the analytic process, and, as long as at least one person knows how to tackle data, and everyone listens to each other, it will work (Oparah et al, 2015: 128).

It is arguable that every type of data brings its own ethical challenges at the analytic stage, as this interviewee asserts:

> "Data analysis is hugely varied. It can be analysing a musical score, or a poem, or qualitative results – the amount of data, I use 'data' very carefully when speaking to arts and humanities people – it could be academic research, interviews, media, newspapers, web data, perhaps all of these things, and each one needs to be treated differently ethically. Analysing someone's poem, particularly if they're a living poet, could cause harm; have you spoken with the poet?"

This interviewee hints at the harm that can be caused when material that was not created specifically for research purposes is used by researchers as data for analysis. This can also apply to quantitative and secondary data. We saw in the last chapter that secondary data raises some specific ethical issues at the data-gathering stage. At the analytic stage, it is necessary to treat secondary data with just as much respect and care as if you had gathered it yourself.

We saw in Chapter 2 that quantitative research such as national censuses can be post-colonially exclusionary through the way questions are framed and asked. This can also apply at the analytic stage of quantitative research. For example, your findings can look very different depending on how you prioritise relative and absolute scores (Bonilla-Silva and Baiocchi, 2008: 141). Wilson (2008: 54) reports that in 2007 four Indigenous people graduated with PhDs from the

University of Alberta in Canada, more than ever before. If one Indigenous person had graduated with a PhD in 2006, the University could have announced a 300% increase in Indigenous doctoral achievement in just one year. Further, they could have compared that with the level of non-Indigenous doctoral achievement, which would not have increased – or only modestly – and so stated that Indigenous scholars were outstripping non-Indigenous scholars at doctoral level. But this would have been a very unethical use of statistics, because the relative figures obscure the reality shown by the absolute figures, which are very small. Also, both sets of figures would have completely ignored the fact that 'the university is surrounded by forty-six First Nations Communities' (Wilson, 2008: 54).

(Please note: I am not suggesting that the University of Alberta did, or ever would, use statistics in this way. This is simply an invented example of how statistics *could* be misused. Ten years on, the University of Alberta has a range of courses, collaborations, and other activities designed with and for Indigenous peoples, and appears to be developing good relationships with its surrounding Indigenous communities.)

Computer software can be very helpful in data analysis. However, it also comes with potential ethical risks. For example, the popular software Statistical Package for Social Scientists (SPSS) enables all sorts of descriptive and inferential calculations to be made. The danger here is that novice researchers may simply run all the calculations, then use those showing statistically significant results. This kind of 'fishing' is unethical and poor research practice. If you are using a 5% confidence interval, and you run 100 tests, by definition five of them are likely to show up as significant. However, they may well not be tests that are appropriate for your type of dataset or that help answer your research questions. Before using quantitative data analysis software, you need to understand the rationale behind the calculations you will make, so that you can choose the appropriate statistical tests for your data and enquiry. The biggest risk with qualitative data analysis software is that the data will not be adequately coded (see above for more on data coding), because then the analysis won't be accurate. Also, personal feelings and biases can have an impact on analysis (Fraser and Jarldorn, 2015: 165).

> "In qualitative data analysis there's a danger that the themes you notice are those that are exciting and controversial rather than necessarily what's dominant. The themes you see may be generated more by your excitement than by what's there."

Some evaluators are concerned about how to minimise the impact of their personal ethics and standpoints on the analytic process (Morris, 2008: 19). Another ethical difficulty at the interpretative stage is when potentially problematic findings are made. Interviewees were keenly aware of this.

"In the analysis, if you have answers you don't like, are you going to include them or not if you can't answer the research question in the way you wanted to?"

"Especially for new researchers who are – student researchers and beginning researchers – really trying to make their place in the world with findings, they want those findings that are going to build their credibility as a researcher. There's a huge amount of pressure, competition etc. So, given all of those forces, researchers either ignore or gloss over data that doesn't fit their assumptions or support the kind of findings that they want to be able to put out there."

"Throwing away correct results that you think might disprove your hypothesis so you're not going to publish. They're obviously actual results other people might be able to use and make sense of but they get binned because you're not going to get a journal impact factor. But it's still research and scientific record, and if you're getting funded to do that work you should probably share it with everybody else. It's not just academic research; it's the whole business side of things, research and development there – the well-known cases of drug companies getting rid of inconvenient results."

As this last interviewee suggests, the ethical imperative here is to record and share all findings, even those that may reduce chances of publication or adversely affect career advancement.

Reflexivity

One key difference between the Euro–Western and Indigenous ethical paradigms, which is relevant to data analysis, is that Euro–Western researchers view knowledge as something held by individuals, while Indigenous researchers think of knowledge as collectively owned (Wilson, 2008: 121). An approach that can help to overcome this epistemological divide is that of reflexivity, which is regarded as useful by Euro–Western and Indigenous researchers working in quantitative and qualitative research in a range of fields (Shimp, 2007: 154; Stahl 2011; Chilisa, 2012: 178; Doucet and Mauthner, 2012: 130; Walter and Andersen, 2016: 50; Rix et al, 2018: 8).

Reflexivity is 'the examination of both the structural and personal conditions which help us understand the knowledge we create' (Dean, 2017: 10–11). This requires us to pay 'attention to the interplay between our multiple social locations and how these intersect with our personal biographies', and to personal, institutional and other such influences on our work, as we analyse our data (Doucet and Mauthner, 2012: 130; Hammersley and Traianou, 2012: 33–4). So it's a complicated business, and can involve some circularity, as this interviewee shows in reflecting on their own interview for this book:

"This research process is very reflective for me. There are lots of things I'm having to say out loud, not just about your research, about my reflexivity, and how this research process is influencing me. So hopefully my contribution will influence the research and at this point the research is influencing me. This is me reflecting out loud!"

Reflexivity may be particularly challenging for quantitative scholars, who are used to working with facts, systems and algorithms. Some commentators have offered helpful suggestions about how reflexivity might be approached. Strauss and Corbin, in their work on grounded theory, propose the 'red flag' approach. This means that any absolutist language, such as 'always', 'never', 'can't' or 'must', is treated as a metaphorical 'red flag' that indicates the need to stand back and consider what is actually going on (Strauss and Corbin, 1998: 97). For Mannay (2016: 24), working across different fields and disciplines can help to provide the necessary distance to enable reflexivity. However, she acknowledges that the 'defamiliarisation' that promotes good reflexive analysis can be uncomfortable for researchers, who 'may be confronted with elements of their lives that they manage to defend from consciousness in their everyday existence' (Mannay, 2016: 111). Stahl posits that reflexivity requires people first to understand their own standpoint, and then to try undertaking analytic work from a different standpoint. For example, a religious person could try analysing as an atheist, a cis person as trans, and so on. Of course this can be made as complex and intersectional as you like: a sporty young white gay male could try analysing as a sedentary older female heterosexual person of colour. Stahl refers to this as a higher level of reflexivity that requires understanding, and being able to critically evaluate, different standpoints including our own. Like Mannay, he acknowledges that this 'can be a deeply uncomfortable process' (Stahl, 2011: 258).

Another option, offered by an interviewee, is what they call a 'debrief', that is, a meeting with someone else who can help you to think reflexively about your data analysis.

"I think it can be seen as a luxury, or as something quite touchy-feely, but actually I think it's also important for you to be able to analyse your data effectively, to be really clear about what your personal involvement with that research topic has been, and I think a debrief is a really effective way of managing that, to straddle that tension. So hopefully then take out those personal prejudices and assumptions and subjectivities."

Conclusion

We have seen that, while collaborative working can be problematic in some ways, in general collaboration raises ethical standards in research. This may be particularly useful during analysis. It seems that other people have a moderating influence and so help us to stay true to our participants and our data.

Another thing to bear in mind is that what is regarded as ethical may change over time.

> "I need to think in ways I didn't 30 years ago about whether what I do with the material is going to be of use or interest to the community – and, if it's not, is that OK? In my part of the world, it comes up a lot; is it OK to ask questions that are simply of interest to academic researchers? One of the things we're discovering is that some of the questions of interest to academic researchers are turning out to be of quite a lot of interest to the people we work with."

The Indigenous researcher Margaret Kovach says that analysis within Indigenous research involves 'observation, sensory experience, contextual knowledge, and recognition of patterns' (Kovach, 2009: 140). These words also apply to Euro-Western analysis, although of course they will mean different things in different paradigms. For example, contextual knowledge in Euro-Western research will refer to individuals' knowledge of contexts such as disciplinary or policy context, while in Indigenous research it will refer to collective knowledge of a holistic context. Nevertheless, while these processes are not the same, they do contain parallels, which may be helpful for collaborative work.

REFLECTIVE QUESTIONS

1. How might your political views or religious beliefs affect your analytic work?
2. If a researcher decides that they have 'interpretative authority', will this solve or create ethical problems? Why?
3. What do you see as the ethical issues around analysing data that you didn't gather yourself?
4. Under what circumstances do you think you could be tempted to 'be economical with the truth' when analysing data? What could you do to prevent this actually happening?
5. Does reflexivity really add anything useful to research? Why?

CHAPTER 10

Ethical reporting

Introduction

In the Euro-Western paradigm, reporting research usually involves some kind of document including words and numbers, perhaps with some illustrative images or diagrams. However, there are many other types of written communication that could be relevant for research, such as computer code, tattoos, chalk on pavements and the sand drawings of Vanuatu. Writing in Vanuatu is done with a finger in sand (or dust or ash) and always accompanies, or is accompanied by, talk. This is not as Euro-Western people might understand illustration; the drawings are geometric patterns and can be used, for example, in explanation, discussion, storytelling, teaching or for sacred purposes. They are not intended to be permanent, any more than spoken words are permanent, and are 'left to be blown away in the breeze' (Zagala, 2004: 32).

Research in Vanuatu may involve sand drawings. This tells us that writing does not have to be permanent to count as relevant in research. We can also begin to see that the boundary between writing and drawing is not firm or impermeable. For example, tattoos are usually thought of by Euro-Western people as decorative (even when script is used) and a matter of individual choice. They are also something that can be commissioned and created on a whim, even (if the tattoo artist is unscrupulous) when the recipient is intoxicated. By contrast, for some Indigenous peoples such as Māori, tattoos are functional, offering specific links to culture, community and ancestors, providing information about the wearer to others and having a strong spiritual dimension, among other things (Pawlik, 2011: 5). This suggests that, although script is not used as such, Māori tattoos may have some functions that are closer to the Euro-Western conception of 'writing' than of 'drawing'.

Euro-Western researchers and scholars tend to think that writing has a single primary function: to transmit information between individual brains. However, much writing for research, even in the Euro-Western paradigm, is in fact multi-functional. Euro-Western researchers use writing to work out what they think, obtain funding, gain prestige, secure employment, teach others and so on. We can see from the examples of Māori tattoos and Vanuatu sand drawings that Indigenous writings can also be multi-functional. This means that the ethics of writing are potentially very complex (Rhodes, 2009: 659).

This chapter focuses primarily on reports in writing. The Indigenous research methods literature touches on reporting in terms of its importance and who should be included, but doesn't seem to cover the mechanics of reporting research within oral traditions. Therefore this chapter draws more from Euro-Western literature. We will look at writing as process and product (Mitchell and Evison, 2006: 74) and as creative and relational. But first, we will consider the issue of languages and ethics, and the question of authorial power.

Language, culture and ethics

English is at present the dominant language of research, education and academic publishing worldwide (Liamputtong, 2010: 214). This is a direct result of colonialism and has created a 'hierarchy of language' (Chilisa, 2012: 154). In some parts of the world, where written language is not used, those who wish to use writing may have to learn to read and write in English (Tindana, Kass and Akweongo, 2006: 7), or another colonial language such as French or Portuguese (Chilisa, 2012: 154). However, it is not ethical to treat English as though it were the only language, or even the only major language, as there are other languages that have millions of speakers, such as Spanish and Mandarin Chinese (Anderson, 2010: 2). Thousands of languages are spoken worldwide, although they are not evenly distributed, and around one in four of the world's languages has fewer than 1,000 speakers (Anderson, 2010: 2). Conversely, there are 23 languages that are each spoken as a first language by over 50 million people, with Chinese, Spanish and English in the top three places, respectively (Simons and Fennig, 2017).

This has implications for the ethics of writing – and, indeed, for the whole activity of research. Language plays a part in constructing people's realities. Different languages contain concepts and discourses that may not be directly or easily translatable between those languages (Richardson, 1997: 88–9; Okalik, 2013: 243). This means that translation from one language to another is not a simple solution, because even where there is a straightforwardly equivalent word, the meanings attached to that word may be different for the native speakers of each language (González and Lincoln, 2006). Also, some ideas and concepts have no direct equivalents, which makes translation a complex and difficult task requiring extensive explanations of context and culture (González and Lincoln, 2006; Tindana, Kass and Akweongo, 2006: 7). Therefore research conducted across more than one language, even with the utmost diligence, can lead to misunderstandings and mistakes (Tindana, Kass and Akweongo, 2006: 7; González and Lincoln, 2006).

There is also an ethical dimension to the prioritisation of spoken versus written language. Trying to represent any aspect of an oral culture in writing is fraught with ethical difficulty (Kovach, 2009: 41). There is a 'cultural and methodological disconnect' because Indigenous peoples respect and protect their oral traditions, while Euro-Western people respect and protect their written traditions (Bowman, Francis and Tyndall, 2015: 345–6). In many Indigenous societies, stories are endowed with similar power to documents in Euro-Western societies, and individuals may be designated as witnesses to significant events, to keep the records in their memories and pass them on to others as appropriate

(Qwul'sih'yah'maht, 2015: 183). A retold story will be recognisable in shape and content to listeners who have heard it before, but the precise words and gestures of the storyteller will be chosen in the moment, to suit the needs that the storyteller perceives their listener(s) to have (Kovach, 2015: 53). This means that it can feel uncomfortable, even dangerous, to fix such stories in writing (Kovach, 2015: 53; Qwul'sih'yah'maht, 2015: 191). Worse still, sometimes stories are stolen from Indigenous people and published without their consent (McGregor, 2018).

The ethical reporter of research needs to acknowledge any of these issues that affect their research and describe their effects on the project. Written outputs may need to be produced in more than one language, either as parallel or as separate texts (McGregor, 2018). Even if most or all readers share the same first language, any data gathered in a different language should be presented in both languages so that those who are able can discern the original meanings (Lincoln and González, 2008: 803). Reporting to anyone from an oral culture should be done face to face, as a presentation (Smith, 2012: 124; Lambert, 2014: 66) (see Chapter 11 for more on research presentation).

Authorial power

Writers have a great deal of power. We don't get it all our own way, because reviewers, editors, publishers and others can influence the content and format of our work. But we choose the words and the order, what to put in and what to leave out of our accounts. Many of the people I interviewed were keenly aware of this.

> "There's a myth that research is a linear process: research questions, literature review, planning, gathering, analysis. It's not. They're all going on in between, but you write it as a linear neat and tidy process. It doesn't reflect all the agonising, false trails, dead ends, quirks and so on."

With power, as always, comes responsibility. It is not possible to write a complete account of any research project. You have to be selective, and there are likely to be ethical considerations in most, if not all, of the decisions you need to take. Also, if we are sufficiently skilled and persuasive writers, we can influence others. Therefore there is an ethical aspect to each decision about how to tell the story of your research.

> "There's a craft in writing a thesis, a golden thread, but you have to not let it get too far away and become a fairy tale. Your storytelling, you could end up writing a myth based on what you think, because you've got an idea in mind that you want to arrive at, not a conclusion, but you've got to keep reminding, going back, not overlooking things. Looking at the negatives, the outliers, testing it against that, where someone didn't agree with what you think is your idea, and being aware of that, and not being worried about showing those in the findings."

In one sense, your data is your lodestone.

> "You're doing it in layers, building, coding, starting to conceptualise, building conceptual frameworks, linking these, coming up with new layers as you see patterns emerging, and it's hard not to lose sight of the links between your conceptual frameworks and what's down in the data. It's too easy to get carried away. There's a story to tell, but how far do you get carried away with the story you think is there, that you've developed in the head, and what's actually in your data?"

Going back to your data can help you to write ethically.

> "Honesty, accuracy, integrity in what you can and can't say. Writing is a craft; you can craft a story by what you start with, what you end with, what bits of data you highlight and what you pass over briefly. I know it's not an uncommon situation where people have the opportunity to write about a particular result and they decide to leave things out."

Yet writing ethically is not an easy task, particularly when data is complex or contradictory. Disciplinary imperatives can complicate this further.

> "Are we good at recognising evidence which doesn't support our argument? How do we deal with conflict in the data? It's the balance between an argument and showing results, and in the humanities that isn't a binary, it's far more grey and murky and muddled."

When you are writing about research, it is important to clarify the status of your data: how it was gathered, why you used that method or methods, any difficulties you encountered or changes of plan. This is an ethical imperative because it helps your readers to make their own decisions about the quality, rigour and ethics of your work. However, it also creates ethical difficulties. For example, some people may not want to write about the problems they faced or the limitations of their research.

> "Today we have a tendency that at the end of the study people write about limitations. It's a rule almost to criticise your study. I think that's a very good thing for people; it's like a safe zone to say out all your black dots in the study. So I think people should pay more notice to this section. They should really write it thoroughly. In most cases I see it as superficial."

> "Sometimes you want to leave out some details about the context or bad things that happened during the study so it looks prettier. A student left out a sentence about the sample. She brought out the limitations of the sample. It was not a bad science sample but in the notes it looked prettier as she wrote it up. I think people are not wanting to write negative things about the process."

Also, writing down the boundaries and limitations of research can create the illusion of a neat and tidy process, which is far from the reality. Writing reflexively is often proposed as a solution but, again, this can serve to conceal the researcher's 'ignorance or confusion' (Pullen and Rhodes, 2008, cited in Rhodes, 2009: 665) or their biases. (See Chapters 1, 6 and 9 for more on reflexivity, and Chapter 6 for more on bias and debiasing.)

> "Sometimes people have an inherent bias around what they decide to use. That goes back to the really basic question about how rigorous and ethical a researcher you are. I think one of the components of that kind of researcher is you're really conscious of your own biases. We all have them, it's not about you don't have them, it's about being conscious of what they are."

Some Euro-Western researchers argue that one way to make research more ethical is to share and cite data as well as written products.

> "If more people started acknowledging data and citing it properly within their research they could start putting that on their CVs and showing the impact they've made with their career of collecting and curating data for research but not necessarily creating a whole lot of papers and texts and things like that. It's allowing scientific output to be more broad than just the paper. Datacite provides a system which has been in place for a few years now but people don't use it; there's not a massive culture of if you're doing secondary reuse of data you have to put it in the paper."

Data sharing would need to be done carefully and with consent from participants or communities. Some Euro-Western and Indigenous researchers have, or have access to, carefully constructed data-sharing protocols which set out the circumstances in which data may (or may not) be shared. BIOTA Africa is a partnership between researchers of sustainability and biodiversity from four European and nine African countries. It has a data-sharing protocol which is overseen by a data management group. This group can restrict access to information in any of eight categories which include 'information on indigenous traditional knowledge or practices' (BIOTA Africa, 2010: 5).

If done ethically, sharing and citing data is an ethical act in itself. For example, it can enable readers to make fuller assessments of the integrity and quality of research reports, and it would enable researchers to reuse and re-analyse the data.

Writing as process

There is a common misconception, at least in the Euro–Western paradigm, that you find something out and then you write it down. In fact the process of writing is part of the process of investigation, in two respects. First, you will be writing throughout your research project, and, second, the act of writing itself helps you to figure out what you want and need to say and how to say it most effectively (Richardson, 1997: 87). There are specific ethical questions to consider as you write, such as the following.

- What is the best way to tell the story of this research?
- How can I represent my participants fairly?
- How can I represent my findings accurately?
- How can I best meet the needs of my readers?

> "What I feel when I'm writing is the constituents that the writing is for have got different interests, so my interests, and the person who's going to read and judge my work, and the people on whom it's based, we've got different agendas. I feel that ethical tension quite a lot."

Qualitative researchers and evaluators may need to think about whether to use quotes from participants. There can be good ethical reasons for this, such as to give your participants a 'voice' in your research output, and to include multiple perspectives. Conversely, using quotes can be unethical, for example if doing so breaches a participant's anonymity, or if you use quotes selectively to support an argument you want to make.

> "In qualitative research we can feel there's a need to put quotes in to back up everything we say. Sometimes we over-use them, and that can be an issue for confidentiality."

> "I started off with all quotes, then took too many out, now I've got the right balance. So that the conclusion you've arrived at, here's the evidence to support it."

So, careful ethical thinking is needed to help you decide whether or not to use quotes. Also, if you decide to use quotes, you need a rationale for which ones to use.

> "When you do your quotes, do you pick out the most exciting ones like a headline?"

> "The reason I was quoting him was that his points were interesting and controversial."

It is good ethical practice to state your rationale, as indeed I have done in the Prologue of this book.

If any of your quotes are in a different language from that in which you are writing, you should give both the original and a translation (Chilisa, 2012: 156). Also, bear in mind that if you have gathered data via social media and promised to maintain your participants' anonymity and confidentiality, you should not use quotes. This is because, if anyone entered such a quote into a search engine, it could immediately identify the source and therefore your participant.

It is also important to note that words are not the only tools researchers have at their disposal in telling the story of their work. Words can convey a great deal, but even so you will give a fuller, clearer picture if you can also include some images or other illustrative media such as sound clips.

Writing as product

If you have to write a specific product, such as a research report, thesis or dissertation, or a journal article, start by finding out what the requirements are, for example, word count and any stylistic requirements such as font type or size. This is good practice and also ethical because it saves you, and potentially others, from unnecessary time and effort.

Some academic disciplines require writing to be done in the third person, which necessitates clumsy linguistic contortions when you are reporting your own work. Indigenous researcher Shawn Wilson (2008: 26–7) persuaded his academic committee to let him write his thesis in the first person. However, some Indigenous peoples are not comfortable with use of the first person in writing (Smith, 2012: 38). There are no clear generalities here, so, if you are unsure, it is best to check whether you should use the first or third person in your writing.

When you're producing a written product, you need to take care to cite other people's work accurately and not plagiarise (see Chapter 7 for more on this). You also need to ask for formal copyright permission if you want to reproduce text, images, music or other creative outputs that were generated by someone else. Copyright law varies between countries, so you need to check out the position where you are, but the basic principles are the same. Creative work is owned by its creator, who holds what is called the 'intellectual property'. Even if the work is in the public domain, such as a photograph on a website, you cannot use it freely unless you are sure it is under a licence such as a Creative Commons license that allows free use. Some writers, photographers, musicians, artists and others are trying to earn their living from their creative work, and reproducing it without their permission, or payment if required, is a form of theft. In most countries, this kind of theft is a legal offence that carries a penalty under criminal law.

In the Indigenous paradigm, permission is needed to tell traditional stories outside their traditional context (Lambert, 2014: 73, 226).

Writing as creative

All writing is creative: a writer puts together words to create sentences, sentences to create paragraphs and paragraphs to create a document that did not previously exist. The writer chooses how they will tell the story of their research in words. Research writing is called non-fiction, but some Euro-Western scholars see it as a form of fiction, and some interviewees agreed.

> "I use fiction for example. Creative non-fiction is one way of approaching difficult ethical issues."

Some Euro-Western scholars have argued that taking a creative approach to research writing is an ethical stance in itself (Rhodes, 2009: 662). Others have argued that a creative approach can be used to solve ethical problems, such as by creating a composite case study from several interview transcripts to avoid identifying individual participants (Piper and Sikes, 2010: 572). Another ethical problem that creative methods can solve is the requirement that some researchers, particularly doctoral students, use a single authorial voice. This implies that the researcher has sole power and their voice should dominate the thesis. Some doctoral candidates have used creative methods to subvert this requirement. For example, Nick Sousanis presented his thesis in the form of a graphic novel, to reduce the primacy of the written word and enable him more effectively to include multiple viewpoints (Sousanis, 2015). Spencer Harrison painted his thesis on the inside and outside of a full-sized circus tent. He also wrote an accompanying thesis in the form of an artist's catalogue that enabled him to include multiple narratives (Harrison, 2014).

For some Indigenous scholars, the use of written stories seems more troubling. In oral cultures, the same story may be told very differently on different occasions. Writing a story down fixes it in a way that may become unhelpful as the context changes (Wilson, 2008: 22). Also, when an Indigenous person is face to face with someone, they can make a judgement about what kind of story that person needs to hear. For some Indigenous peoples, such as the Māori of New Zealand, face-to-face communication equates with ethical communication (Smith, 2012: 124). A written story may be read by anyone, anywhere, and the writer cannot tell whether the story is likely to be useful for each reader (Wilson, 2008: 69). Some Indigenous scholars are also concerned by the Euro-Western tendency to conflate stories with untruths (Wilson, 2008: 97).

When Indigenous researchers do write, they often take a creative approach. For example, Wilson (2008: 8) chose to include personal narrative sections addressed to his sons. Lambert (2014: 5–6) used the metaphor of the crafting of a Micmac potato basket as a metaphor for Indigenous research, and received permission to include some traditional Indigenous stories from around the world to illustrate her points (Lambert, 2014: 73, 110). There are many more examples. These approaches make the writing easier to read and understand, which is an ethical act.

Writing as relational

In the Euro–Western paradigm, writing is often seen as a solitary activity, because it involves one person putting words onto a page or screen. Yet writing for research is highly relational, and so is reading. Some of the Indigenous literature acknowledges this (Wilson, 2008: 9). When you are reading research, you are in relationship with the writer(s). When you are writing for research, you are in relationship with the people you are writing about, the people you are writing with and the people you are writing for. Kovach (2009: 101) argues that these are conceptual, rather than tangible, relationships, although I would suggest that they may be both.

Mostly, the people you are writing about are your participants. Researchers regularly grapple with the ethical difficulty of how best to represent participants.

> "One of my main preoccupations is about how to retain the participants' contribution as a human contribution. I absolutely hate reading research where participants are known as P1 and P2 and P3."

This is perhaps more of a preoccupation for qualitative researchers, although it is no less of an ethical consideration for quantitative or mixed-methods researchers.

In research within small communities, maintaining participants' anonymity in writing can be a challenge. I remember doing research within a big multi-disciplinary team providing children's services. There were several creche workers, kindergarten teachers, midwives and so on, but only one music therapist. Both her work and her contribution to the research were very valuable, and so distinctive that it was impossible to anonymise her data in the report. I dealt with this by talking to her, explaining my dilemma and asking for her views and wishes. I offered to withdraw her data, but she was content to stand by what she said and wasn't worried by the likelihood that others would be able to identify her contributions.

This was research with participants in a professional context, which is often less contentious than some other kinds of research. Zethu Matebeni, in her research with lesbians of colour in South Africa, worked with women who were vulnerable to violence and murder, and who also had to navigate a complex terrain of identity concealment and disclosure. She chose to anonymise participants and use pseudonyms in her research reporting. Some of her participants were happy with this approach, but many, particularly those who had taken the brave step of 'coming out' publicly as lesbians, were not happy about being 'put back in the closet' in this way (Matebeni, 2014: 121). This is a situation where there is no right answer: Matebeni, an insider researcher and an activist within and for her community, had to make a decision about how to write her research, which she knew could jeopardise the well-being of some of her participants whatever she decided. (See Chapter 8 for more on naming participants.)

Participants may also be some of the people you are writing with, although this is less common, at least in the Euro–Western paradigm.

> "Thinking about the PPI [patient and public involvement – a principle of health research in the UK] and 'nothing about us without us' stuff and all that, it's at this stage of writing up and dissemination that the involvement of the participants often falls away."

For this reason, some Euro–Western researchers regard it as an ethical imperative to share their findings and writings in draft with participants, for feedback, before finalising their work. Writing with participants can take a similar approach, as this interviewee suggests:

> "We've done a lot of co-authorship. I've done most of the writing, but then I've shared what I've done with my co-authors, and have incorporated what they've told me about that work."

However, sharing findings with participants doesn't always lead to the outcome a researcher might expect or desire, as this interviewee demonstrates:

> "A researcher I know had this lovely set of findings from two women, and when they saw it, they hated how they thought they came across, and asked that everything be withdrawn. And that was probably hideous for the researcher, especially as I bet she didn't think it represented them in a negative light."

Another interviewee highlights the reproduction of social inequalities within research work as a potential reason for such difficulties:

> "I think again there are potentially challenges in terms of representing groups of voices that are very different from your white middle class which, very broadly, is often the research audience and the vested interests in the research findings. I think all the assumptions and prejudices that go along with that, which you can't get over, we're all human beings but it's just being mindful of them."

Whichever paradigm a researcher works in, failing to give a voice to participants can cause harm to the people the researcher was trying to help (Millett, 2013: 328). Researchers are responsible for reporting their research in ways that will not harm their participants (Parpart, 2010: 25). One highly ethical way to do this is to report to participants (González and Lincoln 2006; Munté, Serradell and Sordé, 2011: 262), yet, as we have seen, this is not always straightforward.

Conclusion

Reporting your research findings is a huge responsibility. As well as the ethical imperative to convey your process and findings as effectively as possible, there is also the point that your descriptive and analytic writing may alter the way in which people experience research more generally (Warren, 2014: 10).

Writing is a particularly powerful act. Some of the more radical Euro-Western scholars of ethics suggest that ethical writing should focus on multiple voices offering contextualised questions, thoughts, possibilities, ambiguities and openness, rather than a single voice giving answers, generalisations, prescriptions and closure (Rhodes, 2009: 667; Warren, 2014: 65; Kuntz, 2015: 79). Some Indigenous scholars work in exactly this way (for example, Wilson 2008; Kovach 2009; Lambert 2014). Yet many Euro-Western researchers, including most doctoral students, are required by discipline and convention to use a single authorial voice.

Whether or not we are able to include multiple voices, reporting ethically requires us to remain aware of our authorial power and of how we choose to wield that power. Working reflexively helps us to act more ethically at all stages of the research process, but is arguably most important as we work to report our research.

REFLECTIVE QUESTIONS

1. How would you like to use your authorial power, and to what ends?
2. How ethical are your aims in reporting? Could you make them more ethical?
3. What can you do in your research work to help counteract the hierarchy of language?
4. If your readers included some people whose language you did not speak, and who did not speak your language, how would you report your research findings?
5. If your participants came from one or more communities with an oral tradition, such that many of them did not read, how would you report your findings to them?

CHAPTER 11

Ethical presentation of research findings

Introduction

The days when researchers presented their work only to each other, or to research funders or evaluation commissioners, are long gone. Contemporary researchers present to, and increasingly with, a wide range of diverse audiences (Pickering and Kara, 2017: 300). This shift has brought with it a range of ethical considerations that are often overlooked. There is little information about ethical approaches to presenting research in either the Euro-Western or the Indigenous literature. Yet presentations may conceal as well as reveal (Tamas, 2009: 617). To take an ethical approach to your presentation, you need to consider what you are hiding as well as what you intend to show.

In the Euro-Western paradigm, the time available for presentations is often very short, which may lead to more concealment than revelation.

> "Time is always limited so you're not opening all your skeletons within your presentations, you just bring out the good stuff."

The presentation is usually made by a researcher to an audience, with a few minutes for questions at the end, at an event created to facilitate such presentations, such as a conference or seminar. In the Indigenous paradigm, research may be presented within existing community methods for information sharing, such as the sharing circle. These can last for many hours, and are dialogic, with everyone present being given a chance to contribute if they wish (Lambert, 2014: 32).

As you present research, you are communicating directly with other people, which brings ethical responsibilities (Warren, 2014: 1). To make presentations ethical, it is essential to know your audience(s) as far as possible, and to make your work accessible for them. The aim is to give people the best chance to understand and retain the information you communicate.

> "Knowing your audience is crucial – without that, how can we determine what we want to say?"

Presenting research involves representing others, which requires considerable ethical sensitivity. As Bannister (1996: 52) says, 'People respond to representations of themselves with reactions ranging from delight to despair.' As a researcher, you can't always predict others' responses to being represented in your work, but you can do your best to represent them fairly and well. There are a number of ways to do this, including (but not limited to): co-presenting, using creative techniques and using social media. These will be discussed in more detail later in this chapter.

The thorny twins of anonymity and confidentiality arise again in relation to representation, particularly for qualitative researchers, as these interviewees suggest:

> "It's the stories that illustrate and give the richness to it, but how do you do that without revealing that person's identity? I think that is the real challenge that qualitative researchers have in presentation and in writing. I've read a lot of different solutions, people have suggested, and none of them really seem adequate to me so I think it's an unresolved issue."

> "You need to think carefully about presenting findings in terms of things like confidentiality. I remember in some qualitative research I did where I was interviewing a tight-knit group, medical consultants in a specific area, they knew each other. In using quotes from one of these characters, he used the term 'to be honest' a lot, so when I quoted from him I took those out because anyone who knew him would know he was saying that."

As we have seen previously, it is necessary to think carefully about the context and content of your own research, consult where necessary and make a considered decision about when and how to offer anonymity and confidentiality. Of course this should be done, as far as possible, at the planning stage of your research (see Chapter 6 for more on this). In the Indigenous paradigm, it is generally seen as ethical to use people's real names, with occasional exceptions for any participant who would prefer a pseudonym (Wilson, 2008: 63). In the Euro-Western paradigm, it is generally seen as ethical to offer anonymity to all participants, although sometimes people have reasons for wanting to be named (Scarth, 2016: 81). Naming research participants can bring researchers into conflict with a REC/ IRB (Wilson, 2008: 86), and REC/IRB requirements for confidentiality can make research work more difficult.

> "I said I would take out identifying details but sometimes it's quite hard to do that."

This particular ethical difficulty can be foreseen in either paradigm, and the ethical solution is to give participants the choice of whether or not they wish to remain anonymous, plus any support they may need in making that choice. Participants have their own reasons for taking part in research (Bell and Salmon, 2011: 88; Cox and McDonald, 2013: 229–30) and are generally better placed than researchers to decide whether or not they want to be named (Scarth, 2016: 86).

Ethical dilemmas around presentation may arise that could not have been foreseen. For example, one interviewee told a story of research involving young people who were same-sex attracted and gender diverse. The findings showed that levels of self-harm and drug use, among other related issues, were much higher among these groups than in the general population of young people.

The researchers identified a risk that their results could confirm some people's prejudices that being lesbian, gay, bisexual or trans was an undesirable, unhealthy life-style. In this case the researchers were careful to frame their results so as to make it clear that the findings were the result of external factors, explicitly including homophobia, biphobia and transphobia in the explanatory narrative.

For the interviewee, that was an ethical way to present the results. However, it is also evidently allied with a specific set of social and political ethics that support diverse sexual orientations among human beings. There are other social and political ethics that do not support such diversity, such as those which argue (as the interviewee recognised) that non-mainstream identities may condemn people to lives of unhappiness, ill-health and stigmatisation. Each position considers the other to be unethical, which demonstrates that not all ethical dilemmas can be entirely resolved.

This chapter is intended to help you find your way through any such dilemmas you may encounter in presenting your research work. It will cover the importance of knowing your audience, ways to make presentations accessible, the pros and cons of co-presenting, using creative methods of presentation and the role of social media.

Know your audience

Of course you can't always be sure, ahead of time, who will be in your audience. Nevertheless, it's worth thinking through who may be present, to help you figure out how to meet their needs. It is best to choose methods of presentation that are likely to help your audience understand your work (Kelleher and Wagener, 2011: 826), rather than picking methods because they suit you.

These questions will help you to think through who your audience may be, and what needs they may have.

- How homogeneous or heterogeneous is your audience?
- What are the likely age range and gender balance?
- What status do these people have in their communities and/or professions?
- Which ethnicities are likely to be represented there?
- What cultural competence(s) do you need to address this audience effectively?
- Do you anticipate any specific communication requirements, such as the need for an interpreter?
- What kinds of responses do you anticipate to the content of your presentation?

More homogeneous audiences are generally easier to present to than more heterogeneous audiences. Evaluation researchers are particularly likely to face heterogeneous audiences, made up of community members, service users, project staff and managers, local politicians or their equivalent and research commissioners and/or funders. We saw in Chapter 5 that evaluation research is an ethical juggling act, and extra balls may be added when it comes to presentation. At this stage, evaluators are particularly likely to experience pressure from stakeholders such as funders, commissioners or managers to play down or omit uncomfortable or politically inexpedient findings (Morris, 2008: 19; Desautels and Jacob, 2012: 440). There are many factors that can influence evaluators in making decisions about how they respond to such pressure. These may include the evaluator's own ethical stance, their perception of the 'competing goods' in the evaluation context (Josselson, 2007: 560) and their need for employment or payment.

As a presenter of research, you have a great deal of power; perhaps more than you realise. As always, power brings with it ethical responsibility, as this interviewee understood:

"It's what you put in and what you leave out that creates the picture in the audience's mind. You have the power to steer them to particular understandings. You can downplay the image, steer the positive, you're interacting with other human beings and telling them a story, I think it's a more powerful way of presenting than reading some academic journal that's dry. You have more responsibility, people trust you more in a face-to-face process; they don't have the same capacity to really critically think about what you're presenting because it's there and gone. You're crafting and creating a picture of results, so you have to be really fair and clear about what you say."

Sometimes your audience includes, or is made up of, your participants. Several interviewees identified the ethical importance of presenting research to participants.

"I think there's also something there about informing your research participants of the outcomes of your research – I think that's good ethical practice."

"Another thing for me is feedback to participants. That's always in those forms. Everyone has to say 'yes', they're going to give feedback, but how you give feedback, what way you give it, how much time you take, what language you give feedback in, is something I feel really strongly is not done well enough and is done irresponsibly in many ways."

"There's a lack of relevant, useful, thought-felt [sic] feedback to people. I still don't know how to do that. I sent a summary to everyone I had an email address for, where I didn't I asked local organisations to print them. I came up with a really nice poster type thing, with photos, bullet points, a map, to say what I'd found in my research. The reaction from people was like I'd won the Nobel prize or something. In my mind it was the bare minimum of a small, little, contribution of feedback to people. The reaction told me how little researchers do that, how little people expect them to do it or to care."

In the Indigenous paradigm, communicating findings to participants may often be an essential stage of the research process (Wilson, 2008: 48; Lambert, 2014: 215–16).

Unless your participants have specific characteristics such as hearing impairment, making ethical presentations to them is no different from making ethical presentations to any other kind of audience. Generally an ethical presentation will use everyday language, include information in at least two formats (for example, spoken and visual) and be engaging for its audience. The exception for everyday language is when you have a homogeneous audience who are familiar with relevant jargon and/or technical terms, in which case you can use such terminology as much as you like.

Making presentations accessible

Once you have identified, as far as possible, the nature and needs of your audience(s), you can start to work on making your presentation accessible for them. Stories are increasingly used as an accessible way to present research findings (Kovach, 2009: 131). Also, the use of visual materials can help people to understand and remember what you tell them (Evergreen, 2014: 18). However, there can be ethical difficulties around using some visual methods in presenting research, such as photographs.

> "I've used photos, of beautiful landscapes, farms, things like that. I think one has to be very careful about how much those photos give away about the people and places you've worked in, and how much they convey about your bias. So I've taken a photo that I think shows X about this landscape, when I've shown that to other people, I've had other things asked. I think the way photos are used can have a big impact on how people receive our research, so there's a point in doing that carefully and responsibly."

Photos of people, too, need careful ethical consideration. In the Euro–Western paradigm, consent is needed. In the Indigenous paradigm, other considerations may apply. For example, some communities do not approve the showing of pictures of people from that community who are now deceased (see Chapter 12 for more on this).

There are many other visual methods that you can use to help make your research more accessible, such as diagrams, infographics, maps and charts. Do choose carefully, though, and make sure that the visual methods you use truly help to communicate your message. As with writing, creating visualisations is a relational process in which you and your audiences work together to create meaning (Kirk, 2016: 22).

It is also important to present in everyday language. If you need to use jargon or technical terms, give clear definitions. Don't present big chunks of text visually

– and if you present any text visually, don't read it out to the audience unless some or all are unable to read it for themselves.

Co-presenting

There is an ethical argument for co-presenting, as this demonstrates the cooperative nature of much research.

> "I guess the thing that's important to me when I'm presenting is acknowledging other people's involvement. So it's a bit like being a humble researcher. I don't want to lessen the research, but for me that's really important. Just because you achieve something, it's acknowledging that that's not down to you alone. So I often will acknowledge out loud the people that were involved, whether other researchers or participants."

Some researchers view it as particularly ethical to involve participants in presentations.

> "You do see at conferences far more of patients and clients being involved in dissemination, speaking at conferences and so on."

> "I hope it would come through in my presentation that it's not just about me, because some researchers do come across like that."

In the Indigenous paradigm, co-presenting fits well with the relational ethic (Bowman, Francis and Tyndall, 2015: 351). That has led this interviewee to expand their approaches to presenting the research they work on with Indigenous people.

> "A lot of it is making sure that different voices are heard in the presentation, and we've chosen ways to present which have made it easier for us all to be involved. So rather than going to theoretical conferences, we've gone to conferences with Indigenous and non-indigenous participants, so that the work we present is of use to all of us, not just to the academic members. Sometimes people we're working with don't want to stand up and talk, but they want to be there, and it's a way of showing support for the researcher. But it's – I've presented at a few conferences where there have been four of us talking, actually I think one was six, we divided it up, it was talky but it felt good."

However, to do this ethically is not always easy. Not all participants will be willing to take part in such a presentation. Those who are willing may not be able, for all sorts of reasons: work, caring responsibilities, inaccessible venues and so on. Money can overcome some of these problems, but funds are not always available. Then it is vital that participants who are willing and able to take part are not treated tokenistically, but are as involved as they want to be in preparing and delivering the presentation. Also, at least in the Euro-Western paradigm, participants should be paid for their time and input, or – as a minimum – should have their expenses covered so they are not effectively subsidising the research (see Chapter 8 for more on paying participants).

Using creative methods

As this interviewee explains, presentation is performative, in that it involves one or more people in front of an audience.

> "I think there is a bit of an issue in presentation. It is a performance and you do have to entertain the crowd a bit, or you've got to try anyway. Often in presentation we want to use visual materials, make things more interesting and lively and evocative, and sometimes that can lead you into displaying a bit more data than you might have done in a publication. It potentially ends up coming across as disrespectful of the participants. You don't want to make your presentations dull and boring and worthy but at the same time you've still got to make sure you don't say too much. I think the urge to perform and be evocative and show in a presentation does sometimes create extra challenges."

Some scholars are making a much more direct link between presentation and performance, by using techniques such as spoken poetry, music, drama and dance to present research findings. This involves quite a specific form of compromise: a reduction in the communication of absolute facts, and a corresponding increase in the communication of emotion (Pickering and Kara, 2017: 306).

> "Presenting is performance. It's about getting your ideas across, keeping people engaged, and that may involve compromise. You cannot show the complexity, the rigour, in detail. And so that can cause ethical issues. I do performative papers which leave open spaces for interpretation quite deliberately, so my processes and methods are not necessarily immediately clear, or not clear at all. There's a question of how do I show that in the context of a short time-scale, so it's a balance between performance and drily reading results. That's something I wrestle with all the time."

Performative presentation engages audiences' emotions as well as their intellect, and so is more engaging and has more impact than conventional styles of research presentation (Kara, 2015: 156). For ethical performative presentation, researchers need to be aware of, and make explicit, the choices and compromises they decide to make as they prepare their presentation (Pickering and Kara, 2017: 307).

Other creative methods may also be useful in presenting research. For example, images and short forms of poetry can convey a great deal in relation to their size. Lambert (2014: 66) makes the point that visual materials, such as posters or brochures, may be useful in presenting research to communities or groups who do not have access to the internet. She also suggests that visual materials such as artworks or maps may be useful in helping to communicate research findings (Lambert, 2014: 66).

The role of social media

Social media is more commonly thought of in relation to dissemination than presentation. However, social media can play a useful role in presentation too. Use of live real-time feeds from platforms such as Twitter extends the presentation beyond the boundaries of the venue. Live presentations can be recorded and uploaded to sites such as YouTube or Vimeo, where comments may be made by viewers. These methods can enable involvement from interested people who can't attend in person.

Also, research conducted using social media may be best presented via social media. The use of social media for presentation can be seen as ethical because it gives participants and other stakeholders time and space to respond (Pickering and Kara, 2017: 306), and so promotes debate that can enrich findings and improve practice.

Conclusion

The ultimate aim of any ethical presentation is to give your audience enough information about your research – or about a part or aspect of your research – so that they can judge it for themselves. This is difficult to do under any circumstances, and trying to do it ethically makes it even harder. Nevertheless, as ethical researchers, we have a responsibility to take as ethical an approach as possible to our presentations.

REFLECTIVE QUESTIONS

1. What could you do to make your presentations more ethical?
2. How do you feel about standing up in front of an audience and presenting your research? How might that affect the quality of your presentations?
3. At your last presentation, how well did you know your audience? Is there anything you could have done to get to know them better?
4. How could you make your next presentation more accessible to your audience?
5. If your views were going to be represented by a researcher, how would you want that to happen?

CHAPTER 12

Ethical dissemination

Introduction

As we saw in the previous chapter, dissemination involves sharing data and publicising research beyond that which you can do in person. Dissemination itself is an ethical imperative for researchers, particularly if the work is resourced from public or charitable funds, as this interviewee was keenly aware.

> "Dissemination is now beyond the confines of academia; you've got new audiences. We need to look at the consequences of our findings on new audiences and how we communicate these. Is there an ethical responsibility to share our results? Yes there is. Do we do it? Probably not all the time. And therefore do we start thinking about academic language and access to results? This is really pressing. If it's about them, they should have the rights to the results. I'd like impact to start to be seen from an ethical point of view, rather than just a government funding type issue. There are ethical issues about sharing results beyond academia particularly if it's government funded."

This is partly because it is ethical to share information and knowledge gained, and partly because it is ethical to make the most possible use of research findings.

> "There's no point doing research unless you take it into policy and practice and make a difference."

There are many ways to disseminate research, and some are more ethical than others, depending on the context. You can disseminate information online; in hard copy; using text, images, video; in academic journals or other formal publications, or by self-publishing; through mainstream media; using social media; through an exhibition or installation; or in a range of other creative ways from graphic novels or zines to interpretative dance (Gaudry, 2015: 257; Kara, 2015: 161). It can be a good idea to use more than one method of dissemination, to increase the accessibility and reach of your findings. The key to ethical dissemination is to figure out who could benefit from knowing about your research, and which methods are most likely to reach those people.

However, there are also some barriers to dissemination that any researcher may encounter. Ethical practice involves finding ways around these barriers. Wide dissemination requires working out who might have an interest in your findings and how to reach them. This chapter will review the barriers to dissemination, and the potential roles of participants in dissemination. It will then discuss the pros and cons of the most common methods and of some creative approaches.

Barriers to dissemination

Failing to share data or to publicise research can cause real harm. In some circumstances, it can even cost lives, such as during outbreaks of viral disease. Yet even in such acute situations, data is not always shared swiftly or freely. For example, during the Ebola outbreak in West Africa in 2014–16, which caused the deaths of over 10,000 people, there were several cases of people and organisations being unwilling to share data about the epidemic (Whitty et al, 2015: 1797). At least some of these were because the researchers concerned were worried that sharing data would jeopardise their ability to publish their findings in academic journals and so boost their careers. Putting your own career before the lives of others – including some of your participants – is one of the more unethical things you can do as a researcher. Even where less is at stake, it is important to share information as early and as much as you can.

> "There is a kind of onus I would say on you, that not everyone appreciates, to release as much as possible for the public good, to reuse and for the scientific good. There's obviously a tension there between people's careers, and progress, and releasing that, so it's getting that balance right."

However, there are ethical issues around data sharing: for example, in most cases only aggregated, anonymised data should be shared, although there are exceptions.

> "I think keeping data confidential is important, but on the other hand we should be more generous in sharing our data, to get more out of it."

So, while data sharing is in one sense an ethical act, these tensions illustrate that dissemination of data is not ethically straightforward. There are similar tensions when it comes to publishing findings. We saw in Chapter 5 that evaluators may come under particular pressure, from one or more stakeholders, to amend or skew findings, usually for political reasons (Williams et al, 2011: 6). If evaluators resist such pressure – or if stakeholders recognise that it is unethical to apply such pressure – evaluation commissioners or funders can choose, instead, not to publish the evaluation results. This would be in direct contravention of Indigenous ethical guidelines (Williams et al, 2011: 6). (It is also in contravention of Euro-Western ethical principles, but not of Euro-Western ethical guidelines as such, because they don't usually mention dissemination.)

It is not only evaluation that is subject to these pressures: they can apply to other forms of commissioned research and to academic research as well.

"One of the committees I'm on is a government committee. There are always tensions when governments commission research and the researchers have to sign a form that says they will only release results if approved by the government ... in the end you can only do so much."

Then there are some specific barriers to dissemination for particular types or elements of research. For example, visual methods raise some unique ethical difficulties. In the Euro–Western paradigm these include questions about anonymity and consent (Rose, 2012: 331). It is hard to maintain people's anonymity if you include photographs of them in your research outputs. Also, it is difficult to obtain fully informed consent for doing this, as it may not be possible to inform participants at the outset about all the ways in which their image might be used and who might look at it, particularly if you intend to make it available online.

Different ethical difficulties arise with using visual methods in the Indigenous paradigm. For example, some Indigenous peoples, such as those in parts of Australia and the Torres Strait Islands, can be very distressed by the publication of photographs of people who have died. It is essential to be aware of this if you use photographs from these communities, as you would need to be prepared to amend or remove those images from your research outputs following the death of any participant: perhaps for a period of mourning, or for good, as specified by the community (Bostock, 1997: 38). This is also, evidently, a major ethical issue for researchers working with secondary or archival data.

"Some people are publishing visual research, there's a whole swathe of issues around doing visual research in online settings and how you deal with taking images. You get a lot of publications on internet research that have no images in at all. We really haven't cracked what to do ethically about saving images and publishing them. There's a whole sphere of research not being done particularly thoroughly just because it is so difficult to find a route through."

There are two big structural ethical fault-lines that act as barriers to dissemination. One is that most formal publication systems are controlled by Euro–Western people and it can be difficult or impossible for Indigenous people to publish within those systems. Another problem here is that research that is unethical from an Indigenous perspective may be published in a journal that recognises only Euro–Western research governance (Moodie, 2010: 820). The second fault-line is that much of academia confers status on publishing in ways that are accessible only to others in academia, such as paywalled journals or expensive monographs.

Where research has been resourced with public or charitable funds, the truly ethical option is usually open publication. However, there may be cases where open dissemination is not advisable. For example, research into escapes from prison by convicted criminals might be very helpful to the prison service, but it could also be helpful to other criminals serving prison sentences who would like to escape. So it is important to think this through, rather than automatically publishing openly.

Open publication usually means publication online that is free for everyone to view or download. Do be aware, though, that this doesn't actually mean it's accessible to everyone. For example, work may be difficult to access if it's hard to find among the ever-increasing billions of web pages.

> "Making sure, if you do disseminate stuff, that people can find it. There are systems out there people can use, and a lot of them are free now, so it's basically using that – whether it be in a journal, then your publishers will take care of that. There are places where you can release your data and supplementary material."

Also, some people have little or no access to the internet (see below for more on this). So, even with open publication, you need to be aware of whom you may be excluding. If you are excluding people who would benefit from your research, you should consider alternative means of dissemination that could reach those people. If you are unsure about how to do this, consulting with participants or their representatives may be helpful.

Dissemination to and with participants

In the Indigenous research literature, disseminating findings to participants, in ways that they can understand and use, is often presented as an ethical imperative (Kovach, 2009: 149; Okalik, 2013: 245; Wilson and Wilson, 2013: 349; Lambert, 2014: 215). Some Euro-Western researchers share this view. For example, this interviewee is clear-sighted about the potential positive impacts:

> "To me, one way to deal with those things, is to be transparent and give something back, that's a way to build goodwill towards research. The next way [sic] someone asks me to participate in a study I'll be more likely to say 'yes OK that's great' and be more positive because I can see that there is a value in the research. That's part of the ethical issues to dissemination."

Another interviewee goes further.

> "We try to get participants involved in the dissemination plan. Either they co-present, or they're involved in writing a plain-language summary and it's given to them to distribute in their communities, or they're involved in the training that results or the media."

These interviewees speak of participants as a homogeneous group, but a third viewpoint widens the discussion.

> "The other thing around dissemination is you have to communicate results to a range of audiences. If I could get a dollar for every time I got an application that said 'present findings in peer-reviewed journal and conferences' – the committee just goes 'no, not good enough'. You have to have a process of offering summary feedback to the group, and you have to disseminate it in a way that makes a difference. There was a case not so long ago in the northern part of Australia that was looking at crocodile attacks, they just said 'academic conferences and peer-reviewed journals', and we were saying 'don't you think it's a public issue?'"

This suggests that in many cases dissemination should be not only to participants, but also to the communities those participants represent. For Indigenous researchers this can offer opportunities for community learning (Smith, 2013: 95). In this context, an ethical approach to dissemination involves working out how to share your findings with your participants and with others, whom they represent, who may have an interest in learning from your research.

> "The research centre I'm involved in involves marginalised people, LGBTI, Hep C, sex workers, Indigenous and so on. The expectation is that you build partnerships with the community, invite them in at the beginning; they form advisory committees around the research question. They're often paid as co-researchers, then they're absolutely critically involved in the dissemination of the research because it's relevant to them, they want to take it back into their communities, co-present to policy makers, politicians, health workers, whatever. It's the whole process of the research that ideally people are participating in, to me that's the most ethical way to do research. I know it's not always possible, not always even appropriate, but to me that's gold standard research."

Many Indigenous researchers would not think of disseminating research without the full involvement of participants (Moloi, 2013: 111). Generally, dissemination to participants and communities is a good idea in Euro-Western research too. However, there are exceptions. The autoethnographer Carolyn Ellis always suggested that her students do this, but 'Then a student, writing about being abused by her brother, convinces me it would cause unraveling of a family system that is, after many long years, intact' (Ellis, 2007: 24). Ellis now acknowledges that there are times when disseminating research can damage the people and relationships researchers are working to support (Ellis, 2007: 24).

Dissemination can be challenging when participants have specific attributes and needs. A creative approach can be useful here. For example, researchers investigating the phenomenon of homelessness in the UK interviewed over 100 people. Two of the problems they faced in disseminating the research were: how to tell the stories of these 'vulnerable and excluded people' (Dahl et al, 2012: 3), and how to disseminate findings to a transient population. They solved these problems by creating a graphic novel, *Somewhere Nowhere: Lives Without Homes*, which they self-published using the online print-on-demand service Lulu. This enabled them to tell stories in a direct way, and to give copies to all the participants they could find.

> "You should disseminate your results to your participants always – that's ethical behaviour I would say."

A differently creative approach was taken by the journal *Research Ethics*, which published an account of a child's experience of taking part in a UK national survey. The child, 10-year-old Freja Edwards, was chosen at random, and her father, John Edwards, happened to be an academic at Keele University. The article is written in the first person, most of it in Freja's words, with a short 'parental perspective' from her father's viewpoint (Edwards and Edwards, 2012: 167). It covers a range of ethical issues from the participant's perspective: the sampling method, the consent process, the difference between the expectations created by the researchers and the reality of the research experience, rewards given for participation, privacy and the ultimate point of the research. There are no references. This method of publication enables a child participant's voice to be heard in a forum where that is very rarely the case. I expect that some readers critiqued the Edwardses' account as anecdotal and therefore pointless. I don't share their view; for me, the ethical content is interesting, and publishing this account was an ethical act.

I have highlighted dissemination to participants here as it features most prominently in the literature. Liamputtong (2010: 225) makes the point that it is also important to disseminate research to those 'who have the authority or power to change policies and practices'. Within an Indigenous community, participants and those in power may well be the same people. In Euro-Western contexts that is unlikely to be the case. I have not found any information in the literature about how best to disseminate research to those with authority or power; this would be a useful topic for study.

Online dissemination

The internet and social media are very useful tools for dissemination.

> "I think it's great that we've got social media to help us with dissemination, that makes it much more accessible, I think that's good."

Placing research findings online, and advertising them through social media, does indeed make them more accessible to many people. However, as so often with digital technologies, this brings new ethical difficulties in its wake. First, not everyone can access the internet or social media. For example, a number of countries in the Middle and Far East block Twitter, Facebook and YouTube, which are the social media most commonly used in much of the world to disseminate research. People in those countries may still be able to access the web page where the research is located online, but if they don't know it's there, they are unlikely to stumble across it among the ever-increasing billions of web pages. Then, in countries that do not block social media, there may be individual differences between people's levels of access to the internet. People in sparsely populated rural, coastal or desert areas may have little or no ability to connect to the internet. There may be financial barriers: people may not be able to afford to pay for the necessary hardware, software and/or connection costs. And there may be skill barriers, as not everyone is able to use digital technologies, or to use them effectively.

Disseminating research online and via social media is a good plan, but it is also important to be aware of, and to state, the limits to that dissemination. Where this means that a chunk of your intended audience is likely to miss out on your findings, you will need to look for other ways in which your research can reach those people.

Another potential problem with online dissemination is that the internet never forgets. This has implications for the status of consent given by participants.

> "I think risks of people's reputations and what you say about communities and people you've worked with. Confidentiality, anonymity, especially with the internet and the way things can be shared."

Generally, consent is given in the present; it is very hard for a participant to know how they may feel in years to come. Yet, once information is placed in the public domain, it can become impossible to remove it, particularly if (as with most research) it has been made available for download. So it is very important for researchers to think this through as far as they can, and to present as full a picture as possible to participants when asking for their consent (Mannay, 2016: 114).

Formal publication

Research can be formally published in outputs such as academic journals and book chapters. Academic journals are perhaps the most common method of formally publishing research. Around 2.5 million scientific, technical and medical journal articles are published each year (Ware and Mabe, 2015: 6), plus more in the arts and humanities. Reputable journals use systems of editorial control and peer review to try to ensure quality, yet erroneous and unethical articles are regularly published, some of which are later retracted (see Chapter 7 for more on this). On the whole, this is despite the best efforts of reviewers, editors and publishers. However, sometimes editors decide to publish research that evidently included unethical practice, on the basis that the harm has already been done, so any potential benefit might as well be gained (Hunter, 2012: 67). In my view this is ethically questionable, as refusal to publish is surely a significant deterrent to researchers who may be considering unethical practice.

Another ethical issue around formal publication is the way in which authors are named. This varies between disciplines. For example, in economics, authors of journal articles are named in alphabetical order, while in sociology the author who made the largest contribution is named first (Sarsons, 2017: 2). The system used in economics has an adverse impact on women's career prospects in academia, which are unaffected by the system used in sociology (Sarsons, 2017: 3).

Journal editors and publishers are sometimes reluctant to name participants who have co-authored journal articles, even when they explicitly wish to be named (Sinha and Back, 2014: 483–4). Yet, ethically, there may be an argument for naming participants more prominently, or even instead of, academics, as this interviewee explains:

> "Another thing in this big grant I was on was we produced a lot of material; even though I was the PI [principal investigator], my name wasn't on a lot of those. We didn't use the scientific model where the PI is on everything – that's a colonising way of doing things. We were trying to overturn or to shift research roles. We wanted to say the community members are the researchers here, the academic members are not the primary researchers. Really important in terms of decolonising knowledge, for the academics to be in the background or non-existent in the co-authoring."

Conversely, senior academics may offer 'gift authorship' to colleagues who have done no work on an article, as part of the complex network of favours that underpins academia (Martin, 2013: 75). Worse still, senior academics may take credit for the work of doctoral students and junior staff by adding their own names to articles to which they have made no contribution. This is a form of plagiarism (Martin, 2013: 74).

There is a prevailing myth that most journal articles are rarely read. In fact, as long as an article is accessible online, it is likely to be quite widely read (Ware and Mabe, 2015: 44). Book chapters are much less widely read because you have to get hold of the hard copy, academic books are often prohibitively expensive, libraries have limited capacity, inter-library loans can take a long time and so on. So, the most ethical publishing option for journal articles is an open access journal, because that can be read by anyone who has internet access. This can cause difficulties for academics who are required to publish in high-impact journals to meet performance assessment targets, as most of those are still paywalled, although an increasing number of open access journals do have high-impact factors, so this may change in time. However, it does not seem that publishing in an open access journal leads to more citations (Pringle, 2017), so as yet there is no incentive for academia to change its ways.

The companion website (http://policypress.co.uk/resources/kara-ethics) for this book holds a range of resources on the ethics of formal publishing.

Using creative methods

Indigenous methods of dissemination are often inherently creative. For example, these methods may include the use of stories, arts, crafts or metaphors (Blodgett et al, 2013: 328; Rix et al, 2018: 11). In the Euro–Western paradigm, creative methods can be particularly useful for disseminating complex research, such as research using mixed-methods or transformative approaches, and for reaching a wider section of the public than traditional methods do (Kara, 2015: 161, 168). Research has been disseminated using methods such as film, quilting, art installations and exhibitions, graphic novels, animations and drama. Used well, creative methods can make research more accessible and appealing (Pickering and Kara, 2017: 307), as this interviewee found:

> "I made a map, people loved the map, wanted to use it in their reports."

One approach in the Euro–Western paradigm that is deemed to be creative is knowledge exchange, that is, knowledge being shared between people rather than being given by one person to others. Ward et al researched this phenomenon and found that it was not, as dissemination is often portrayed, linear and deterministic, but fluid, dynamic and 'an integral part of the process of change' (Ward et al, 2012: 302). The aim of these researchers was to formulate a conceptual framework of knowledge exchange for use as a practical tool in putting research findings into practice, but they were able to produce only a descriptive rather than a conceptual framework. They found that knowledge exchange was difficult to research empirically because it is hard to observe and dependent on context and interpersonal relationships (Ward et al, 2012: 303). It is notable that, here, Euro–Western researchers seem to be problematising an ethical aspect of research that many Indigenous researchers regard as a central principle: that community knowledge is communally owned (Kovach, 2009: 145; Lambert, 2014: 215).

The role of mainstream media

For some research, this is the best way to reach interested people. It is certainly a good way to reach a lot of people, which means that it appeals to many researchers.

> "Everyone who does interesting research hopes to get media coverage."

However, as we saw in Chapter 6, journalistic ethics are not the same as research ethics. Another implication is that, in handing over your findings to a journalist, you relinquish editorial control. There are pros and cons here, as this interviewee explains:

"Make sure your research is accurately represented if you can because you know how journalists can be in terms of reporting on findings, they like to be sensationalist. Some people might like that to promote their work and get in the papers, others might want to get the right findings out there and not little snapshots that don't show the whole picture."

Decide ahead of time which is more important to you: wide dissemination that may be inaccurate, or accurate dissemination that will not be so wide? It is rare to be able to have both, though if you have contacts in the media, an institutional press office or access to media training, that may help.

Conclusion

In general, publication and dissemination of research findings is an ethical act, particularly if research is funded from the public purse. However, there are times when it is more ethical not to publish and disseminate. For example, if a forensic science researcher discovered a particularly effective way to dispose of a dead body, it would not be sensible to publish that information because of the risk of its misuse. In 2011 the US government intervened to ask two high-profile, high-impact academic journals to modify a research article before publication. The research was on the bird flu virus and the US government feared that misuse of the findings could cause a dangerous pandemic (Kuhlau et al, 2013: 7). This generated a heated international discussion about the relationship between scientific openness and public safety.

There are no hard-and-fast rules about when findings should or should not be published. However, it is important to think carefully about whether your findings could be misused by other people. As long as they could not, then your research should be disseminated.

REFLECTIVE QUESTIONS

1. Why do you think it is important to share the methods and findings of research?
2. Why do you think it is important to share data?
3. How would you disseminate information to people who have little or no internet access, such as rough sleepers, elderly people who have never been online or those in rural or coastal/island areas where there is no internet coverage?
4. Do you think it can ever be ethical to publish your work in a paywalled journal? Why?
5. Are there ways in which you could use and disseminate Indigenous research or theory more than you do at present?

CHAPTER 13

Ethical aftercare

Introduction

In the Euro–Western paradigm, the potential need for research aftercare is rarely recognised or discussed.

> "I just think that's a great question! Because it never comes up! I think it's a great question and it's one I'm going to think about for some of my ethics training and lecturing. You're right, the research is done, the researchers leave, the participants might get a two-page summary and that's the last they hear of it."

> "Do we have a duty of care for any audience? Or should we only be considering the ethics of the research? A medical thing will say 'we'll give you a counsellor for three months if you need it'; I could see an art exhibition having that effect, only on a small percentage but ethically every member of that audience needs to be cared for. This comes into practicalities: is it possible to resource? If there hasn't been a case, is it 'reasonable risk'? These are issues that perhaps aren't being thought about. All I would say at this stage is, they should be thought about, so there are no surprises."

Some Euro–Western researchers do think about aftercare, at least to some extent. For example, some ethnographers advocate 'friendship as method' (Tillmann-Healy 2001, cited in Ellis, 2007) and acknowledge that, if this is the case, 'there is no leaving the field' (Ellis, 2007: 13). However, this seems mostly to happen at an individual level rather than with any team or institutional encouragement.

> "Making sure that people know what happens with the research, that's always been important to me. It has been before I knew what participatory research was – don't just parachute in and parachute out. Even if they weren't involved in writing or interpretation, that they get to see what's produced at the end as a minimum. I've got my own invisible minimum requirements, then those might expand and extend depending on the nature of the project."

By contrast, in the Indigenous paradigm, aftercare is often part of the standard long-term commitment to relational community-based life and work (Smith, 2012: 16). Some Indigenous communities aver that researchers 'hold seven generations of ethical responsibility to those they study. They must consider the long-term legacy of what they do' (Kouritzin and Nakagawa, 2018: 10).

This could help to explain why the literature suggests that researchers using a Euro-Western paradigm while working in countries with Indigenous populations may be more likely to pay attention to aftercare for participants. For example, Cluver et al, gathering evidence for social work interventions in families with AIDS in South Africa, report that one researcher repeatedly saved a young girl's life when her mother refused to do so. The researcher took the girl to hospital, bought her food so that she could take her medication, rang her twice a day to make sure she took her medication, arranged a foster carer for her and kept in touch by letter after the research project ended (Cluver et al, 2014: 46). Some of the interviewees for this book, none of whom was an Indigenous researcher themselves, also recognise the importance of aftercare for some participants.

> "It's certainly something we do more in our centre. The way we do research is to build relationships with communities and they go for years, so the aftercare is maintenance of a relationship that goes on."

> "It's not always possible to maintain relationships where you're speaking to people every week, but I think it's important to acknowledge relationships, to acknowledge that there was an important research-based friendship, and sometimes there are deeper friendships than that as well. I think it's very very important to try to maintain some sort of connection, even if it's only once a year when you say 'hello, how are you, it was great working with you, miss you', that kind of thing. Everything we do as researchers is part of a wider context and we're all human beings. Maintaining those relationships after a project is a way of acknowledging the humanity of the work that you do."

Nevertheless, at least in the Euro-Western paradigm, the concept of aftercare is in its infancy. Some interviewees were uncomfortable at the prospect.

> "Most people seem to provide signposting – that does seem to be the standard approach. That's what I do, and I certainly wouldn't feel comfortable about having ongoing contact with a participant."

One approach within the Euro-Western paradigm is to try to act ethically when ending contact with a participant. For example, researchers are advised to 'make endings as clear and pain-free as possible' (Boynton, 2017: 155–6). Another approach is to question the principle, often drummed into qualitative researchers during their training, that they should build rapport with participants. This can lead to blurred boundaries between relationships created and maintained for research, and genuine friendships, which can result in negative consequences for researchers and participants alike (Duncombe and Jessop, 2012: 118). (See Chapter 8 for more on friendship in research.)

Aftercare is potentially a particular issue for researchers working with more vulnerable participants, such as those with physical or learning disabilities or mental health problems. Writing of mental health service users and their involvement in research, Hamilton (2009: 221) says:

> "Involvement can be a very significant experience for service users and relationships with others in the team can become very important to user researchers. Researchers should be careful that service users are not simply dropped at the end of a project, and at the least should remain available to them after their formal involvement has ended."

This interviewee makes a similar point:

> "One of the other ethics committees I'm on is disability specific. I'm really conscious that people working with severe physical or communication disabilities, and having a researcher coming and spending three months with them, doing an activity, really adds to their life. What happens when it finishes? I've worked in intellectual disability as a researcher; people think they've made a friend, the researcher is there to do research. It's really important right at the beginning for researchers to think about the relationship they have with participants. It really makes a difference to people's lives, and then you disappear. You really have to think about what you're presenting, and what you're offering, and what kind of thing you'll do when it's finished. I know people who continue relationships regardless, but it's not common, because people go on and get their next funded project."

This chapter argues that aftercare is a vital component of ethical research, and provides some pointers for how to provide appropriate aftercare. Aftercare may include care of participants and their communities, of data and findings and of researchers ourselves (Thomas, 2013: 96).

Aftercare for participants

Your responsibilities to research participants do not end when the data has been gathered, or when it has been analysed, or when an output has been produced.

> "The crucial thing is to communicate with participants. For example, we make interviews and people have given their time. I prefer to send them reports – for me that's a rule – a thank you letter with your results."

Your responsibilities may not even end after the last piece of work has been published. There may be occasions when participants want to revisit the research in some way years, even decades, after the substantive work on the project is over.

It is common in the Euro-Western paradigm for participants to be given assurances that they can withdraw their data if they become uncomfortable about the research. This is usually done by means of a unique code given to the participant that they can use to withdraw their data if they wish. However, there seems to be no guidance for researchers, from IRBs/RECs or elsewhere, about a time-scale for participant withdrawal. The lack of such guidance can cause difficulties for researchers. For example, the South African researcher Zethu Matebeni conducted ethnographic research with lesbians of colour in Johannesburg. These women are at high risk of 'corrective' rape and murder, so many of them are highly selective about when, how and to whom they reveal their lesbian identity. Matebeni was an insider researcher and activist who thought very carefully about how to negotiate consent. She decided to use consent forms to set a boundary between research work and other activist and humane actions within her community (Matebeni, 2014: 122). These forms, in line with good practice, included a statement that participants could withdraw from the research at any stage. To Matebeni's surprise, 18 months after she had finished gathering data, two of her participants (who did not know each other) asked to withdraw from her research. The reason each person gave was that they were undergoing gender reassignment from female to male, and so had come to identify as trans men rather than lesbians (Matebeni, 2014: 117). Matebeni understood and agreed to their wishes, although she found the process difficult, as she was well underway with analysis and writing. While she could easily decide not to include any quotes from those participants, or any examples based on the data they had given, she found it much harder – ultimately, impossible – to disentangle the impact their input had made on her interpretative work (Matebeni, 2014: 119). This interviewee sums up the problem:

> "Even if someone withdraws their data, they are still in your head."

On the basis of the evidence, it would seem sensible to explain to participants the potential limits to their withdrawal. For example, wording on an information sheet or consent form could be as follows.

You are free to withdraw your data from this study at any time and without giving a reason. If you withdraw your data before we begin our analysis, scheduled for [date], we will destroy your data or return it to you and we will not make use of it in any way. If you withdraw your data after that point, we will remove all references stemming from, or including text or images contained in, your data from our work. Please note that whether you withdraw your data before or after we have begun our analysis, your contribution will inevitably influence our thinking. After our work, or any part of it, has been submitted for publication or examination, we will not be able to withdraw your data from the study.

As Matebeni's example shows, for insider researchers, responsibility to participants evidently continues after the research is done, because participants are also colleagues, families, neighbours and friends. But even for outsider researchers, working on topics that are not so personally sensitive, there is a responsibility here.

"The kinds of research that I have done, or have supervised other people to do, are not about sensitive issues, really, for the most part. So I think the aftercare issue is probably not as present in my field. I encourage my students to do, not so much in the 'care' kind of thing, more about respect, appreciation, acknowledgement and giving something back. So if you've gone into an organisation or school or some other setting that has cooperated with your study, at the planning stage I encourage them to offer a summary of the findings – something that's not in academic language, a white paper or a webinar or a talk or a brown-bag lunch meeting or training for the staff or something – so there's some way of translating what you've found from the research back to the people who contributed. I think people who have done that, it's really appreciated."

As we saw in Chapter 11, some researchers regard it as ethical to share their findings and writings in draft with participants before finalising their work. Bannister (1996) tells a cautionary tale based on his research with the Australian army band Kapooka, which could not be anonymised as it was the only one of its kind. Band members gave their consent to take part in Bannister's research, and were uninterested in commenting on drafts of his academic publications. However, when one of his pieces was published in the *Australian Defence Force Journal*, which was read by band members' peers and superiors, some of them became unhappy with how they had been represented, even though it was exactly the same as in the drafts they had been offered to review. This is an interesting example of how researchers need not only to know their audiences (see Chapter 10 for more on this) but also to consider how those audiences may interact with the participants they have represented. Bannister had to undertake some fairly onerous aftercare in responding to telephone calls and letters from participants who had become unhappy about the way they had been represented (Bannister, 1996: 54–5). This shows that simply sharing drafts of your work with participants may not be enough to prevent ethical problems at a later stage.

Perhaps one key difference between the Euro–Western and Indigenous paradigms is that in the Euro–Western paradigm relationships with participants, gatekeepers and other stakeholders are created and/or built on in the service of research. This approach is routinely taught to novice researchers. Some Euro–Western researchers are uncomfortable with it (Duncombe and Jessop, 2012: 110), although they are in a tiny minority. The Indigenous literature suggests that, conversely, for most Indigenous people, research is conducted in the service of relationships (Wehipeihana et al, 2013: 281). This means that aftercare is particularly important in Indigenous research, not only for its primary participants, but potentially also for ancestors, land, communities – all of the entities with which an Indigenous researcher is in relationship. As Kouritzin and Nakagawa (2018: 10) explain: 'Research should control the remainder of researchers' human relationships for a lifetime; relationships should be inescapable, not be entered into lightly.'

Aftercare for communities

In most research projects participants are representative of wider communities. These communities may be geographically located, or communities of interest, or people with a common cause such as a particular illness, job or social problem. As a researcher, you have responsibilities to these wider communities, and those responsibilities include aftercare, as this interviewee explains:

> "After my Masters research, I was very glad I could leave that project knowing there were people who could carry on with the work I'd done and the relationships I'd built. I was with an institute that was well established, well funded and would be there for a long time after me. It was still hard to leave; you've always got unfinished business. That experience I've taken into my PhD, where I'm only working in communities where there are existing organisations or bodies who can keep those relationships and ideas alive. I feel very strongly about that as an ethical responsibility researchers should be taking."

The next quote, by contrast, highlights an example of lack of Euro–Western researchers' care and aftercare for the community of mothers of autistic children.

> "The example that comes to mind, from years ago, was the research suggesting that autism was a product of refrigerator mothers. That had a terrible effect on the mothers of autistic children, personally and on the way they were judged. We still get it sometimes, still get this thing that something terrible must have gone on in the parenting; they must have been a cold-hearted monster in some way to produce an autistic child. It's largely gone but there are still echoes of it. That would be a pretty good example of research going ethically wrong at some point, and aftercare would be part of it. In a sense it's a theory, a hypothesis; it would also be wrong to shut down argument and criticism and theories and discussion, but something more should have been thought about, what effect this was going to have. It had a bad effect for a long time."

And the next interviewee's awareness has been heightened by working with Indigenous communities.

> "I think the other thing which is really really important, in ways that it was not when I started doing this work 35 years ago, is thinking about where the material is going to go when it's done. Thinking about appropriate archiving, about making sure that material is given back to the community in an appropriate form, whatever exactly that means. Really really important now."

This is supported in the Indigenous research literature, too. For example:

> I don't know if outside research about our community ever comes back to the regular community. I think they are supposed to provide their final documents, but that is as far as it goes. For the most part because of that, there is still quite a bit of negativity regarding researchers and research, because it is not shared. They could share by coming back to do community presentations. That would be great. (Gillen, 2014: 142)

So, to take an ethical approach, first identify the community or communities that your participants represent. Then, where possible, ask them what kind of aftercare they would like, and how you can best deliver that to them. Be sure to keep your promises.

Even this won't prevent all ethical difficulties. Chris Colvin, a white American, spent two years in Cape Town conducting ethnographic research with the Khulumani Support Group for survivors of political violence. During his ethnographic work, he volunteered for the group, doing administrative tasks as a way of giving something back (Colvin, 2014: 65). This led group members to see him as a member of the executive committee rather than a researcher, and he frequently had to remind them of his research role. An unexpected consequence arose, a year after Colvin had finished his fieldwork, when some members of the executive committee asked him to stand for election as the chairperson, because there was a difference of opinion in the group over the strategy their activism should take (Colvin, 2014: 68). Colvin declined, on the basis that it was not appropriate for a white American to lead a group of South African survivors of political violence. However, they asked again, at which point Colvin decided that he needed to reduce his level of contact with the group (Colvin, 2014: 68). This is an interesting example of the way in which an ethical action, such as volunteering in order to give something back, can lead to further ethical dilemmas. It also demonstrates the need to pay careful attention to aftercare in community-based research.

Aftercare for data

Conventionally, data is used for research, then stored securely, never to be looked at again. Secure storage is one form of aftercare for data, and in some cases it will be the most appropriate form, such as where your data is personally or commercially sensitive. However, as we saw in Chapter 8, there is now increasing recognition that an ethical approach to most data is to use and reuse it as much as possible. Therefore, another form of aftercare is to publish your data. If you have given your participants assurances of anonymity or confidentiality, you will need to ensure that those assurances are upheld in any published version of your data.

You can simply upload your data to any website, but that won't make it easy for people to find unless it has a 'global persistent identifier' such as a DOI (which stands for 'digital object identifier' – you'll see these for some recent journal articles in the bibliography of this book) or a 'Handle'. DOIs can be obtained from DataCite, an organisation specifically set up to provide these identifiers, or from The Dataverse Project, which also offers Handles. The Dataverse Project supports repositories known as 'dataverses', which contain datasets, including descriptive metadata and data files, and may themselves contain other dataverses. Some institutions have their own dataverses, and Harvard University in the US has a dataverse that is open to all researchers, worldwide, from any discipline, to deposit their data.

Having a global persistent identifier for your dataset makes it possible for you, and others, to search, reuse and cite your data. It also means that you can put links to your data in other outputs, such as journal articles or reports, so that readers can look at your data themselves if they wish to do so.

Aftercare for findings

There is a question about whether consent to use research data is given forever (or 'in perpetuity', as the lawyers would say) or whether it is given for a specific period of time. There are a number of reasons why you might consider seeking consent for a specific period of time. To begin with, views on ethics change.

> "What is ethically sound today might change and does change over time. What people are agreeing and signing up to now may change. A lot of that is out of your control, but it's understanding the importance of acknowledging it and saying it out loud, checking that out. Something about asking if it's OK, and will it still be OK in five years' time and if not is there something I need to do about that?"

Then, if your research is published online and freely available, anyone can find it indefinitely. This means that participants may come back to you at any time and ask to revisit the research. In some circumstances, researchers may even need to make provision for their successors and/or descendants to take over this responsibility after they die.

We can see that it is not always clear where a research project ends (Matebeni, 2014: 122). Does a project end when a report has been written? When a budget has been spent? When the research is spoken of for the last time?

> "Your findings might get picked up again in future and people might contact you, such as the press etc."

To some extent this depends on the paradigm in which you are working. We saw in Chapter 12 that some Indigenous peoples, such as those from parts of Australia and the Torres Strait Islands, can be very distressed by images of people who have since died, particularly those from their own communities. In research using such images, then, aftercare may be needed until the last participant depicted has died and the necessary consequent action, as required by that participant's community, has been completed.

Aftercare can also mean doing whatever is possible to help to ensure that the research findings are used to inform policy and/or practice. This is generally acknowledged as an ethical imperative for researchers and evaluators, although it is not always easy. For example, Cluver et al report meetings with non-governmental organisations and government departments, policy forums, politicians, funders, communities, hospitals and schools; presentations on three continents; interviews with journalists and podcasts; giving 'the same talk so often that it becomes a blur' (Cluver et al, 2014: 52). Other researchers may have the opposite problem and struggle to find an outlet for their findings. Also, publicised findings are vulnerable to non-use or misuse (Morris, 2008: 20–1).

It is also possible, particularly in the Euro–Western paradigm, that others will use your findings in ways you did not intend or foresee.

> "I got quite nervous quite quickly about how something like that can go off and become everyone's property. All the concerns are magnified if you start to think about disseminating and things going beyond your own control."

This is not necessarily unethical, even if you disagree with what others are doing. People's understandings of issues develop over time, so each case needs careful consideration on its own merits. Also, while it is important to take care of your findings as far as possible, when you publish your work you have to let go of it to some extent.

> "In a way you often have to accept that you don't have the central role that you might think you have. Participants, funders, other stakeholders will pick up what you've done and use it in ways you didn't anticipate or wouldn't yourself. How much do you chase after your findings saying 'that's not what I meant'? Or do you just let them go in the world?"

Ultimately, it is ethical to do what you can to ensure the research findings *are* used; you can't always have the final say on *how* they are used.

Conclusion

This chapter has argued for the importance of aftercare for participants and communities, data and findings. In the Euro–Western paradigm, with its budgets and deadlines, aftercare can seem like an irrelevance when everyone is rushing on to the next project. Yet this is not only unethical but also counter-productive. As the Indigenous experience shows, failing to provide appropriate aftercare gives researchers a bad name and leaves participants feeling reluctant to take part in future research.

Aftercare for researchers is just as important, as we need to take care of ourselves too. This will be covered in the next chapter, on researcher well-being.

REFLECTIVE QUESTIONS

1. Think of a situation, whether as a result of research or otherwise, when you would have liked aftercare in some form but didn't get it. How did you feel?
2. Can a researcher really provide aftercare for all their participants? If not, why not?
3. This chapter has covered aftercare for participants, communities, data and findings, and the next chapter will cover aftercare for researchers. What else might need aftercare? How could that be provided?
4. How could you provide aftercare for participants and findings of research conducted and disseminated entirely online?
5. Thinking about your own research or evaluation, what more could you do to ensure your findings or recommendations are implemented in practice?

CHAPTER 14

Researcher well-being

Introduction

Few ethical codes or guidelines mention researcher well–being, and most textbooks don't cover this either (Boynton, 2017: 168; Velardo and Elliott, 2018: 311).

> "There's an interesting thing around the ethical risks to researchers themselves. There's been an ongoing debate; it's now in the new draft national statement, around care for the researchers. When we're ethically reviewing a project, what's in place for the researcher? If you're talking to 25 women around their experiences of sexual assault, it's distressing, particularly if you really relate to a couple of people, or you're talking to people whose relatives have committed suicide. I was talking to someone in the post-natal ward where babies were dying and she had to work with parents around autopsy and things like that. That's an ethical obligation for ethics committees, I think, to focus much more on the care of researchers."

RECs/IRBs ask about researcher well–being more than they used to, but even so they are mostly concerned with the physical safety of researchers, rather than taking a more holistic approach.

> "In our committee we do ask about researcher welfare, we do ask about lone worker policies, often with social workers, because they're already putting themselves in those dangers anyway and they have those policies in place. The research isn't adding a great deal to the dangers of their lives. We would turn down some students doing that kind of thing – it would depend on the experience of the person – we do think about it but probably more the physical than the emotional dangers."

Yet there are real emotional risks to researchers. The literature emphasises emotional risk to those doing qualitative work (Qwul'sih'yah'maht, 2015: 193–4; Velardo and Elliott, 2018: 312–13), although quantitative researchers may also face emotional risk. This is because the risks to researchers vary, depending on the type and location of the research. Some research is very low risk, such as desk research into a topic that isn't particularly emotive for the researcher. Some is very high risk, such as qualitative or quantitative research in conflict or disaster zones. Most falls between these two extremes.

There are a range of factors other than risk that may affect the well-being of researchers. Personal attributes such as ethnicity, sexual orientation or age may interact with research work in negative (or positive) ways. Being an Indigenous researcher can be stressful because of the need to answer to different systems of knowledge and values (Kovach, 2009: 164) (see below for more on this). Whichever paradigm you work in, research can be quite isolating, and can bring you into conflict with others in your community (Hornung, 2013: 144; Passingan, 2013: 363; Steere, 2013: 385; Boynton, 2017: 192). Even if a researcher works within an organisation or community, there is no guarantee that they will be supported in their work (Boynton, 2017: 188).

Different aspects of research may be more or less stressful for different researchers. Some will find data gathering a joy but dread having to analyse that data, while for others data gathering can be terrifying and data analysis blissful. Also, this can vary for the same researcher between different projects. More holistic approaches, such as participatory or community-based research, can be very stressful for some Euro-Western researchers (Pollard and Evans, 2015: 44–5). Conversely, it can be very stressful for some Indigenous researchers to have to work within the Euro-Western paradigm (Absolon in Kovach, 2009: 151; Smith, 2012: 132–5). All this means that researchers need to be accountable to themselves, as well as others, by practising self-care. This is recognised in both the Euro-Western and Indigenous literatures (Wilson, 2008: 123; Boynton, 2017: 193).

This chapter advocates a holistic approach to researcher well-being. However, for the purposes of discussion, I am going to break that down into components. The components are: physical, emotional, mental, spiritual and relational well-being.

Physical well-being

As researchers, we have the right to be physically safe in our work. The part of research that may hold the most risks to physical safety is the data-gathering stage. Here, again, the level of risk will vary, depending on the type and location of the research. Collecting survey responses on an iPad in a public place is fairly low risk, while conducting interviews in participants' homes may be higher risk. Doing ethnography in prisons, or restless urban areas, or with extreme sportspeople, may be higher risk still. However, qualitative research is not inherently more dangerous than quantitative research. For example, survey researchers in parts of South Africa may be at risk from riots, gangs or lions (Cluver et al, 2014: 41). And, as already mentioned, research in conflict or disaster zones can be one of the riskiest options. Even where risks seem comparatively low, researchers may be in danger. For example, Giulio Regeni, an Italian doctoral student at Cambridge University in the UK, went to Cairo, Egypt in late 2015 to study labour unions. Cairo has a large international academic community and Regeni spoke Arabic. In early 2016 he was kidnapped, tortured for several days and then killed (Bibbo, 2017). There are several theories about why this happened, but nobody knows for sure.

If you do research for an organisation, it may have a health and safety policy, or procedures, designed to help keep you safe. However, there is evidence that some research organisations don't use their health and safety regulations to help keep researchers safe while they're gathering data (Bahn and Weatherill, 2013: 25). If specialist research organisations can't be relied on to take such precautions, it must be even less likely that generalist organisations employing researchers will have, and use, appropriate policies and procedures. And of course some researchers work outside institutional structures.

This means that the onus is on you, the researcher, to figure out how to keep yourself physically safe in your work. This should be done as part of the research planning process, with funds allocated where necessary (Bahn and Weatherill, 2013: 33; Boynton, 2017: 172). It is important to base your decisions on evidence, rather than stereotypes or suppositions (Boynton, 2017: 170). Bahn and Weatherill focused on researchers working in participants' houses, where there may be hazards such as aggressive pets, or loose rugs or toys on the floor to trip over. They developed a seven-point checklist to help researchers identify and manage risk.

1. Has a mobile phone call-in system been established?
2. Is the researcher experienced in working with these types of participants?
3. Can researchers work in pairs?
4. Can researchers be given personal alarms?
5. If data is to be gathered in participants' homes, are other colleagues aware of researchers' whereabouts, and can researchers plan an exit strategy, for example parking in the street for an easy getaway?
6. Is debriefing support or counselling available?
7. What types of safety training are needed? (Bahn and Weatherill, 2012: 33)

Boynton (2017: 179–81) offers a much longer checklist, including items such as access to buildings, safety of your property and use of equipment. These kinds of checklists offer useful templates for some of the kinds of things you need to think about when working out how to stay physically safe while gathering data for your research.

Emotional well-being

The perceptive reader will have noticed that point 6 in Bahn and Weatherill's checklist, above, refers to emotional, rather than physical, well-being. Researchers, like most workers, have to undertake 'emotional labour', or the management of emotion within a work environment (Hochschild, 1983: 7). For example, the data-gathering phase can be emotionally demanding, as these interviewees explain.

> "I think it's a really big deal, especially with social research with the kind of emotional ties you develop with people and places. I don't think we pay enough attention in academia to that; sometimes academia is far too clinical and removed from the relationships we develop as researchers. Particularly so in my field, a lot of natural scientists are quite happy to pretend that relationships don't exist and we do our science in a social vacuum. A very close friend went to Zambia, did research there for six months, had a terrible time, was not prepared for the emotional and political mess she got herself in. I think it's a big deal. We don't take care of it well enough. There's an ethical concern and issue which needs more attention."

> "I had a lot of difficulty getting approval for a study where I was interviewing women who'd had very traumatic births. I wanted to interview women where the baby had died. Ethics committees were very reluctant to give me that permission. I did get it in the end, but the harm had already been done; I'm not sure the interview itself was ever likely to add to that harm. You don't stir it up, it's there anyway. I've not seen any evidence that it harmed – it harmed me, I didn't like doing it, I was upset at the end of it, but I don't think it harmed the people I was doing it with. There were also assumptions in those interviews that a dead baby is worse than a seriously handicapped one, but the mothers who were every day facing this, every day they got up and went through the same trauma again and again, looking after this blind, seriously mentally handicapped child. Some come to a way of dealing with that and others don't, but it was funny that the committees didn't balk at that, but did balk at me interviewing the ones whose child had died. In the interviews, you couldn't see the join. I guess harm to yourself is something you don't think about so much, but it certainly wasn't a happy period for me doing those interviews."

However, this is not the whole story. Even the more procedural parts of research, such as applying for ethical approval or preparing and coding data, can come with an emotional burden attached (Monaghan, O'Dwyer and Gabe, 2013: 73; Moncur, 2013: 1883). And in some cases, as this interviewee suggests, all stages of the research process can take an emotional toll:

> "Again, from the researcher's point of view, the continued exposure to very distressing material when you're analysing and report-writing can have an impact, so we all have a responsibility to try and safeguard against that."

Some of the literature suggests ways of managing emotional well-being that can be arranged, or requested, by researchers. Such suggestions include: advance preparation, peer support, support from managers, working reflexively, seeking counselling and making sure you take time off (Moncur, 2013: 1885; Boynton, 2017: 182, 193). (See Chapter 6 for more on advance preparation, and Chapters 1, 6 and 9 for more on working reflexively.) Others recommend changes to systems and institutions to ensure that researchers' emotional well-being is protected. These recommendations include changes to university support systems, researchers' training and the processes of RECs/IRBs (Velardo and Elliott, 2018: 316).

Mental well-being

Doing research can be very stressful at times. Even if the project itself is comparatively low stress, pressures of work or from other aspects of life can make research feel stressful. Working ethically can induce stress, as when facing a problem that has no entirely ethical solution.

One particular stress factor can be receiving feedback on your work, whether that comes from participants, commissioners, funders, peer reviewers, journal editors, colleagues, supervisors or managers. Unfortunately, feedback can be negative or even derogatory. Indigenous researchers are particularly vulnerable to this when they are aiming to publish in Euro-Western academic journals, many of whose reviewers don't recognise the value or even the existence of the Indigenous paradigm (Kovach, 2009: 83–4; Chilisa, 2012: 55–6). Even when feedback is fair, balanced and constructive, it can also be disheartening, demoralising, even depressing. Yet feedback is a very valuable resource. A good way to manage this stress factor is a threefold process, as follows.

1. Give yourself time to digest and understand the feedback.
2. Remember that it is human nature to hear the negatives much more loudly than the positives (negativity bias – see Chapter 6 for more on cognitive biases), and work to counteract that.
3. Consider the extent to which the feedback can help you to improve your work.

Giving feedback can also be stressful, especially if you don't know how the recipient will react. A good way to manage this stress factor is to ensure that you give good-quality feedback and give it well. Feedback should focus on the work, not the worker, be constructive rather than negative and offer specific suggestions for ways in which the author can improve the text (Hames, 2013: 4). These suggestions should focus on the author's intentions and the content of their typescript, rather than on the way in which the reviewer would write about the topic (Hames, 2013: 4).

Suggestions for ways of managing work-related stress include: changing your working practices; taking a break or a holiday; improving skills through training (and stress management is one skill you could consider here); taking more exercise; and seeking counselling (Graveling et al, 2008: ii–ix).

Spiritual well-being

Several Indigenous researchers describe research as a ceremony or ritual (Wilson, 2008; Meyer, 2013: 252). For some Indigenous peoples, it seems that research is about more than fact finding: 'It is an expression of ritual, renewal, insight, relationship, and life' (Meyer, 2013: 252). Also, ritual may be used within Indigenous research (Smith, 2013: 96). There are occasional mentions of research as ritual in the Euro-Western literature (for example, Romanyshyn, 2013: 137), but here it appears as a fringe interest, whereas in the Indigenous literature it is often presented as a core concern.

As we saw in Chapter 2, most Indigenous peoples take a holistic view of life (Moloi, 2013: 109). Community or tribe, relationships with the land and with ancestors, well-being of people and the environment, all these things and others are experienced as interrelated and inseparable. This makes it hard for these Indigenous peoples when they find that they need to interact with Euro-Western people, who believe that it is possible to separate out elements of life and research them separately, and have built institutions and social and political systems on that basis. For most Indigenous peoples, spiritual well-being is as important as any other kind of well-being (Wilson, 2008: 89), and indeed cannot be separated from other aspects of being and knowing (Bartlett et al, 2015: 287). Spiritual well-being for Indigenous peoples usually involves staying connected, or reconnecting, with their land, their community and their ways of life (Chilisa, 2012: 3; Walker, 2013: 306–7).

For Euro-Western researchers, who emphasise the individual, spiritual well-being depends on each person's beliefs. A fundamentalist atheist may reject the very concept of spiritual well-being. For people of faith, spiritual well-being may involve attending places of worship and following the tenets of their faith as best they can in daily life. For agnostics and some atheists (and quite possibly some people of faith as well), spiritual well-being may involve practices such as mindfulness, yoga and spending time in nature. Most Euro-Western researchers are used to, and comfortable with, keeping their spiritual life private from most of their colleagues and generally separate from their research work. The desire of many Indigenous peoples to integrate spirituality into research, just as they integrate spirituality into all aspects of their lives, is at odds with Euro-Western academic ways (Walker, 2013: 305).

For some Indigenous researchers, being forced to work in the Euro-Western paradigm, with its compartmentalisation of topics and linear approach to work, constitutes academic imperialism and epistemic violence (Walker, 2013: 302). It would also be difficult for some Euro-Western researchers to work in the Indigenous paradigm, particularly if they are unable to 'adjourn disbelief and, in the pause, consider alternative possibilities' (Kovach, 2009: 29). However, there are examples of Indigenous and Euro-Western researchers collaborating respectfully and effectively across the boundary between the two paradigms (Ball and Janyst, 2008: 46; Pipi in Wehipeihana et al, 2013: 285–6). For the spiritual well-being of all of us, however we define that, it seems that the best approach may be to work within our own paradigm, while retaining both awareness of and respect for the other paradigm, and being willing to engage with ideas and collaborate with researchers from that other paradigm when possible and appropriate.

Relational well-being

Relational well-being implies harmonious interpersonal relationships; not necessarily conflict free (that would be unrealistic), but where conflict is managed constructively. This idyllic situation is, unfortunately, rare in Euro-Western professional life. Most people have professional relationships that are harmonious enough, yet there is a sizeable minority of people who do not experience relational well-being at work.

Bullying and harassment are, sadly, prevalent in universities around the world, affecting up to 25% of university staff (Lipsett, 2005). While anyone can become a victim of bullying, you are more likely to be a victim if you are from a minority ethnic background, have a disability, or are from the LGBTI+ community (Boynton, 2017: 183). For example, Róisin Ryan-Flood is an openly lesbian researcher who studies queer lives. Simply as a result of her identity and choice of subject, she has received harassment by telephone while working in two different universities (Ryan-Flood, 2010: 196). Even more sadly, little is done to address this problem within academia (Boynton, 2017: 185). And, of course, bullying and harassment are not limited to academia but can occur anywhere. Nor are researchers only victims; researchers can be bullies and harassers too (Boynton, 2017: 190). Bullying and harassment affect not only the relationship between the bully or harasser and the victim, but also the victim's self-esteem and mental health (Boynton, 2017: 184), which will have knock-on effects within their wider network of relationships.

If you are the unfortunate victim of bullying or harassment, there are some actions you can take (and I am indebted to Boynton, 2017: 187 for these suggestions).

- Keep a diary of incidents, including copies of relevant documents such as print-outs of emails.
- Check your organisation's policies for anything related to bullying or harassment and invoke them if that seems appropriate.
- Look online for anti-bullying or harassment support groups and organisations that might help you.
- If you feel safe to do so, seek support from your line manager, supervisor or equivalent, or from their line manager.
- Seek support from trusted friends, family and/or colleagues.

You can consider taking official action, such as making a formal complaint within the organisation, or seeking legal advice from outside the organisation. This may be worth doing; it may resolve the problem and in the process help you and other people too. At the same time, it can be very stressful and isn't guaranteed to resolve the problem. So, think carefully before taking official action, because this is a situation where organisational rules and/or the law may conflict with ethical principles.

If possible, join a trade union, as they can help to support you in the workplace if you become a victim of bullying or harassment. (Don't wait until you need them, though, as some unions won't help until you've been a member for a set period of time, such as one month.)

Conclusion

For most researchers, however much they love their subject, it is a means to an end: to earn a living, or to enhance a career, or to achieve necessary social change. The need to succeed in such endeavours can, at times, lead researchers to take more risks than is sensible. Cluver et al (2014: 49) identify some of the difficult ethical issues that this can raise for research commissioners and managers:

> I don't think I had properly thought through the power and economic relations between a university teacher, their students and local staff. Could people really say no to fieldwork when their career or their livelihood might depend on it? To what extent were we responsible for their safety?

Lack of care for researcher well-being is unethical in itself, and also can lead to unethical research practices (Benson, 2015). Researchers often feel that they have to be professional, strong and competent, which means not asking for help even when their research experiences have been so upsetting that they are suffering from post-traumatic stress (Cluver et al, 2014: 49–50).

> "On some of the projects I've done we've been looking at sexual abuse. You need to be sure that whoever is going to be doing that fieldwork is happy, willing, able to do that and is going to be supported."

Having an investment in the topic of your research can help you to keep going when times are hard (Kovach, 2009: 109), and so helps to maintain or improve well-being. Doing what it takes to translate research into practice can be difficult for Euro-Western researchers. However, it is worth making the effort, partly because it is ethical to do so and partly because it is rewarding for researchers when their research is put to use (Cluver et al, 2014: 53). This too can improve researcher well-being.

REFLECTIVE QUESTIONS

1. What factors affect your well-being as a researcher, both negatively and positively?
2. What could you do to reduce the impact of the negative factors and increase the impact of the positive factors?
3. During data gathering, whose well-being is more important, that of participants or that of researchers? Why?
4. Are there places you would not go to do research? If so, where, and why not?
5. Are there groups or types of people you would not do research with? If so, who, and why not?

CHAPTER 15

Conclusion

Ermine et al write of an 'ethical space'. This conceptual space 'between the Indigenous and Western worlds' (Ermine et al, 2004: 19) 'provides a venue within which to articulate the possibilities and challenges of bringing together different ways of coming to knowledge and applying this theory to the practice of research' (Ermine et al, 2004: 16). Chilisa, too, writes of a 'space in between' the Euro-Western and Indigenous paradigms. This space:

> involves a culture-integrative research framework. This is a tapestry, a mosaic of balanced borrowing of less hegemonic Euro-Western knowledge and its democratic and social justice elements and combining it with the best of the democratic, liberatory, and social justice essentialized indigenous knowledge and subgroups' knowledges. (Chilisa, 2012: 25)

This book has attempted to work within that ethical space in between by balancing the Euro-Western and Indigenous paradigms alongside each other, with the aim of finding out what may be learned from their differing approaches to research ethics.

It is ethical to question 'the hegemonic role of colonialism ... in the construction of knowledge' (Chilisa, 2012: 123). This hegemony is evident in academia in so many ways:

- the colonised curriculum, in which no Indigenous scholars are represented (le Grange, 2016: 6);
- the colonisation of methodology, such that Indigenous research methods are judged by Euro-Western standards (Wilson, 2008: 30);
- the colonisation of process, such that Indigenous researchers are forced to justify their long-established approach to research in more recent Euro-Western terms (Wilson, 2008: 30–1);
- research still being done by Euro-Western researchers, using Euro-Western methods, on Indigenous peoples, communities and lands (Kovach, 2009: 28; Rix et al, 2018: 7); and so on.

This is massively unethical, so another aim of this book has been to question, and perhaps make a small contribution to dismantling, that hegemony.

Most Indigenous researchers do not separate ethics from research as a whole (Kovach, 2009: 142). Yet the Euro-Western system of research ethics regulation is not going to go away any time soon. Some would argue that it should not. But it does need to change, to become more flexible and accessible, to be more aware of its own limitations and blind spots and to pay attention to the whole of research, not just data gathering. Crucially, the system of research ethics regulation needs to encourage and support researchers and evaluators to consider ethical issues at each stage of the research process. Further, ethical scrutiny should not confine its gaze to research methods, but should also focus on the ethical dimensions of relevant professions, institutions, societies, disciplines, cultures and so on as they interact with the research in question (Williams, 2016: 544). This should not only apply to the research governance system but also to researchers and evaluators; research managers, commissioners and funders; research-active communities and organisations; and users of research. These authors express it well:

> Rather than relying on the deceptive assurances of ethical codes, our institutions, organizations, regulatory regimes, and research disciplines should encourage theoretically informed, self-critical, perceptive approaches to moral matters that stimulate the moral imagination, recognize ethical issues, develop analytical skills, elicit a sense of moral obligation and personal responsibility – and that tolerate disagreement and ambiguity. (Israel, Allen and Thomson, 2017: 306)

There is a sense in which we will always fail in our ethical responsibilities as researchers (Warren, 2014: 188). We cannot design a perfectly ethical research project, write a report that accurately represents all the messy particularities of our work or present our findings in a way that meets all the needs of every audience member. But this does not absolve us of the responsibility to try to act as ethically as we can. As Ball and Janyst (2008: 48) remind us: 'The overall goal is to strengthen all our capacities to engage in research with integrity and respect as allies in co-creating knowledge that is socially useful.'

I am accountable, for what I have written here, to the people whose work I have learned from and cited and to the people who read this book. I could have written a book on research ethics without any reference to Indigenous literature – and if I hadn't attended the July 2016 seminar mentioned in the prologue I would have done so. I now understand that excluding Indigenous literature serves to maintain the imbalance of power between Euro-Western and Indigenous peoples (Kovach, 2009: 42, drawing on the work of Potts and Brown, 2005). I can't imagine that my one book, in this huge and busy world, will do much to redress that imbalance of power. It certainly does not tell any kind of 'whole story'. Yet I hope that it may act as a stepping-stone on the long, long journey towards a world where people from different cultures are better able to understand and value each other's viewpoints.

Appendix: People interviewed for this book

NB: Each designation below was chosen by the interviewee concerned. All had general experience of research ethics. Also, four said they had current or previous experience of serving on a REC/IRB, which they drew on in their interview. A fifth taught ethics, and a sixth helped with others' ethics applications.

1. UK social work lecturer
2. Social science researcher at an Estonian university
3. UK mature doctoral student in ethics
4. Freelance researcher and writer in sociology, New Zealand
5. Associate professor at a UK university
6. Associate professor at a Japanese university
7. Senior lecturer in management at a post-1992 university, UK
8. Academic researcher at a Canadian post-secondary institution
9. Research support worker in a UK university
10. Australian researcher
11. Research fellow at a UK university
12. Qualitative methodologist and independent scholar in the US
13. Reader in sociology at a UK university
14. PhD student from South Africa doing social–ecological research
15. UK-based independent researcher
16. Academic in philosophy and applied ethics from Mexico
17. Research support worker for UK universities
18. Lecturer in psychology in Scotland

References

Note: all URLs accessed 20 May 2018.

ABS (Australian Bureau of Statistics) (undated) *Statement of intent*.

Agbebiyi, A. (2013) Tiers of gatekeepers and ethical practice: researching adolescent students and sexually explicit online material. *International Journal of Social Research Methodology* 16(6) 535–40. DOI: 10.1080/13645579.2013.823290.

AIATSIS (2012) *Guidelines for ethical research in Australian indigenous studies*. Australian Institute of Aboriginal and Torres Strait Islander Studies.

Alkin, M. (2013) Context-sensitive evaluation. In Alkin, M. (ed) *Evaluation roots: a wider perspective of theorists' views and influences*, 283–92. Thousand Oaks, CA: Sage.

Alldred, P. and Gillies, V. (2012) Eliciting research accounts: re/producing modern subjects? In Miller, T., Birch, M., Mauthner, M. and Jessop, J. (eds) *Ethics in qualitative research* (2nd edn) 140–56. London: Sage.

Anderson, S. (2010) *How many languages are there in the world?* Washington, DC: Linguistic Society of America.

Ascione, G. (2016) *Science and the decolonization of social theory: unthinking modernity*. London: Palgrave Macmillan.

Australian Government (2007) *Australian code for the responsible conduct of research*.

Back, L. (2015) *Academic diary*. London: Goldsmiths Press.

Bahn, S. and Weatherill, P. (2013) Qualitative social research: a risky business when it comes to collecting 'sensitive' data. *Qualitative Research* 13(1) 19–35.

Ball, J. and Janyst, P. (2008) Enacting research ethics in partnerships with Indigenous communities in Canada: 'Do it in a good way'. *Journal of Empirical Research on Human Research Ethics* 33–51. DOI: 10.1525/jer.2008.3.2.33.

Bannister, J. (1996) Beyond the ethics committee: representing others in qualitative research. *Research Studies in Music Education* 6 50–8.

Barad, K. (2007) *Meeting the universe halfway: quantum physics and the entanglement of matter and meaning*. Durham, NC: Duke University Press.

Barnett, C. and Camfield, L. (2016) Ethics in evaluation. *Journal of Development Effectiveness* 8(4) 528–34. DOI: 10.1080/19439342.2016.1244554.

Bartlett, C., Marshall, M., Marshall, A. and Iwama, M. (2015) Integrative science and two-eyed seeing: enriching the discussion framework for healthy communities. In Hallström, L., Guehlstorf, N. and Parkes, M. (eds) *Ecosystems, society and health: pathways through diversity, convergence, and integration*, 280–326. Montreal: McGill-Queen's University Press.

Beckett, J. (2009) A survivor-led evaluation of a survivor-led crisis service. In Sweeney, A., Beresford, P., Faulkner, A., Nettle, M. and Rose, D. (eds) *This is survivor research*, 153–4. Ross-on-Wye: PCCS Books.

Bell, K. and Salmon, A. (2011) What women who use drugs have to say about ethical research: findings of an exploratory qualitative study. *Journal of Empirical Research on Human Research Ethics* 6(4) 84–98. DOI: 10.1525/jer.2011.6.4.84.

Benson, M. (2015) On Goffman: ethnography and the ethics of care. *The Sociological Review*, https://www.thesociologicalreview.com/information/blog/on-goffman-ethnography-and-the-ethics-of-care.html.

Bibbo, B. (2017) Giulio Regeni murder: 'It's not yet the time to grieve'. Al Jazeera, 2 February, http://www.aljazeera.com/indepth/features/2017/01/killed-giulio-regeni-170129080239822.html.

Biber, D., Conrad, S. and Leech, G. (2002) *Student grammar of spoken and written English*. Harlow: Pearson Education Limited.

BIOTA Africa (2010) Data sharing protocol, http://www.biota-africa.org/downloads/BIOTA_AFRICA_Data_sharing_protocol_20100609.pdf.

Blackfoot Gallery Committee, The (2013) *The story of the Blackfoot people: Niitsitapiisinni*. Richmond Hill, Ontario: Firefly Books.

Blalock, N. (2015) More than me. In Jolivétte, A. (ed) *Research justice: methodologies for social change*, 57–62. Bristol: Policy Press.

Blodgett, A., Coholic, D., Schinke, R., McGannon, K., Peltier, D. and Pheasant, C. (2013) Moving beyond words: exploring the use of an arts-based method in Aboriginal community sport research. *Qualitative Research in Sport, Exercise and Health* 5(3) 312–31.

Bond, T. (2012) Ethical imperialism or ethical mindfulness? Rethinking ethical review for social sciences. *Research Ethics* 8(2) 97–112.

Bonilla-Silva, E. and Baiocchi, G. (2008) Anything but racism: how sociologists limit the significance of racism. In Zuberi, T. and Bonilla-Silva, E. (eds) *White logic, white methods: racism and methodology*, 137–51. Lanham, MA: Rowman & Littlefield Publishers, Inc.

Bostock, L. (1997) *The greater perspective: protocol and guidelines for the production of film and television on Aboriginal and Torres Strait Islander communities*. Australia: Special Broadcasting Service.

Bowman, N., Francis, C. and Tyndall, M. (2015) Culturally responsive Indigenous evaluation: a practical approach for evaluating Indigenous projects in tribal reservation contexts. In Hood, S., Hopson, R. and Frierson, H. (eds) *Continuing the journey to reposition culture and cultural context in evaluation theory and practice*, 335–59. Charlotte, NC: Information Age Publishing.

Boynton, P. (2017) *The research companion: a practical guide for those in the social sciences, health and development* (2nd edn). Abingdon: Routledge.

Brady, G. and Brown, G. (2013) Rewarding but let's talk about the challenges: using arts based methods in research with young mothers. *Methodological Innovations Online* 8(1) 99–112. DOI: 10.4256/mio.2013.007.

Brant-Castellano (2004) Ethics of Aboriginal research. *Journal of Aboriginal Health* 1(1) 98–114.

Bray, R. (2014) Layers of watching and protection in research with children. In Posel, D. and Ross, F. (eds) *Ethical quandaries in social research*, 27–40. Cape Town, SA: HSRC Press.

Brearley, L. and Hamm, T. (2009) Ways of looking and listening: stories from the spaces between Indigenous and non-Indigenous knowledge systems. In Grierson, E. and Brearley, L. (eds) *Creative arts research: narratives of methodologies and practices*, 33–54. Rotterdam, Netherlands: Sense Publishers.

Brunger, F. and Wall, D. (2016) 'What do they really mean by partnerships?' Questioning the unquestionable good in ethics guidelines promoting community engagement in Indigenous health research. *Qualitative Health Research* 26(13) 1862–77. DOI: 10.1177/1049732316649158.

Bryman, A. (2016) *Social research methods* (5th edn). Oxford: Oxford University Press.

Bull, J. (2016) A two-eyed seeing approach to research ethics review: an Indigenous perspective. In van den Hoonaard, W. and Hamilton, A. (eds) *The ethics rupture: exploring alternatives to formal research ethics review*, 167–86. Toronto: University of Toronto Press.

Carpenter, D. (2018) Ethics, reflexivity and virtue. In Iphofen, R. and Tolich, M. (eds) *The SAGE handbook of qualitative research ethics*, 35–50. London: Sage.

Cartland, J., Ruch-Ross, H. and Mason, M. (2012) Engaging community researchers in evaluation: looking at the experiences of community partners in school-based projects in the US. In Goodson, L. and Phillimore, J. (eds) *Community research for participation: from theory to method*, 169–84. Bristol: Policy Press.

Castleden, H., Sylvestre, P., Martin, D. and McNally, M. (2015) 'I don't think that any peer review committee … would ever "get" what I currently do': how institutional metrics for success and merit risk perpetuating the (re)production of colonial relationships in community-based participatory research involving Indigenous peoples in Canada. *The International Indigenous Policy Journal* 6(4), http://ir.lib.uwo.ca/iipj/vol6/iss4/2. DOI: 10.18584/iipj/2015.6.4.2.

CDC (2014) *Practical strategies for culturally competent evaluation*. Atlanta, GA: Centers for Disease Control and Prevention.

Cerulo, K. (2010) Mining the intersections of cognitive sociology and neuroscience. *Poetics* 38 115–32. DOI: 10.1016.j.poetic.2009.11.005.

Chambers, R. (1992) *Political theory and societal ethics*. Buffalo, NY: Prometheus Books.

Chevalier, J. and Buckles, D. (2013) *Participatory action research: theory and methods for engaged enquiry*. Abingdon: Routledge.

Chilisa, B. (2012) *Indigenous research methodologies*. Thousand Oaks, CA: Sage.

Chouinard, J. and Cousins, J. (2007) Culturally competent evaluation for Aboriginal communities: a review of the empirical literature. *Journal of MultiDisciplinary Evaluation* 4(8) 40–57.

Christie, C. and Alkin, M. (2013) An evaluation theory tree. In Alkin, M. (ed) *Evaluation roots: a wider perspective of theorists' views and influences* (2nd edn), 11–57. Thousand Oaks, CA: Sage.

Citro, C., Martin, M. and Straf, M. (eds) (2009) *Principles and practices for a federal statistical agency* (4th edn). Washington DC: The National Academics Press.

Cluver, L. et al (2014) The cost of action: large-scale, longitudinal quantitative research with AIDS-affected children in South Africa. In Posel, D. and Ross, F. (eds) *Ethical quandaries in social research*, 41–56. Cape Town, SA: HSRC Press.

Colnerud, G. (2014) Ethical dilemmas in research in relation to ethical review: an empirical study. *Research Ethics* 10(4) 238–53. DOI: 10.1177/1747016114552339.

Coltart, C., Henwood, K. and Shirani, F. (2013) Qualitative secondary analysis in austere times: ethical, professional and methodological considerations. *Forum: Qualitative Social Research* 14(1) Art. 18, http://nbn-resolving.de/urn:nbn:de:0114-fqs1301181.

Colvin, C. (2014) Who benefits from research? Ethical dilemmas in compensation in anthropology and public health. In Posel, D. and Ross, F. (eds) *Ethical quandaries in social research*, 57–74. Cape Town, SA: HSRC Press.

Connell, R. (2007) *Southern theory*. Cambridge: Polity Press.

Coombes, B. (2013) Indigenism, public intellectuals, and the forever opposed – or, the makings of a 'Hori Academic'. In Mertens, D., Cram, F. and Chilisa, B. (eds) *Indigenous pathways into social research: voices of a new generation*, 71–88. Walnut Creek, CA: Left Coast Press.

Coulthard, G. (2014) From wards of the state to subjects of recognition? Marx, Indigenous peoples, and the politics of dispossession in Denendeh. In Simpson, A. and Smith, A. (eds) *Theorizing native studies*, 56–98. Durham, NC and London: Duke University Press.

Cox, S. and McDonald, M. (2013) Ethics is for human subjects too: participant perspectives on responsibility in health research. *Social Science & Medicine* 98 224–31. DOI: 10.1016/j.socscimed.2013.09.015.

Cram, F., Chilisa, B. and Mertens, D. (2013) The journey begins. In Mertens, D., Cram, F. and Chilisa, B. (eds) *Indigenous pathways into social research: voices of a new generation*, 11–40. Walnut Creek, CA: Left Coast Press.

Crane, A. and Matten, D. (2016) *Business ethics: managing corporate citizenship and sustainability in the age of globalization*. Oxford: Oxford University Press.

Croskerry, P., Singhal, G. and Mamede, S. (2013a) Cognitive debiasing 1: origins of bias and theory of debiasing. *BMJ Quality & Safety* 22 ii58–ii64. DOI: 10.1136/bmjqs-2012-001712.

Croskerry, P., Singhal, G. and Mamede, S. (2013b) Cognitive debiasing 2: impediments to and strategies for change. *BMJ Quality & Safety* 22 ii65–ii72. DOI: 10.1136/bmjqs-2012-0001713.

Crossen-White, H. (2015) Using digital archives in historical research: what are the ethical concerns for a 'forgotten' individual? *Research Ethics* 11(2) 108–9. DOI: 10.1177/1747016115581724.

Czymoniewicz-Klippel, M., Brijnath, B. and Crockett, B. (2010) Ethics and the promotion of inclusiveness within qualitative research: case examples from Asia and the Pacific. *Qualitative Inquiry* 16(5) 332–41.

Dahl, S., Morris, G., Brown, P., Scullion, L. and Somerville, P. (2012) *Somewhere nowhere: lives without homes*. Salford: Salford Housing and Urban Studies Unit.

Datta, L. (2016) Who pays the piper: funding sources and evaluation's contribution to equity. In Donaldson, S. and Picciotto, R. (eds) *Evaluation for an equitable society*, 153–68. Charlotte, NC: Information Age Publishing, Inc.

de Vries, J. and Henley, L. (2014) Staying silent when we should speak up: informed consent and the interface between ethics as regulation and ethics in practice. In Posel, D. and Ross, F. (eds) *Ethical Quandaries in Social Research*, 75–92. Cape Town, SA: HSRC Press.

Dean, J. (2017) *Doing reflexivity: an introduction*. Bristol: Policy Press.

Denzin, N. (2005). Emancipatory discourses and the ethics and politics of interpretation. In Denzin, N. and Lincoln, Y. (eds) *The SAGE Handbook of Qualitative Research* (3rd edn), 933–58. Thousand Oaks, CA: Sage.

Derry, S., Pea, R., Barron, B., Engle, R., Erickson, F., Goldman, R., Hall, R., Koschmann, T., Lemke, J., Sherin, M. and Sherin, B. (2010) Conducting video research in the learning sciences: guidance on selection, analysis, technology and ethics. *The Journal of the Learning Sciences* 19 3–53. DOI: 10.1080/10508400903452884.

Desautels, G. and Jacob, S. (2012) The ethical sensitivity of evaluators: a qualitative study using a vignette design. *Evaluation* 18(4) 437–50. DOI: 10.1177/1356389012461192.

Dingwall, R. (2016) The social costs of ethics regulation. In van den Hoonaard, W. and Hamilton, A. (eds) *The ethics rupture: exploring alternatives to formal research ethics review*, 25–42. Toronto: University of Toronto Press.

Doucet, A. and Mauthner, N. (2012) Knowing responsibly: ethics, feminist epistemologies and methodologies. In Miller, T., Birch, M., Mauthner, M. and Jessop, J. (eds) *Ethics in qualitative research* (2nd edn), 122–39. London: Sage.

Dreger, A. (2015) *Galileo's middle finger: heretics, activists, and the search for justice in science*. New York: Penguin Press.

Dresser, R. (2015) What subjects teach: the everyday ethics of human research. *Wake Forest Law Review* 50 301–41.

Dunbar-Ortiz, R. (2014) *An Indigenous peoples' history of the United States*. Boston, MA: Beacon Press.

Duncombe, J. and Jessop, J. (2012) 'Doing rapport' and the ethics of 'faking friendship'. In Miller, T., Birch, M., Mauthner, M. and Jessop, J. (eds) *Ethics in Qualitative Research* (2nd edn), 108–21. London: Sage.

Edwards, S. (2013) Editorial: From research governance to research integrity: What's in a name? *Research Ethics* 9(1) 3–5. DOI: 10.1177/1747016113479276.

Edwards, F. and Edwards, J. (2012) The experience of taking part in a national survey: a child's perspective – Freja Edwards, aged 10 years. *Research Ethics* 8(3) 165–8. DOI: 10.1177/1747016112451087.

Edwards, R. and Mauthner, M. (2012) Ethics and feminist research: theory and practice. In Miller, T., Birch, M., Mauthner, M. and Jessop, J. (eds) *Ethics in Qualitative Research* (2nd edn), 14–28. London: Sage.

Ellis, C. (2007) Telling secrets, revealing lives: relational ethics in research with intimate others. *Qualitative Inquiry* 13(1) 3–29.

Emmerich, N. (2013) Between the accountable and the auditable: ethics and ethical governance in the social sciences. *Research Ethics* 9(4) 175–86. DOI: 10.1177/1747016113510654.

Ermine, W., Sinclair, R. and Jeffery, B. (2004) *The ethics of research involving Indigenous peoples: report of the Indigenous Peoples' Health Research Centre to the Interagency Advisory Panel on Research Ethics*. Regina, SK: Indigenous Peoples' Health Research Centre, http://iphrc.ca/pub/documents/ethics_review_iphrc.pdf.

ETS Wales and YMCA Wales (2012) *Code of occupational ethics for the Youth Service in Wales*, http://www.etswales.org.uk/resource/g_2_Code_of_Occupational_Ethics_Feb_2012_Eng.pdf.

Evergreen, S. (2014) *Presenting data effectively: communicating your findings for maximum impact*. Thousand Oaks, CA: Sage.

Fanelli, D. (2009) How many scientists fabricate and falsify research? A systematic review and meta-analysis of survey data. *PloS one* 4(5) e5738.

Fanelli, D., Costas, R., Fang, F., Casadevall, A. and Bik, E. (2017) Why do scientists fabricate and falsify data? A matched-control analysis of papers containing problematic image duplications. Pre-print. DOI: 10.1101/126805.

Fiennes, C. (2015) We don't all need to throw wellingtons. *Third Sector* January 36–9.

First Nations IGC (2014) Ownership, control, access and possession (OCAP™): the path to First Nations information governance. Ottawa: The First Nations Information Governance Centre.

Fitzpatrick, T. (2008) *Allied ethics and social problems: moral questions of birth, society and death*. Bristol: Policy Press.

Fleming, S. (2013) Social research in sport (and beyond): notes on exceptions to informed consent. *Research Ethics* 9(1) 32–43. DOI: 10.1177/1747016112472872.

Foster, V. (2016) *Collaborative arts-based research for social justice*. Abingdon: Routledge.

Fraser, H. and Jarldorn, M. (2015) Narrative research and resistance: a cautionary tale. In Strega, S. and Brown, L. (eds) *Research as resistance: revisiting critical, Indigenous, and anti-oppressive approaches* (2nd edn), 153–75. Toronto: Canadian Scholars' Press Inc.

García, R., Melgar, P. and Sordé, T. in conversation with Cortés, L., Santiago, C. and Santiago, S. (2013) From refusal to getting involved in Romani research. In Mertens, D., Cram, F. and Chilisa, B. (eds) *Indigenous pathways into social research: voices of a new generation*, 367–80. Walnut Creek, CA: Left Coast Press.

Gaudry, A. (2015) Researching the resurgence: insurgent research and community-engaged methodologies in 21st-century academic inquiry. In Strega, S. and Brown, L. (eds) *Research as resistance: revisiting critical, Indigenous, and anti-oppressive approaches* (2nd edn), 221–42. Toronto: Canadian Scholars' Press Inc.

Gawrylewski, A. (2007) Glossary of retractions. *The Scientist*, http://www.the-scientist.com/?articles.view/articleNo/24765/title/Glossary-of-retractions/.

Gentelet, K., Basile, S. and Asselin, H. (2017) 'We have to start sounding the trumpet for things that are working': an interview with Dr Marlene Brant-Castellano on concrete ways to decolonize research. *ACME: An International Journal for Critical Geographies*, https://acme-journal.org/index.php/acme/article/view/1423.

Gerver, M. (2013) Exceptions to blanket anonymity for the publication of interviews with refugees: African refugees in Israel as a case study. *Research Ethics* 9(3) 121–39. DOI: 10.1177/1747016113481176.

Gillen, S. (2014) Steps along the journey: voices from the Flathead Indian Reservation, Montana. In Lambert, L. (ed) *Research for Indigenous survival: Indigenous research methodologies in the behavioral sciences*, 141–4. Lincoln, NE: University of Nebraska Press.

Gillies, V. and Alldred, P. (2012) The ethics of intention: research as a political tool. In Miller, T., Birch, M., Mauthner, M. and Jessop, J. (eds) *Ethics in qualitative research* (2nd edn), 43–60. London: Sage.

Goddard, S. (2009) Research and evaluation in East Berkshire. In Sweeney, A., Beresford, P., Faulkner, A., Nettle, M. and Rose, D. (eds) *This is survivor research*, 161–2. Ross-on-Wye: PCCS Books.

Gontcharov, I. (2013) Methodological crisis in the social sciences: the New Brunswick Declaration as a new paradigm in research ethics governance? *Transnational Legal Theory* 4(1) 146–56. DOI: 10.5235/20414005.4.1.146.

González, E. and Lincoln, Y. (2006) Decolonizing qualitative research: non-traditional reporting forms in the academy. *Forum: Qualitative Social Research* 7(4) September.

González-López, G. (2011) Mindful ethics: comments on informant-centered practices in sociological research. *Qualitative Sociology* 34 447–61.

Graveling, R., Crawford, J., Cowie, H., Amati, C. and Vohra, S. (2008) *A review of workplace interventions that promote mental wellbeing in the workplace*. Edinburgh: Institute of Occupational Medicine.

Gray, B., Hilder, J., Macdonald, L., Tester, R., Dowell, A. and Stubbe, M. (2017) Are research ethics guidelines culturally competent? *Research Ethics* 13(1) 23–41.

Greene, J. (2013) Making the world a better place through evaluation. In Alkin, M. (ed) *Evaluation roots: a wider perspective of theorists' views and influences*, 208–17. Thousand Oaks, CA: Sage.

Grinyer, A. (2009) The ethics of the secondary analysis and further use of qualitative data. *Social Research Update* 56: Summer 2009. University of Surrey.

Grover, J. (2010) Challenges in applying Indigenous evaluation practices in mainstream grant programs to Indigenous communities. *The Canadian Journal of Program Evaluation* 23(2) 33–50.

Grugulis, I. and Stoyanova, D. (2011) The missing middle: communities of practice in a freelance labour market. *Work, Employment and Society* 25(2) 342–51. DOI: 10.1177/0950017011398891.

Guillemin, M. and Gillam, L. (2004) Ethics, reflexivity, and 'ethically important moments' in research. *Qualitative Inquiry* 10(2) 261–80.

Hames, I. (2013) *COPE ethical guidelines for peer reviewers*. Committee on Publication Ethics, https://publicationethics.org/.

Hamilton, A. (2016) Research ethics review and compliatorianism: a curious dilemma. In van den Hoonaard, W. and Hamilton, A. (eds) *The ethics rupture: exploring alternatives to formal research ethics review*, 335–52. Toronto: University of Toronto Press.

Hamilton, S. (2009) Money. In Wallcraft, J., Schrank, B. and Amering, M. (eds) *Handbook of service user involvement in mental health research*. Chichester: Wiley-Blackwell.

Hammersley, M. and Traianou, A. (2012) *Ethics in qualitative research: controversies and contexts*. London: Sage.

Harrison, S. (2014) *Not a freak show, growing up gay in rural Ontario: an arts-informed inquiry*. PhD thesis, University of Toronto.

Hernandez, A. (2013) I never really had any role models. In Mertens, D., Cram, F. and Chilisa, B. (eds) *Indigenous pathways into social research: voices of a new generation*, 59–70. Walnut Creek, CA: Left Coast Press.

Hesse-Biber, S. (2014) A re-invitation to feminist research. In Hesse-Biber, S. (ed) *Feminist research practice: a primer*, 1–13. Thousand Oaks, CA: Sage.

Hochschild, A. (1983) *The managed heart: commercialization of human feeling*. Berkeley, CA: University of California Press.

Hornung, F. (2013) Indigenous research with a cultural context. In Mertens, D., Cram, F. and Chilisa, B. (eds) *Indigenous pathways into social research: voices of a new generation*, 133–52. Walnut Creek, CA: Left Coast Press.

Howell, C., Cox, S., Drew, S., Guillemin, M., Warr, D. and Waycott, J. (2014) Exploring ethical frontiers of visual methods. *Research Ethics* 10(4) 208–13. DOI: 10.1177/1747016114552685.

Hunter, D. (2012) Editorial: the publication of unethical research. *Research Ethics* 8(2) 67–8. DOI: 10.1177/1747016112445959.

Hunter, D. (2017) Non-negligent harm, clinical trials and the NHS: should research ethics committees be activists? *Research Ethics* 13(1) 2–3.

Husband, C. (ed) (2016) *Research and policy in ethnic relations: compromised dynamics in a neoliberal era*. Bristol: Policy Press.

Ignacio, G. (2013) Being and becoming an Indigenous social researcher. Mertens, D., Cram, F. and Chilisa, B. (eds) *Indigenous pathways into social research: voices of a new generation*, 153–69. Walnut Creek, CA: Left Coast Press.

Iphofen, R. (2011) *Ethical decision-making in social research: a practical guide*. Basingstoke: Palgrave Macmillan.

Israel, M. (2015) *Research ethics and integrity for social scientists* (2nd edn). London: Sage.

Israel, M. (2018) Ethical imperialism? Exporting research ethics to the global South. In Iphofen, R. and Tolich, M. (eds) *The SAGE handbook of qualitative research ethics*, 89–102. London: Sage.

Israel, M., Allen, G. and Thomson, C. (2017) Australian research ethics governance: plotting the demise of the adversarial culture. In van den Hoonaard, W. and Hamilton, A. (eds) *The ethics rupture: exploring alternatives to formal research ethics review*, 285–316. Toronto: University of Toronto Press.

Jennings, S. (2012) Response to Schrag: what are ethics committees for anyway? A defence of social science research ethics review. *Research Justice* 8(2) 87–96.

Johnson, J. (2013) Becoming an Indigenous researcher in Interior Alaska: sharing the transformative journey. In Mertens, D., Cram, F. and Chilisa, B. (eds) *Indigenous pathways into social research: voices of a new generation*, 189–202. Walnut Creek, CA: Left Coast Press.

Jolivétte, A. (2015) Radical love as a strategy for social transformation. In Jolivétte, A. (ed) *Research justice: methodologies for social change*, 5–12. Bristol: Policy Press.

Jones, H. (2015) *Negotiating cohesion, inequality and change: uncomfortable positions in local government*. Bristol: Policy Press.

Josselson, R. (2007). The ethical attitude in narrative research: principles and practicalities. In Clandinin, D. (ed) *Handbook of narrative inquiry*, 537–66. Thousand Oaks, CA: Sage.

Judd, J. (1996) Irish butt of English racism for more than eight centuries. *Independent* 20 March, http://www.independent.co.uk/news/irish-butt-of-english-racism-for-more-than-eight-centuries-1342976.html.

Kahneman, D. (2011) *Thinking, fast and slow*. London: Allen Lane.

Kara, H. (2015) *Creative research methods in the social sciences: a practical guide*. Bristol: Policy Press.

Kara, H. (2017) *Research and evaluation for busy practitioners: a time-saving guide* (2nd edn). Bristol: Policy Press.

Keith-Spiegel, P. and Koocher, G. (2005) The IRB paradox: could the protectors also encourage deceit? *Ethics & Behavior* 15(4) 339–49.

Kelleher, C. and Wagener, T. (2011) Ten guidelines for effective data visualization in scientific publications. *Environmental Modelling & Software* 26(2011) 822–7.

Kirk, A. (2016) *Data visualisation: A handbook for data driven design*. London: Sage.

Koitsiwe, M. (2013) Prospects and challenges of becoming an Indigenous researcher. In Mertens, D., Cram, F. and Chilisa, B. (eds) *Indigenous pathways into social research: voices of a new generation*, 261–75. Walnut Creek, CA: Left Coast Press.

Kouritzin, S. and Nakagawa, S. (2018) Toward a non-extractive research ethics for transcultural, translingual research: perspectives from the coloniser and the colonised. *Journal of Multilingual and Multicultural Development* (online pre-print). DOI: 10.1080/1434632.2018.1427755.

Kovach, M. (2009) *Indigenous methodologies: characteristics, conversations, and contexts*. Toronto: University of Toronto Press.

Kovach, M. (2015) Emerging from the margins: Indigenous methodologies. In Strega, S. and Brown, L. (eds) *Research as resistance: revisiting critical, Indigenous, and anti-oppressive approaches* (2nd edn), 43–64. Toronto: Canadian Scholars' Press Inc.

Kuhlau, F., Höglund, A., Eriksson, S. and Evers, K. (2013) The ethics of disseminating dual-use knowledge. *Research Ethics* 9(1) 6–19. DOI: 10.1177/1747016113478517.

Kukutai, T. and Taylor, J. (2016) Data sovereignty for Indigenous peoples: current practice and future needs. In Kukutai, T. and Taylor, J. (eds) *Indigenous data sovereignty: toward an agenda*, 1–22. Canberra: Australian National University Press.

Kuntz, A. (2015) *The responsible methodologist: inquiry, truth-telling, and social justice.* Walnut Creek, CA: Left Coast Press.

LaFrance, J. and Nichols, R. (2010) Reframing evaluation: defining an Indigenous evaluation framework. *The Canadian Journal of Program Evaluation* 23(2) 13–31.

Lambert, L. (2014) *Research for Indigenous survival: Indigenous research methodologies in the behavioral sciences.* Lincoln, NE: University of Nebraska Press.

Land, C. (2015) *Decolonizing solidarity: dilemmas and directions for supporters of Indigenous struggles.* London: Zed Books.

le Grange, L (2016) Decolonising the university curriculum. *South African Journal of Higher Education* 30(2) 1–12. DOI: 10.20853/30-2-709.

Leavy, P. (2017) *Research design: quantitative, qualitative, mixed methods, arts-based, and community-based participatory research approaches.* New York: The Guilford Press.

Lederman, R. (2016) Fieldwork double-bound in human research ethics reviews: disciplinary competence, or regulatory compliance and the muting of disciplinary values. In van den Hoonaard, W. and Hamilton, A. (eds) *The ethics rupture: exploring alternatives to formal research ethics review*, 43–72. Toronto: University of Toronto Press.

Leone, L., Stame, N. and Tagle, L. (2016) Exploring ethical issues and conditions for institutionalizing evaluation in the public sector. *Evaluation* 22(2) 149–67. DOI: 10.1177/1356389016640626.

Liamputtong, P. (2010) *Performing qualitative cross-cultural research.* Cambridge: Cambridge University Press.

Lifelong Learning UK (2009) Community development national occupational standards – introduction and overview, http://www.cdnl.co.uk/wp-content/uploads/2015/04/CDNOS-Guide1.pdf.

Lincoln, Y. and González, E. (2008) The search for emerging decolonizing methodologies in qualitative research: further strategies for liberatory and democratic inquiry. *Qualitative Inquiry* 14(5) 784–805. DOI: 10.1177/1077800408318304.

Lipsett, A. (2005) Bullying rife across campus. *Times Higher Education* September 16, https://www.timeshighereducation.com/news/bullying-rife-across-campus/198392.article.

LoBiondo-Wood, G., Haber, J. and Singh, M. (2014) Rigour in research. In LoBiondo-Wood, G., Haber, J., Cameron, C. and Singh, M. (eds) *Nursing research in Canada: methods, critical appraisal, and utilization* 306–30. Toronto: Elsevier Canada.

London, L. and Macdonald, H. (2014) Transnational excursions: the ethics of Northern anthropological investigations going South. In Posel, D. and Ross, F. (eds) *Ethical quandaries in social research*, 93–110. Cape Town, SA: HSRC Press.

MacDonald, J. and Bourke, R. (2017) Reflecting on evaluation practice by considering an educative values-engaged approach: how would it have changed this utilisation-focused evaluation? *Evaluation Matters* (3) 130–155. DOI: 10.18296/em.0024.

Macfarlane, B. (2009) *Researching with integrity: the ethics of academic enquiry*. Abingdon: Routledge.

McGregor, D. (2014) Lessons for collaboration involving traditional knowledge and environmental governance in Ontario, Canada. *AlterNative* 10(4) 340–53.

McGregor, D. (2018) Peer-review commissioned by Policy Press, May.

McKemmish, S., Faulkhead, S., Iacovino, L. and Thorpe, K. (2010) Australian Indigenous knowledge and the archives: embracing multiple ways of knowing and keeping. *Archives and Manuscripts* 38(1) 27–50.

McLellan, E., MacQueen, K. and Neidig, J. (2003) Beyond the qualitative interview: data preparation and transcription. *Field Methods* 15(1) 63–84. DOI: 10.1177/1525822X02239573.

Mannay, D. (2016) *Visual, narrative and creative research methods: application, reflection and ethics*. Abingdon: Routledge.

Markham, A. (2012) Fabrication as ethical practice. *Information, Communication & Society* 1–20. DOI: 10.1080/1369118X.2011.641993.

Markless, S. and Streatfield, D. (2013) *Evaluating the impact of your library* (2nd edn). London: Facet Publishing.

Marlowe, J. and Tolich, M. (2015) Shifting from research governance to research ethics: a novel paradigm for ethical review in community-based research. *Research Ethics* 11(4) 178–91. DOI: 10.1177/1747016115579536.

Martin, B. (2013) Countering supervisor exploitation. *Journal of Scholarly Publishing* 45(1) 74–86.

Matebeni, Z. (2014) My best participants' informed consent. In Posel, D. and Ross, F. (eds) *Ethical Quandaries in Social Research*, 111–24. Cape Town, SA: HSRC Press.

Mathison, S. (2016) Confronting capitalism: evaluation that fosters social equity. In Donaldson, S. and Picciotto, R. (eds) *Evaluation for an equitable society*, 83–107. Charlotte, NC: Information Age Publishing, Inc.

Mertens, D. (2013) Social transformation and evaluation. In Alkin, M. (ed) *Evaluation roots: a wider perspective of theorists' views and influences*, 229–40. Thousand Oaks, CA: Sage.

Mertens, D., Cram, F. and Chilisa, B. (eds) (2013) *Indigenous pathways into social research: voices of a new generation*. Walnut Creek, CA: Left Coast Press.

Meyer, M. (2013) The context within: my journey into research. In Mertens, D., Cram, F. and Chilisa, B. (eds) *Indigenous pathways into social research: voices of a new generation*, 249–60. Walnut Creek, CA: Left Coast Press.

Mfecane, S. (2014) Friends in the field. In Posel, D. and Ross, F. (eds) *Ethical quandaries in social research*, 125–39. Cape Town, SA: HSRC Press.

Millett, R. (2013) Lens from the 'bottom of the well'. In Mertens, D., Cram, F. and Chilisa, B. (eds) *Indigenous pathways into social research: voices of a new generation*, 317–31. Walnut Creek, CA: Left Coast Press.

Mitchell, S. and Evison, A. (2006) Exploiting the potential of writing for educational change at Queen Mary, University of London. In Ganobcsik-Williams, L. (ed) *Teaching academic writing in UK higher education: theories, practices and models*, 68–84. Basingstoke: Palgrave Macmillan.

Moloi, K. (2013) An African narrative: the journey of an Indigenous social researcher in South Africa. In Mertens, D., Cram, F. and Chilisa, B. (eds) *Indigenous pathways into social research: voices of a new generation*, 101–21. Walnut Creek, CA: Left Coast Press.

Monaghan, L., O'Dwyer, M. and Gabe, J. (2013) Seeking university research ethics committee approval: the emotional vicissitudes of a 'rationalised' process. *International Journal of Social Research Methodology* 16(1) 65–80.

Moncur, W. (2013) The emotional wellbeing of researchers: considerations for practice. Conference paper. Session: Ethics in HCI, at CHI 2013: Changing Perspectives, Paris, France.

Moodie, S. (2010) Power, rights, respect and data ownership in academic research with Indigenous peoples. *Environmental Research* 110 (2010) 818–20. DOI: 10.1016/j.envres.2010.08.009.

Moore, H. (2010) Forms of knowing and un-knowing: secrets about society, sexuality and God in northern Kenya. In Ryan-Flood, R. and Gill, R. (eds) *Secrecy and silence in the research process: feminist reflections*, 30–41. Abingdon: Routledge.

Morris, M. (2008) *Evaluation ethics for best practice: cases and commentaries*. New York: The Guilford Press.

Morris, M. (2015) Research on evaluation ethics: reflections and an agenda. In Brandon, P. (ed) *Research on evaluation: new directions for evaluation*, 31–42. Hoboken, NJ: Wiley.

Morris, M. and Morris, J. (2016) The importance of virtue ethics in the IRB. *Research Ethics* 12(4) 201–16.

Morrow, E., Boaz, A., Brearley, S. and Ross, F. (2012) *Handbook of service user involvement in nursing and healthcare research*. Chichester: Wiley-Blackwell.

Munro, I., Harwood, M., Hlywka, J., Stephen, A., Doull, J., Flamm, W. and Adlercreutz, H. (2003) Soy isoflavones: a safety review. *Nutrition Reviews* 61(1) 1–33.

Munté, A., Serradell, O. and Sordé, T. (2011) From research to policy: Roma participation through communicative organization. *Qualitative Inquiry* 17(3) 256–66. DOI: 10.1177/1077800410397804.

Nicholls, S., Brehaut, J. and Saginur, R. (2012) Social science and ethics review: a question of practice not principle. *Research Ethics* 8(2) 71–8. DOI: 10.1177/1747016112445435.

Noon, M. (2018) Pointless diversity training: unconscious bias, new racism and agency. *Work, Employment and Society* 32(1) 198–209.

Nordling, L. (2017) San people of Africa draft code of ethics for researchers. *Science* 17 March. DOI: 10.1126/science.aal0933.

Okalik, L. (2013) Inuujunga: the intricacy of Indigenous and Western epistemologies in the Arctic. In Mertens, D., Cram, F. and Chilisa, B. (eds) *Indigenous pathways into social research: voices of a new generation*, 239–48. Walnut Creek, CA: Left Coast Press.

Oparah, J., Salahuddin, F., Cato, R., Jones, L., Oseguera. T. and Matthews, S. (2015) By us, not for us: black women researching pregnancy and childbirth. In Jolivétte, A. (ed) *Research justice: methodologies for social change*, 117–37. Bristol: Policy Press.

Oransky, I. and Marcus, A. (2010) Why write a blog about retractions? http://retractionwatch.com/2010/08/03/why-write-a-blog-about-retractions/.

Palfrey, C., Thomas, P. and Phillips, C. (2012) *Evaluation for the real world: the impact of evidence in policy making.* Bristol: Policy Press.

Parpart, J. (2010) Choosing silence: rethinking voice, agency and women's empowerment. In Ryan-Flood, R. and Gill, R. (eds) *Secrecy and silence in the research process: feminist reflections*, 15–29. Abingdon: Routledge.

Passingan, S. (2013) A native Papua New Guinea researcher. In Mertens, D., Cram, F. and Chilisa, B. (eds) *Indigenous pathways into social research: voices of a new generation*, 353–65. Walnut Creek, CA: Left Coast Press.

Patterson, M., Jackson, R. and Edwards, N. (2006) Ethics in Aboriginal research: comments on paradigms, process and two worlds. *Canadian Journal of Aboriginal Community-Based HIV/AIDS Research* 1(1) 47–62.

Pawlik, D. (2011) Maori's ritual body embellishments. *Journal of Martial Arts Anthropology* 11(4) 6–11.

Perry, K. (2011) Ethics, vulnerability, and speakers of other languages: how university IRBs (do not) speak to research involving refugee participants. *Qualitative Inquiry* 17(10) 899–912.

Pickering, L. (2018) Paternalism and the ethics of researching with people who use drugs. In Iphofen, R. and Tolich, M. (eds) *The SAGE handbook of qualitative research ethics*, 411–25. London: Sage.

Pickering, L. and Kara, H. (2017) Presenting and representing others: towards an ethics of engagement. *International Journal of Social Research Methodology* 20(3) 299–309. DOI: 10.1080/13645579.2017.1287875.

Piper, H. and Sikes, P. (2010) All teachers are vulnerable but especially gay teachers: using composite fictions to protect research participants in pupil–teacher sex-related research. *Qualitative Inquiry* 16(7) 566–74.

Pollard, K. and Evans, D. (2015) Theorising service user involvement from a researcher perspective. In Staddon, P. (ed) *Mental health service users in research: critical sociological perspectives*, 39–51. Bristol: Policy Press.

Posel, D. (2014) In depth, out of my depth: research and care in the field of HIV and AIDS research. In Posel, D. and Ross, F. (eds) *Ethical quandaries in social research*, 153–67. Cape Town, SA: HSRC Press.

Posel, D. and Ross, F. (2014) Opening up the quandaries of research ethics: beyond the formalities of institutional ethical review. In Posel, D. and Ross, F. (eds) *Ethical quandaries in social research*, 1–26. Cape Town, SA: HSRC Press.

Potts, K. and Brown, L. (2015) Becoming an anti-oppressive researcher. In Strega, S. and Brown, L. (eds) *Research as resistance: revisiting critical, Indigenous, and anti-oppressive approaches* (2nd edn) 17–41. Toronto: Canadian Scholars' Press Inc.

Pringle, J. (2017) Do open access journals have impact? *Nature* blog post 13 July, http://www.nature.com/nature/focus/accessdebate/19.html.

Puebla, C. (2014) Indigenous researchers and epistemic violence. In Denzin, N. and Giardina, M. (eds) *Qualitative inquiry outside the academy*, 164–78. Walnut Creek, CA: Left Coast Press.

Qwul'sih'yah'maht (Robina Anne Thomas) (2015) Honouring the oral traditions of the Ta't Mustimuxw (Ancestors) through storytelling. In Strega, S. and Brown, L. (eds) *Research as resistance: revisiting critical, Indigenous, and anti-oppressive approaches* (2nd edn) 177–98. Toronto: Canadian Scholars' Press Inc.

Recuber, T. (2016) From obedience to contagion: discourses of power in Milgram, Zimbardo, and the Facebook experiment. *Research Ethics* 12(1) 44–54. DOI: 10.1177/17470161115579533.

RESPECT (2004) *RESPECT Code of practice for socio-economic research*. Falmer: RESPECT project.

Rhodes, C. (2009) After reflexivity: ethics, freedom and the writing of organization studies. *Organization Studies* 30(6) 653–72. DOI: 10.1177/0170840609104804.

Richardson, L. (1997) *Fields of play: constructing an academic life*. New Brunswick, NJ: Rutgers University Press.

Rix, E., Wilson, S., Sheehan, N. and Tujague, N. (2018) Indigenist and decolonizing research methodology. In Liamputtong, P. (ed) *Handbook of research methods in health social sciences* (online pre-print). Singapore: Springer.

Robinson, A. et al (2011) Mixed methods data collection in dementia research: a 'progressive engagement' approach. *Journal of Mixed Methods Research* 5(4) 330–44.

Rodriguez-Lonebear, D. (2016) Building a data revolution in Indian country. In Kukutai, T. and Taylor, J. (eds) *Indigenous data sovereignty: toward an agenda*, 253–72. Canberra: Australian National University Press.

Romanyshyn, R. (2013) *The wounded researcher: research with soul in mind*. New Orleans, LA: Spring Journal, Inc.

Ronagh, M. and Souder, L. (2015) The ethics of ironic science in its search for spoof. *Science and Engineering Ethics* 21 1537–49. DOI: 10.1007/s11948-014-9619-8.

Rose, G. (2012) *Visual methodologies: an introduction to researching with visual materials* (3rd edn). London: Sage.

Ross, F. and Grant, J. (2014) Ethical entailments: publics and responsibilities in social research. In Posel, D. and Ross, F. (eds) *Ethical quandaries in social research*, 168–82. Cape Town, SA: HSRC Press.

Rowe, S., Alexander, N., Clydesdale, F., Alebaum, R., Atkinson, S., Black, R., Dwyer, J., Hentges, E., Higley, N., Lefevre, M., Lupton, J., Miller, S., Tancredi, D., Weaver, C., Woteki, C. and Wedral, E. (2009) Funding food science and nutrition research: financial conflicts and scientific integrity. *Nutrition Review* 67(5) 264–72. DOI: 10.1111/J.1753-4887.2009/00188.x.

Russell, L. (2005) Indigenous knowledge and archives: accessing hidden history and understandings. *Australian Academic and Research Libraries* 36(2) 161–71. DOI: 10.1080/00048623.2005.10721256.

Ryan-Flood, R. (2010) Keeping mum: secrecy and silence in research on lesbian parenthood. In Ryan-Flood, R. and Gill, R. (eds) *Secrecy and silence in the research process: feminist reflections*, 188–99. Abingdon: Routledge.

San (2017) *San code of research ethics*. Kimberley, SA: South African San Institute.

Sands, M. (2009) Empowerment under permit: Canterbury and District Mental Health Forum Service User Evaluation (SUE) project. In Sweeney, A., Beresford, P., Faulkner, A., Nettle, M. and Rose, D. (eds) *This is survivor research*, 154–7. Ross-on-Wye: PCCS Books.

Sarsons, H. (2017) Gender differences in recognition for group work. *Harvard University* working paper version 6, https://scholar.harvard.edu/sarsons/publications/note-gender-differences-recognition-group-work.

Sawlani, S. (2013) Inter-minority prejudice in the UK and East Africa. *Media Diversified* 13 September, https://mediadiversified.org/2013/09/13/inter-minority-racism-in-the-uk/.

Scarth, B. (2016) Bereaved participants' reasons for wanting their real names used in thanatology research. *Research Ethics* 12(2) 80–96. DOI: 10.1177/1747016115599569.

Schrag, Z. (2011) The case against ethics review in the social sciences. *Research Ethics* 7(4) 120–31.

Schrag, Z. (2016) Ethical pluralism: scholarly societies and the regulation of research ethics. In van den Hoonaard, W. and Hamilton, A. (eds) *The ethics rupture: exploring alternatives to formal research ethics review*, 317–34. Toronto: University of Toronto Press.

Schwandt, T. and Gates, E. (2016) What can evaluation do? An agenda for evaluation in service of an equitable society. In Donaldson, S. and Picciotto, R. (eds) *Evaluation for an equitable society*, 67–81. Charlotte, NC: Information Age Publishing, Inc.

Scougall, J. (2006) Reconciling tensions between principles and practice in Indigenous evaluation. *Evaluation Journal of Australasia* 6(2) 49–55.

Scrivens, M. (2016) The last frontier of evaluation: ethics. In Donaldson, S. and Picciotto, R. (eds) *Evaluation for an equitable society*, 11–48. Charlotte, NC: Information Age Publishing, Inc.

Sensoy, Ö. and DiAngelo, R. (2012) *Is everyone really equal? An introduction to key concepts in social justice education.* New York: Teachers College Press.

Sherwood, J. (2013) An Aboriginal health worker's research story. In Mertens, D., Cram, F. and Chilisa, B. (eds) *Indigenous pathways into social research: voices of a new generation*, 203–17. Walnut Creek, CA: Left Coast Press.

Shimp, C. (2007) Quantitative behavior analysis and human values. *Behavioural Processes* 75: 146–55.

Simons, G. and Fennig, D. (eds) (2017) *Ethnologue: languages of the world* (20th edn). Dallas, TX: SIL International, https://www.ethnologue.com/statistics/size.

Simpson, A. (2014) *Mohawk interruptus: political life across the borders of settler states.* Durham, NC: Duke University Press.

Singer, P. (2016) *Ethics in the real world: 86 brief essays on things that matter.* Melbourne, Victoria: The Text Publishing Company.

Sinha, S. and Back, L. (2014) Making methods sociable: dialogue, ethics and authorship in qualitative research. *Qualitative Research* 14(4) 473–87. DOI: 10.1177/1468794113490717.

Slavin, R. (2008) What works? Issues in synthesizing educational program evaluations. *Educational Researcher* 37(1) 5–14.

Smith, C. (2013) Becoming a Kaupapa Māori researcher. In Mertens, D., Cram, F. and Chilisa, B. (eds) *Indigenous pathways into social research: voices of a new generation*, 89–99. Walnut Creek, CA: Left Coast Press.

Smith, L. (2012) *Decolonizing methodologies* (2nd edn). London: Zed Books.

Sousanis, N. (2015) *Unflattening.* Cambridge, MA: Harvard University Press.

Spates, K. and Gichiru, W. (2015) Starting where you are: how race can constrain researchers within the research setting. *The Qualitative Report* 20(11) 1922–34.

Stahl, B. (2011) Teaching ethical reflexivity in information systems: how to equip students to deal with moral and ethical issues of emerging information and communication technologies. *Journal of Information Systems Education* 22(3) 253–60.

Stark, L. (2012) *Behind closed doors: IRBs and the making of ethical research.* Chicago: The University of Chicago Press.

Steere, V. (2013) Interpreting the journey: where words, stories formed. In Mertens, D., Cram, F. and Chilisa, B. (eds) *Indigenous pathways into social research: voices of a new generation*, 381–93. Walnut Creek, CA: Left Coast Press.

Strauss, A. and Corbin, J. (1998) *Basics of qualitative research: techniques and procedures for developing grounded theory* (2nd edn). Thousand Oaks, CA: Sage.

Strega, S. and Brown, L. (2015) Introduction: from resistance to resurgence. In Strega, S. and Brown, L. (eds) *Research as resistance: revisiting critical, indigenous, and anti-oppressive approaches* (2nd edn) 1–16. Toronto: Canadian Scholars' Press Inc.

Tamas, S. (2009) Sketchy rendering: seeing an other. *Qualitative Inquiry* 15(3) 607–17.

Taylor, C. and White, S. (2000) *Practising reflexivity in health and welfare: making knowledge.* Buckingham: Open University Press.

TCPS2 (2014) *Tri-Council policy statement: ethical conduct for research involving humans.* Canadian Institutes of Health Research, Natural Sciences and Engineering Research Council of Canada, Social Sciences and Humanities Research Council of Canada.

Thomas, A. (2013) The process that led me to become an Indigenous researcher. In Mertens, D., Cram, F. and Chilisa, B. (eds) *Indigenous pathways into social research: voices of a new generation,* 41–57. Walnut Creek, CA: Left Coast Press.

Tikly, L. and Bond, T. (2013) Towards a postcolonial research ethics in comparative and international education. *Compare: A Journal of Comparative and International Education* 43(4) 422–42. DOI: 10.1080/03057925.2013.797721.

Tindana, P.O., Kass, N. and Akweongo, P. (2006) The informed consent process in a rural African setting: a case study of the Kassena–Nankana district of northern Ghana. *IRB: Ethics and Human Research* 28 1–9.

Tolich, M. (2016) Are qualitative research ethics unique? In Tolich, M. (ed) *Qualitative ethics in practice,* 33–47. Walnut Creek, CA: Left Coast Press.

Tolich, M. and Ferguson, K. (2014) Measuring the impact of the New Brunswick Declaration. *Cross-Cultural Communication* 10(5) 183–8. DOI: 10.3968/4639.

Tolich, M. and Marlowe, J. (2017) Evolving power dynamics in an unconventional, powerless ethics committee. *Research Ethics* 13(1) 42–52.

Traore, I. (2013) Indigenous researcher's thoughts: an experience from research with communities in Burkina Faso using participatory methods. In Mertens, D., Cram, F. and Chilisa, B. (eds) *Indigenous pathways into social research: voices of a new generation,* 171–88. Walnut Creek, CA: Left Coast Press.

UK Statistics Authority (2009) *Code of practice for official statistics.* London: UK Statistics Authority.

US Government (undated) *Statement of commitment to scientific integrity by principal statistical agencies.*

van den Hoonaard, W. (2013) The social and policy contexts of the New Brunswick Declaration on research ethics, integrity, and governance: a commentary. *Journal of Empirical Research on Human Research Ethics* 8(2) 104–9. DOI: 10.1525/jer.2013.8.2.104.

van den Hoonaard, W. and Tolich, M. (2014) The New Brunswick Declaration of research ethics: a simple and radical perspective. *Canadian Journal of Sociology* 39(1) 87–97.

van den Hoonaard, W. and van den Hoonaard, D. (2013) *Essentials of thinking ethically in qualitative research.* Walnut Creek, CA: Left Coast Press.

van Wyk, I. (2014) The ethics of dislike in the field. In Posel, D. and Ross, F. (eds) *Ethical quandaries in social research,* 199–213. Cape Town, SA: HSRC Press.

Velardo, S. and Elliott, S. (2018) Prioritising doctoral students' wellbeing in qualitative research. *The Qualitative Report* 23(2) 311–18.

Walker, P. (2013) Research in relationship with humans, the spirit world, and the natural world. In Mertens, D., Cram, F. and Chilisa, B. (eds) *Indigenous pathways into social research: voices of a new generation,* 299–315. Walnut Creek, CA: Left Coast Press.

Walter, M. and Andersen, C. (2016) *Indigenous statistics: a quantitative research methodology*. Abingdon: Routledge.

Walton, M. and Hassreiter, S. (2014) Real friends and fake friends: research relationships in an era of global social media. In Posel, D. and Ross, F. (eds) *Ethical quandaries in social research*, 228–49. Cape Town, SA: HSRC Press.

Ward, V., Smith, S., House, A. and Hamer, S. (2012) Exploring knowledge exchange: a useful framework for practice and policy. *Social Science & Medicine* 74 297–304.

Ware, M. and Mabe, M. (2015) *The STM Report: an overview of scientific and scholarly journal publishing*. The Hague, Netherlands: International Association of Scientific, Technical and Medical Publishers.

Warren, J. (2014) *Music and ethical responsibility*. Cambridge: Cambridge University Press.

Weeks, S. (2014) Insider, outsider: marriage proposals, advocacy and other ethical quandaries in law and society research. In Posel, D. and Ross, F. (eds) *Ethical quandaries in social research*, 140–52. Cape Town, SA: HSRC Press.

WEF (2018) *Young Scientists' Code of Ethics*. Geneva: World Economic Forum.

Wehipeihana, N. (2008) Indigenous evaluation: a strategic objective of the Australasian Evaluation Society. *Journal of the Australasian Evaluation Society* 8(1) 40–4.

Wehipeihana, N., Pipi, K., Kennedy, V. and Paipa, K. (2013) Hinerauwhāriki: tapestries of life for four Māori women in evaluation. In Mertens, D., Cram, F. and Chilisa, B. (eds) *Indigenous pathways into social research: voices of a new generation*, 277–97. Walnut Creek, CA: Left Coast Press.

Westall, A. (2009) Value and the third sector: working paper on ideas for future research. *Third Sector Research Centre Working Paper 25*. University of Birmingham: Third Sector Research Centre.

Whitney, D. and Trosten-Bloom, A. (2010) *The power of appreciative inquiry: a practical guide to positive change* (2nd edn). Oakland, CA: Berrett-Koehler Publishers, Inc.

Whitty, C., Mundel, T., Farrar, J., Heymann, D., Davies, S. and Walport, M. (2015) Providing incentives to share data early in health emergencies: the role of journal editors. *Lancet* 386 1797–8. DOI: 10.1016/S0140-6736(15)60931-X.

Wilkes, L., Cummings, J. and Haigh, C. (2014) Transcriptionist saturation: knowing too much about sensitive health and social data. *Journal of Advanced Nursing* 71(2) 295–303. DOI: 10/1111/jan.12510.

Williams, E., Guenther, J. and Arnott, A. (2011) Beyond informed consent: how is it possible to ethically evaluate Indigenous programs? Paper presented to the NARU Public Seminar Series, Darwin, 23 November 2011, http://www.covaluator.net/docs/S1.3_beyond_informed_consent.pdf (no longer available online).

Williams, L. (2016) Ethics in international development evaluation and research: what is the problem, why does it matter and what can we do about it? *Journal of Development Effectiveness* 8(4) 535–52. DOI: 10.1080/19439342.2016.1244700.

Wilson, S. (2008) *Research is ceremony: Indigenous research methods.* Halifax and Winnipeg: Fernwood Publishing.

Wilson, S. and Wilson, A. (2013) *Neyo way in ik issi*: a family practice of Indigenist research informed by land. In Mertens, D., Cram, F. and Chilisa, B. (eds) *Indigenous pathways into social research: voices of a new generation*, 333–52. Walnut Creek, CA: Left Coast Press.

Winston, B. (1998) 'The camera never lies': the partiality of photographic evidence. In Prosser, J. (ed) *Image-based research: a sourcebook for qualitative researchers*, 60–8. London: RoutledgeFalmer.

Yantio, D. (2013) Drawn from the traditions of Cameroon: lessons from twenty-one years of practice. In Mertens, D., Cram, F. and Chilisa, B. (eds) *Indigenous pathways into social research: voices of a new generation*, 123–31. Walnut Creek, CA: Left Coast Press.

Zagala, S. (2004) Vanuatu sand drawing. *Museum International* 56(1–2) 32–5.

Zerubavel, E. (1997) *Social mindscapes: an invitation to cognitive sociology.* Cambridge, MA: Harvard University Press.

Zuberi, T. and Bonilla-Silva, E. (2008) Telling the real tale of the hunt: toward a race conscious sociology of racial stratification. In Zuberi, T. and Bonilla-Silva, E. (eds) *White logic, white methods: racism and methodology*, 329–41. Lanham, MD: Rowman & Littlefield Publishers, Inc.

Index

national censuses 28–9, 40
reflexivity 118
quotes, use of 106, 126–7

R

racism, institutional 51–2
reading, ethical 90–1
reciprocity 26, 27
recolonisation 17
recording data 106–7
record-keeping, and context setting 89–90
recruitment of researchers 74
Red Cross 13
'red flag' approach 118
reflexivity 16–17, 59, 82, 117–18
Regeni, Giulio 162–3
regulation *see* research ethics regulation
relational accountability 25–6
relational well-being 167–8
relationships
  and power 27
  reciprocity 26, 27
  relational accountability 25–6
  relational well-being 167–8
  researcher-participant friendships 101–3
  see also aftercare
reporting research findings 121–31
  authorial power 123–5
  language 122–3
  planning stage 76
  writing as creative 128–9
  writing as process 126–7
  writing as product 127–8
  writing as relational 129–30
Research and Policy in Ethnic Relations:
  Compromised Dynamics in a Neoliberal Era
  (Husband) 4
research design 73–4
researcher-participant friendships 101–3
researcher well-being 161–9
  emotional 163–5
  mental 165
  physical 162–3
  planning stage 77–8
  relational 167–8
  spiritual 166–7
Research Ethics Application Database
  (TREAD) 47
research ethics committees (RECs) *see* ethics
  committees
research ethics regulation 43–55
  formal ethics approval 47–8
  governance 43–7
  and other types of ethics 48–55
research governance 43–7
research integrity 46

Research Methods Festival, Bath 2
research planning *see* planning research
respect 9, 92–3
RESPECT Code (EU) 37
Retraction Watch 88–9, 110
rigour 82–3
risk management
  of institutions 2, 47–8, 54
  of participants 61
  of researcher 77–8, 162–3
ritual, research as 166
Roma peoples 78
Ryan-Flood, R. 167

S

safety of researchers 162–3
sampling 96–7
San people 47
Schrag, Z. 49
Scougall, J. 59
Scrivens, M. 66
secondary data 75, 97–8, 115, 143
secret knowledge 101
Sensoy, Ö 51
service users 61–3, 153
sharing data 107, 125
Singer, P. 4
Singhal, G. 81–2
Smith, C. 48, 83
Smith, G. 4
Smith, L.T. 10
social ethics 14, 27
social justice approach 9
social media
  data gathering 105–6, 127
  dissemination of research 146–7
  presentation of research 140
social theories 24
software 116
Sousanis, N. 128
South Africa
  ethical guidelines 39
  research in 74, 129–30, 152, 154, 157
Southern theory 24
South Sea Islanders 28–9
South Sudan 11–12, 13, 14
spiritual knowledge 23
spiritual well-being 166–7
spoken language 122–3
Stahl, B. 118
stakeholder involvement 61–3
Statistical Package for Social Scientists (SPSS)
  116
statistics 115–16
Steere, V. 92
storage of data 111, 157–8